CRITICAL ISSUES IN INTERNATIONAL REFUGEE LAW

This volume of original essays examines key cutting edge areas of international refugee law, including strategies for interpretative harmony, the rights of refugees and the standard of proof in complementary protection. Each topic is examined from a theoretical and a practical perspective in order to find solutions to the many legal issues and concerns which currently confront this area of law, and to seek ways to advance the field as a whole.

JAMES C. SIMEON is an Assistant Professor in the School of Public Policy and Administration, Faculty of Liberal Arts and Professional Studies, a Centre for Refugee Studies (CRS) Scholar, and a Faculty Associate with the Centre for Support of Teaching (CST) at York University, Toronto, Canada. His teaching and research interests are in the fields of public management, public administration, public policy and administration and international human rights law, international refugee law, and international humanitarian and criminal law.

CRITICAL ISSUES IN INTERNATIONAL REFUGEE LAW

Strategies Toward Interpretative Harmony

EDITED BY

JAMES C. SIMEON

CAMBRIDGE
UNIVERSITY PRESS

CAMBRIDGE UNIVERSITY PRESS
Cambridge, New York, Melbourne, Madrid, Cape Town, Singapore,
São Paulo, Delhi, Dubai, Tokyo, Mexico City

Cambridge University Press
The Edinburgh Building, Cambridge CB2 8RU, UK

Published in the United States of America by Cambridge University Press, New York

www.cambridge.org
Information on this title: www.cambridge.org/9780521199520

First published 2010

Printed in the United Kingdom at the University Press, Cambridge

A catalogue record for this publication is available from the British Library

Library of Congress Cataloguing in Publication data
Critical issues in international refugee law : strategies toward interpretative
harmony / [edited by] James C. Simeon.
p. cm.
Includes bibliographical references and index.
ISBN 978-0-521-19952-0
1. Political refugees–Legal status, laws, etc. 2. Asylum, Right of.
I. Simeon, James C. II. Title.
K3274.C75 2010
342.08′3–dc22
2010023744

ISBN 978-0-521-19952-0 Hardback

Contents

Contributors

NERGIS CANEFE (Ph.D. York, 1998, D.Jur candidate, Osgoode Hall Law School) is Associate Professor of Political Science at York University, and Associate Director at Centre for Refugee Studies. She taught at London School of Economics, UK, and, Istanbul Bilgi and Bogazici Universities in Turkey prior to her appointment at York in 2003, and is currently an adjunct faculty member at Istanbul Bilgi University's Faculty of Law. Her areas of expertise are minority rights, diaspora politics, nationalism and forced migration studies, critical citizenship studies, and, crimes against humanity. Her publications appeared in journals including Refuge, Citizenship Studies, Nations and Nationalism, Balkanologie, Turkish Studies, Rethinking History and South East European Politics and Society. She published a co-edited volume *Turkey and the European Integration* (2004) and a sole-authored volume in Turkish titled *Citizenship, Identity and Belonging: Limits of Turkish Nationalism* (2006).

Her new edited volume with William Safran titled *The Jewish Diaspora as a Paradigm: Politics, Religion and Belonging* is forthcoming. She is currently working on her second Turkish book titled *Sovereign Utopias: Roots of Political Violence in Peripheral Nationalisms*, and a new edited volume titled *Political Violence and Citizenship in Turkey: Fear, Sacrifice and Social Responsibility*. At Osgoode Hall Law School, she is completing her dissertation titled "Substantive Norms Debate in International Law: A Legal Pluralistic Analysis of Crimes Against Humanity," under the supervision of Craig Scott, Harry Arthurs and Les Jacobs.

GEOFF GILBERT is a Professor of Law, School of Law and the Human Rights Centre, and the Director of LL.M. in International

Human Rights and Humanitarian Law at the University of Essex and he is the Editor-in-Chief of the *International Journal of Refugee Law*. He is author of "Current Issues in the Application of the Exclusion Clauses" in Feller, Türk and Nicholson, *Refugee Protection in International Law* (2003), part of UNHCR's Global Consultations, and founding Director of Studies for UNHCR annual Thematic Refugee course for judges, government officials and UNHCR staff at the International Institute for Humanitarian Law, Sanremo, Italy, since 2005. He was Specialist Advisor to the Joint Parliamentary Committee on Human Rights in its inquiry into the treatment of asylum seekers, 2006–07. In 2009, he was elected a Bencher of the Middle Temple, London, United Kingdom.

ELSPETH GUILD is Professor of European Migration Law at the Radboud University Nijmegen, awarded a Jean Monnet Chair in 2009. She is also a visiting professor at the London School of Economics and the College of Europe Bruges. In addition to her academic activities, she is a partner at the London law firm Kingsley Napley and a senior research fellow at the Centre for European Policy Studies in Brussels. Her most recent monograph is entitled *Security and Migration in the 21st Century* (2009).

KATE JASTRAM is a Lecturer in Residence at Berkeley Law, University of California, where she teaches refugee, human rights, and humanitarian law, and is also an Affiliated Scholar at the Chief Justice Earl Warren Institute on Race, Ethnicity, and Diversity. She has been a legal advisor to the UNHCR in Geneva and Washington, D.C., and has served as an expert on asylum issues for the United States Commission on International Religious Freedom.

She is the co-author of "Family Unity and Refugee Protection" in Feller, Türk and Nicholson, *Refugee Protection in International Law* (2003), part of UNHCR's Global Consultations. In 2005, she was a co-recipient of the Arthur C. Helton Human Rights Award, awarded by the American Immigration Lawyers Association in recognition of outstanding service in advancing the cause of human rights.

JANE MCADAM, Associate Professor, is the Director of International Law Programs and Mooting in the Faculty of Law at the University of New South Wales (Australia) and Director of the International Refugee and Migration Law project at the Faculty's Gilbert + Tobin Centre of Public Law. She is also a Research Associate of the Refugee Studies Centre at the University of Oxford. Professor McAdam is the author of *Complementary Protection in International Refugee Law* (2007); co-author with Guy S Goodwin-Gill of *The Refugee in International Law* (3rd edn, 2007); and the editor of *Forced Migration, Human Rights and Security* (2008).

Professor McAdam's current research projects are funded by the Australian Research Council. The first examines climate-induced displacement and international law; the second, a joint project with two historians, examines the history of medico-legal border control in the Asia-Pacific region. Professor McAdam is the Associate Rapporteur of the Convention Refugee Status and Subsidiary Protection Working Party for the International Association of Refugee Law Judges; Vice-President of the Refugee Advice and Casework Service in Sydney; and an advisor to UNHCR on legal aspects of climate-induced displacement.

JUSTICE TONY NORTH was educated at Melbourne University (BA, LL.B (Hons)) and the University of London (LL.M). He joined the Victorian Bar in 1976 and was appointed a Queen's Counsel in 1989. In 1995 he was appointed a Justice of the Federal Court of Australia.

In 2001, Justice North was the trial judge in the Tampa case, the most publicised recent Australian refugee case (*Victorian Council for Civil Liberties Incorporated* v. *Minister for Immigration and Multicultural Affairs* [2001] FCA 1297) about 400 Iraqi and Sri Lankan asylum seekers who had been rescued at sea by the *MV Tampa* were refused entry into Australia by the Australian Government. Justice North ordered that the government allow the asylum seekers to land in Australia.

Justice North has a special interest in refugee law and served as President of the International Association of Refugee Law Judges (IARLJ) from 2005 to 2009.

He has spoken and written widely on refugee law matters. In the most recent article "Towards Convergence in the Interpretation of the Refugees' Convention," vol 25, *Australian Year Book of International Law*, p. 105, he advocated the establishment of an international judicial commission for the authoritative determination of refugee law issues under the *1951 Convention Relating to the Status of Refugees*. He was a signatory to the Michigan Guidelines on Protection Elsewhere adopted on January 3, 2007.

JUSTICE ALBIE SACHS, on turning six, during World War II, received a card from his father expressing the wish that he would grow up to be a soldier in the fight for liberation.

His career in human rights activism started at the age of seventeen, when as a second-year law student at the University of Cape Town, he took part in the Defiance of Unjust Laws Campaign. Three years later he attended the Congress of the People at Kliptown where the Freedom Charter was adopted. He started practice as an advocate at the Cape Bar aged 21. The bulk of his work involved defending people charged under racist statutes and repressive security laws. Many faced the death sentence. He himself was raided by the security police, subjected to banning orders restricting his movement and eventually placed in solitary confinement without trial for two prolonged spells of detention.

In 1966 he went into exile. After spending eleven years studying and teaching law in England he worked for a further eleven years in Mozambique as law professor and legal researcher. In 1988 he was blown up by a bomb placed in his car in Maputo by South African security agents, losing an arm and the sight of an eye.

During the 1980s working closely with Oliver Tambo, leader of the ANC in exile, he helped draft the organisation's Code of Conduct, as well as its statutes. After recovering from the bomb he devoted himself full time to preparations for a new democratic Constitution for South Africa. In 1990 he returned home and as a member of the Constitutional Committee and the National Executive of the ANC took an active part in the negotiations which led to South Africa becoming a constitutional democracy. After the first democratic election in 1994 he was appointed by President Nelson Mandela to serve on the newly established Constitutional Court.

In addition to his work on the Court, he has travelled to many countries sharing South Africa's experience in healing divided societies. He has also been engaged in the sphere of art and architecture, and played an active role in the development of the Constitutional Court building and its art collection on the site of the Old Fort Prison in Johannesburg. His term on the Constitutional of Court will end on October 11, 2009.

JAMES C. SIMEON is an Assistant Professor in the School of Public Policy and Administration, Faculty of Liberal Arts and Professional Studies, a Centre for Refugee Studies (CRS) Scholar, at York University, Toronto, Canada. Immediately before joining the faculty at York University, he served as the first Executive Director of the International Association of Refugee Law Judges (IARLJ), www.iarlj.nl, the foremost international professional association of its kind. He currently serves as the Coordinator of the IARLJ Inter-Conference Working Party Process. He has been awarded an International Opportunities Fund (IOF) grant from the Social Science and Humanities Research Council of Canada (SSHRC) for a collaborative research project with co-applicant Kate Jastram, Berkeley Law, University of California at Berkeley, and collaborators Geoff Gilbert, School of Law, University of Essex, Jane McAdam. Faculty of Law, University of New South Wales, and Guy Goodwin-Gill, Senior Research Fellow, All Souls College, University of Oxford. The title of the comparative research project is "War Crimes and Refugee Status."

Foreword

On 1 and 2 May 2008, at York University, some magic happened at the Research Workshop on Critical Issues in International Refugee Law. The participants left with brains buzzing with ideas and stimulation, better informed, and with a sense of challenge for further inquiry. But we also left with a feeling of inspiration.

In the two days of intense discussion there was a wonderful sense of engagement and uplift with a group all focused on the constructive development of this most important area of the law. These outcomes are not so common in meetings of legal discourse. How and why did it happen that way?

Clearly, the careful selection of the topics for discussion was a central element in the success of the workshop. As the papers in this collection demonstrate, the workshop program reflected some of the most challenging contemporary issues in refugee law.

We first explored the divergence between states' practices in the interpretation of the Convention and considered the question of whether uniformity in interpretation was a desirable, let alone an achievable, goal. Then, we examined the developments of protection outside and beyond the Convention grounds by reference to various forms of subsidiary or complementary protection which have been evolving to meet needs not catered for by the Convention.

On the second day, the workshop considered the effect of the spread of terrorism and, in particular, the events of 9/11 on the application of the Convention, and, especially, the consequence of these developments on the interpretation of the exclusion provisions in Article 1F of the Convention.

Then, in an undoubted highlight of the workshop, Justice Albie Sachs told his own story of being a refugee when he was engaged as an ANC freedom fighter against the apartheid regime. He related this experience, together with his other life experiences, to his work experiences as one of the original judges of the Constitutional Court of South Africa. This moving presentation explored the significant issue of the usually unspoken, and often unacknowledged, influences on the process of judicial or quasi-judicial decision making.

Finally, we addressed the emerging jurisprudence concerning economic, social and cultural claims as a basis for refugee applications and the search for a principled basis for such applications among competing approaches.

The vigorous and searching debate on these topics was largely the result of the careful selection of a small number of eminent participants from across a number of different disciples. In this respect the workshop was an unusual, if not unique, event. The workshop was designed to bring academia, the judiciary and government together in discussion.

This concept of collaboration between academics, judges, and government representatives was without doubt an inspired one. Credit must go to David Dewitt, Associate Vice-President Research (Social Sciences & Humanities) and Professor of Political Science, Centre for International & Security Studies, York University, for the focus at York University on collaboration between academics and the "outside world."

We were privileged to have Chief Justice Lutfy of the Federal Court of Canada as well as two Canadian Federal Court judges at the workshop. Judges also came from Malawi, Germany, Australia, South Africa, the UK and the United States and represented a wide cross-section of judicial opinion and approaches from both common law and civil law jurisdictions. The academic contributors also came from varied backgrounds including Japan, the UK, Australia and the United States. Participants included several senior members of the Canadian Ministry of Justice and Ministry of Foreign Affairs and International Trade. The learning contained in this collection reflects the diversity of the participants.

The exchange between participants was particularly productive because of the format of the workshop. After each key presentation a substantial time was allocated for discussion. The chair of each session managed the participants so that almost everybody made a contribution in each session. This was made possible because the number of participants was limited to around thirty, and the participants were chosen not only for their eminence in their field, but also their capacity to interact within the workshop's format.

The credit for making this happen must centrally go to James Simeon, Assistant Professor, School of Public Policy and Administration, Atkinson Faculty of Liberal and Professional Studies and Centre for Refugee Studies, York University. He was able to make York University's collaborative concept come to life as a result of his own work over the last fifteen years. This work has spanned and linked academia and the judiciary in refugee law. From 1994 to 2005 he was a Member and Coordinating Member of the Immigration and Refugee Board of Canada following a career in academia. Then from 2005 to 2006 he was the first Executive Director of the International Association of Refugee Law Judges (IARLJ). In this role he coordinated the training of refugee law decision makers and judges around the world in pursuit of the Association's main objective of providing a common understanding of refugee law. He was responsible for extending the work of the Association into Africa and establishing the African Chapter. As Executive Director, James met many of the judges who ultimately were invited to participate in the workshop. In his present role at York University he has been able to connect the world of judges and the world of academics in refugee law.

The contributions included in this collection form a body of work that will make a significant contribution to current thinking on issues related to refugee law. It is an honour and a thrill to be part of this very special collaboration. I hope those who read this book will not only benefit from the high quality of the contributions, but will share in the excitement of the collaboration which occurred at the workshop.

Justice Tony North
Federal Court of Australia
Immediate Past President, IARLJ
President, IARLJ, 2005–2009

Acknowledgements

This book would not have been possible without the dedicated effort, support, and encouragement of many different people at various phases of this project as well as our broader research endeavour, the Research Workshop on Critical Issues in International Refugee Law, upon which this book rests. First and foremost, I should like to thank each of the contributors for agreeing to have their work published in this collection. Every one of them made a significant contribution to the success of our Research Workshop on Critical Issues in International Refugee Law that was held at York University on May 1 and 2, 2008. (For a complete description and other details on our research workshop we invite you to visit our Critical Issues in International Refugee Law (CIIRL) website at www.yorku.ca/ciirl/.) This exciting and stimulating research workshop featured some of the world's leading jurists, academics and government officials in the field of international refugee law. All of the contributors' works published in this book owe their genesis to our 2008 Research Workshop on Critical Issues in International Refugee Law held at York University.

Our inaugural Research Workshop on Critical Issues in International Refugee Law was the result of the combined and collective efforts of a number of faculty, staff and graduate and undergraduate students at York University. Most of these individuals served on our Research Workshop Organizing Committee. First among this dedicated group of professional scholars and academics and research administrators were Professor Nergis Canefe, Michele Millard, the Coordinator of the Centre for Refugee Studies, Professor Obiora Okafor, and Professor Sasha Baglay. Subsequently, Sarah Whitaker, Senior Research Officer, and later still, Elizabeth Monier-Williams,

Research Communications Officer, both from the Office of the Vice-President Research and Innovation, joined this group. Robert Denault, then Learning Technology Specialist with the Office of Computing Technology and e-Learning Services (OCTES), Atkinson Faculty of Liberal and Professional Studies, also joined our group and took on the important task of designing and engineering our Research Workshop website. Others joined our Research Workshop Organizing Committee, as required, such as Amy April, Manager, University Events and Visitor Relations, Office of University Events and Community Relations, York University.

A number of highly energetic and devoted graduate students also made a significant and essential contribution to our Research Workshop Organizing Committee and to the overall success of our Research Workshop. Graduate Assistants Karen Vanderwillik and Hicham Safieddine, both Masters students in the Department of Political Science, Faculty of Arts, at the time, and Helen Wong, a particularly gifted organizer in the Masters of Public Policy, Administration and Law (MPPAL) programme in the School of Public Policy and Administration, Atkinson Faculty of Liberal and Professional Studies, and Irene Connie Tumwebaze, who was a Masters of Environmental Studies student at the time, all put in an exceptional effort to ensure that our Research Workshop ran smoothly and without any logistical snags.

A number of Osgoode Hall Law School students were also hired under the RAY [Research at York] Job Program to assist us with note taking during the Research Workshop as well as supporting the work of our academic review commentators during and after the Research Workshop. We are all very grateful for the important contribution that the Osgoode Hall Law School students, Neha Chugh, Grace Wang and Tara Raissi, made to the success of our Research Workshop. Neha Chugh, in particular, stood out in terms of her exceptional service on our Research Workshop Organizing Committee and during the Research Workshop.

The Research Workshop on Critical Issues in International Refugee Law would not have been possible without the strong support of a number of senior officials at York University. These included the following individuals who immediately gave their support for our research workshop: Susan McGrath, Director of the Centre of

Refugee Studies; Rhonda Lenton, who was the Dean of the Atkinson Faculty of Liberal and Professional Studies at the time and is now the Associate Vice-President Academic; Robert Drummond, who was the last Dean of the Faculty of Arts and is now a University Professor in the Department of Political Science, Faculty of Liberal Arts and Professional Studies; Rodney Webb, Associate Vice-President Academic at the time of the Research Workshop; Ian Greene, then Master of McLaughlin College and the founding Director of the MPPAL Programme; Craig Scott, Faculty of Law, Osgoode Hall Law School and the Director of the Nathanson Centre on Transnational Human Rights, Crime and Security; and, David Dewitt, Associate Vice-President Research and Innovation, Social Sciences and Humanities.

We also received the full support of the Director of my School of Public Policy and Administration, Joanne Magee, as well as the Dean of Osgoode Hall Law School, at the time, Patrick Monahan, and who is now the Vice-President Academic and Provost of York University, for our Research Workshop. In addition, Ros Woodhouse, Director, Centre for Support of Teaching (CST), was generous in providing her time and advice on how the Research Workshop might be structured in order to maximize the dialogue and discussion among participants and the generation of new innovative ideas in international refugee law from our research workshop deliberations.

I should like to acknowledge the exceptional support and assistance of Professor Kelly Thomson, then Associate Dean, Research, Atkinson Faculty of Liberal and Professional Studies, and Kay Li, Research Officer, then with the Office of the Dean, Atkinson Faculty of Liberal and Professional Studies. I should also like to thank both of them for playing such an important role at our Pre-Research Workshop meeting that helped to launch several broader international collaborate comparative research projects that came out of our Research Workshop.

I should also like to thank the President and Vice-Chancellor of York University, Mamhoud Shoukri, for taking the time to prepare a video address that was presented to open our Research Workshop on Critical Issues in International Refugee Law and is posted on our CIIRL research workshop website. Although President Shoukri was unable to be with us in person, his warm greetings, strong support and encouragement were felt for the full duration of our two-day Research Workshop.

In addition, a number of renowned and extraordinarily talented legal scholars in the field international refugee law, from outside York University, and whose contributions are found within the chapters in this collection, made superb contributions to our Research Workshop on Critical Issues in International Refugee Law. I must first extend my special thanks to Professor Jane McAdam, Faculty of Law, University of New South Wales, for her immediate endorsement for the idea of holding our Research Workshop and for her enthusiastic support and advice throughout the planning and organizing of our Research Workshop and, of course, for her contribution for this volume. I must also extend my heartfelt thanks to Professor Guy Goodwin-Gill, Senior Research Fellow, All Souls College, University of Oxford, for kindly agreeing to present the official opening address at our research workshop and for his guidance and advice on how our Research Workshop in Critical Issues in International Refugee Law could, in fact, be realized. We are extremely grateful that Professor Goodwin-Gill was not only able to deliver his official opening address, that helped to set the overall tone for our research workshop, but for also participating in the discussions for the full duration of our Research Workshop and our Post-Research Workshop meeting. Without Professor Goodwin-Gill's presence the Research Workshop would not have achieved the same measure of success.

I had the very good fortune to meet Professors Kate Jastram and Geoff Gilbert at the International Institute of Humanitarian Law (IIHL) in Sanremo, Italy, in the fall of 2007 at the course that they co-taught on "Refugee Law and Human Rights." No finer pair of instructors has ever presented a course of this nature that is geared specifically for working professionals in these highly specialized fields of public international law. The participants at this IIHL and UNHCR jointly sponsored course, included: national governmental officials, intergovernmental officials, NGO representatives, academics, refugee law practitioners and judges. By the end of the course not only did I, and the rest of the course participants, have an chance to get to know both Professors Jastram and Gilbert, but I had the opportunity to ask whether they would be willing to participate in our Research Workshop on Critical Issues in International Refugee

Law. I was most grateful and pleased, of course, that they both agreed to do so.

I should also like to acknowledge that I relied heavily on Professor Jastram's advice on how the Research Workshop should be organized, structured and operated. I am most happy to state that following our Research Workshop, Professor Jastram and I were co-applicants on a major international collaborative comparative research project entitled, "War Crimes and Refugee Status," that was awarded funding from the International Opportunities Fund (IOF) of the Social Science and Humanities Research Council of Canada (SSHRC). I am also pleased to note that Professors Guy Goodwin-Gill, Geoff Gilbert, and Jane McAdam are also our collaborators on this international collaborative research project.

A number of other gifted and world renowned legal scholars in the field of international refugee law also served as academic review commentators and also provided their advice and guidance throughout the planning and preparations for our research workshop. Professor Obiora Okafor, Osgoode Hall Law School, served as the academic review commentator for our first session that featured Professor Guy Goodwin-Gill's official opening remarks and Chief Justice Allan Lutfy's, Federal Court (Canada), judicial commentary. Professor Elspeth Guild, Radboud University, Nijmegen, The Netherlands, and Partner, Kingsley Napley, London, served as the academic review commentator for the second session that featured Professor Jane McAdam's academic paper and Justice Professor Harald Dorig's, Vice-President, Senate for Asylum and Migration Law, Federal Administrative Court, Republic of Germany, and Justice Caroline Layden-Stevenson's, Federal Court (Canada), judicial commentaries. Professor Audrey Macklin, Faculty of Law, University of Toronto, was the academic review commentator for Professor Geoff Gilbert's third session academic paper and Justice Geoffrey Care's, now retired and formerly the Chairman of the United Kingdom's Immigration Appeal Tribunal, and High Court Justice in Zambia, and the founding President of the International Association of Refugee Law Judges (IARLJ), judicial commentary. Professor Macklin also generously provided her time and advice on how our Research Workshop should be organized and funded. And, finally, Professor Sharryn Aiken, Faculty of Law, Queen's University,

Kingston, Ontario, Canada, served as the academic review commentator for the fourth session, where Professor Kate Jastram presented her academic paper and three judges provided their commentaries on her paper. The judicial commentators were Juan Osuna, then Acting Chairman of the United States Board of Immigration Appeal (BIA), US Department of Justice, Justice Esme Chombo, High Court of Malawi, and Justice Anne Mactavish, Federal Court (Canada).

We were very fortunate in having a number of the world's leading high court and superior court jurists at our research workshop. First among these was Justice Tony North, now immediate-past President of the International Association of Refugee Law Judges, who kindly agreed to serve as the chair of our Research Workshop. Indeed, Justice North was one of the first persons that I approached with the idea for the Research Workshop and I was most thankful and appreciative that he readily agreed to lend his support to this scholarly endeavour and, despite an extremely busy schedule, to chair our research workshop. In addition, Chief Justice Allan Lutfy and Justice Professor Harald Dorig not only served as judicial commentators at our research workshop, but took on the additional task of chairing one of the four sessions at our research workshop. Another outstanding world renowned jurist presented the keynote address at our research workshop, Justice Albie Sachs, Constitutional Court, Republic of South Africa. Justice Albie Sachs presented an incredibly moving keynote address at our research workshop. We are most grateful that he agreed to present the substance of the remarks of his keynote address at our research workshop in our collection for this volume.

A number of other talented and gifted academics, government officials and NGO representatives participated in our research workshop, including: Professor Osamu Arakaki, Department of Law, Shigakukan University, Japan; Jospeh Rikhof, Senior Counsel, Crimes Against Humanity and War Crimes Section, Ministry of Justice, Government of Canada and Adjunct Professor, Faculty of Law, University of Ottawa; Jessie Thomson, Senior Advisor, Humanitarian Affairs and Disaster Response Group, Ministry of Foreign Affairs and International Trade, Government of Canada; Professor Robert Latham, Director, Centre for International and Security Studies, York University; and, Susan Davis, Executive Vice-President, Canadian Council for Israel and Jewish Advocacy (CIJA).

Our research workshop was generously supported financially by not only internal sources of funding at York University, but also a number of external sources of funding such as the Canadian International Development Agency (CIDA), the Canadian Department of Justice, the Law Foundation Ontario (LFO), SSHRC, the Consul General of The Netherlands in Toronto, and the Japan Foundation Toronto. Without their financial support our Research Workshop and this book would not have been possible.

It was a distinct honour and pleasure to work with so many outstanding and accomplished individuals on the publication of this volume, which was the direct outcome of our highly successful Research Workshop on Critical Issues in International Refugee Law. It was also deeply fulfilling, as well as inspiring, to have the participants at our research workshop express their willingness to continue to collaborate on ongoing international and comparative research projects on international refugee law. Indeed, a number of new international collaborative research projects have come out of our research workshop and are currently underway. There are also plans to hold future Research Workshops on Critical Issues in International Refugee Law, likely on a biennial, basis on the most pressing legal issues and concerns confronting international refugee law today.

Finally, I would be remiss if I did not also acknowledge the contribution of the staff at Cambridge University Press for their support and assistance on this publication. In this regard, I should like to extend our special thanks to Finola O'Sullivan, Editorial Director, Law, Richard Woodham, Assistant Editor, Law, and Brenda Burke, Senior Publishing Assistant, Law, Cambridge University Press. I should especially like to thank Finola O'Sullivan who expressed an interest in this project from the outset and who was particularly helpful in dealing with various issues that arose at different points throughout the stages of the development of the full manuscript for this publication.

Introduction: the research workshop on critical issues in international refugee law and strategies towards interpretative harmony

James C. Simeon

I INTRODUCTION

It is perhaps trite to note that one of the most pressing humanitarian issues of our time is the plight of those who seek asylum from severe human rights abuse amounting to persecution. The latest annual report of the United Nations High Commissioner for Refugees (UNHCR) indicates that there are 42 million people who are uprooted in the world today.[1] Amongst this staggering total of "people of concern" to the UNHCR are some 15.2 million refugees including 872,000 asylum seekers with pending cases.[2] The UNHCR further estimates that in 2008 some 839,000 individual applications were submitted for refugee status and that 9 percent of those claims were made at UNHCR offices.[3]

It is worth noting that the number of asylum seekers making individual claims for refugee status in 2008 rose for a second year in row, up by 28 percent, and that the Republic of South Africa was the largest single recipient of individual refugee status claims estimated at the incredible number of some 207,000 applications. The United

[1] UNHCR, *2008 Global Trends: Refugees, Asylum seekers, Returnees, Internally Displaced and Stateless Persons*. 16 June 2009, p. 2, "2008 in Review – Statistics at a Glance," www.unhcr.org/4a375c426.pdf. (accessed August 10, 2009) UNHCR, "UNHCR annual report shows 42 million people uprooted worldwide," Press Release June 16, 2009, www.unhcr.org/cgi-bin/texis/vtx/search?page=search&docid=4a2fd52412d&query=42 Million Uprooted#hit2. (accessed August 10, 2009).

[2] *Ibid.* Of the 15.2 million refugees, 10.5 million fall under the UNHCR's mandate and some 4.7 million Palestinian refugees are the responsibility of the United Nations Relief and Works Agency for Palestine Refugees in the Near East (UNRWA).

[3] *Ibid.*

States of America came in a distant second, with 49,600 refugee status claims, a mere one-quarter of the number that were received by South Africa. France, with 35,400 claims, and Sudan, with 35,100 claims, came in at third and fourth respectively.[4] It is also interesting to point out that the Federal Republic of Germany was the only country in the Global North to be listed as a major refugee-hosting country in 2008 with 582,700 refugees.[5] The number of refugees in the world today is truly astounding[6] as are the challenges for those who are seeking to address the plight of all persons who are fleeing severe affronts to their most fundamental human rights and dignity as human beings.

It was within this disturbing global reality and background that a Research Workshop on Critical Issues in International Refugee Law was conceived and held at York University, Toronto, Canada, on May 1 and 2, 2008. The research workshop was premised on the notion that refugee law decision-makers and, in particular, judges at the appellate levels are being confronted with ever more sensitive and complex legal issues in refugee law, whether at the national, regional or international level. In short, judges, irrespective of their jurisdiction, are now faced with a broad range of difficult and problematic legal issues in asylum law. For instance, security considerations have reached unprecedented levels since the horrific events of September 11, 2001 and have had a profound impact on the number of new asylum applications received by countries in the Global North. It has been noted that the "securitization" of the asylum systems across industrialized states has had a significant affect on the application and interpretation of the *1951 Convention* and *1967 Protocol relating to the Status of Refugees*.[7] Given the overriding emphasis on security and

4 UNHCR, "UNHCR annual report shows 42 million people uprooted worldwide," Press Release June 16, 2009, www.unhcr.org/cgi-bin/texis/vtx/search?page=search&docid=4a2fd52412d&query=42MillionUprooted#hit2. (accessed August 10, 2009).

5 *Ibid.* The others listed by the UNHCR are Pakistan (1.8 million); Syria (1.1 million); Iran (980,000); Jordan (500,400); Chad (330,500); Tanzania (321,900); and Kenya (320,600).

6 Gil Loescher, writing in the early 1990s, observed that:"Over the past decade and a half, the number of refugees in the world has increased alarmingly. The total rose from 2.8 million in 1976 to 8.2 million in 1980 to nearly 18 million at the end of 1992. It is likely that the number will exceed 20 million during this decade. In addition, at least another 20 million people are displaced inside their own country." *Beyond Charity: International Cooperation and the Global Refugee Crisis.* (Oxford University Press, 1993), p. 5.

7 *Convention relating to the Status of Refugees,* Geneva, 28 July 1951, in force 22 April 1954, 1989 UNTS 137 and the *Protocol relating to the Status of Refugees*, New York, 31 January 1967, in force 4 October 1967, 19 UNTS 6223, 6257.

the concomitant tightening and the stricter enforcement of border controls, further limiting the access to asylum, states parties, it has been argued, have also adopted a more liberal application and interpretation of Article 1F, the exclusion clauses, of the *1951 Convention* and *1967 Protocol*.[8] Moreover, further developments in international law have raised the possibility, if not created a positive obligation, for state parties to the *1951 Convention* and/or *1967 Protocol* and the international community to prosecute those who have committed international crimes.[9] In addition, with a number of jurisdictions consolidating Convention refugee status with complementary or subsidiary forms of international protection, this has raised a number of questions and concerns regarding overlapping and competing forms of international protection, evidentiary burdens, and the standards of proof for those who are fleeing serious human rights violations.[10] Furthermore, serious violations of economic, social and cultural rights have increasingly formed the bases for those seeking international protection. These types of claims for Convention refugee status have raised legal issues regarding what, if any, infringement on a person's right to health services, education, to practise their profession or to earn a livelihood, or to live in a reasonably safe and a toxic-free environment may form the basis of a claim to international protection.[11] These examples illustrate the growing complexity and the current challenges facing asylum and refugee status adjudicators and, especially, high court and superior court judges, as they address

[8] See Geoff Gilbert's chapter in this volume and James C. Simeon: "Exclusion Under Article 1F(a) of the 1951 Convention in Canada," *International Journal of Refugee Law*, 21 (2) (July 2009), 194–195.

[9] See the *Report of the International Criminal Court to the United Nations for 2007/2008*, A/63/323, 22 August 2008, 63th Session of the United Nations General Assemby. www.icc-cpi.int/NR/rdonlyres/60963BCD-D0D7–4DA3-B8CA-BB80EDD49C70/278593/ICCA63323En.pdf. (accessed September 10, 2009). Matthew Smith, "The Relevance of the Work of the International Criminal Court to Refugee Status Determination," *International Journal of Refugee Law*, 20 (1) (2008), 166–185. Jelena Pejic,"Article 1F(a): The Notion of International Crimes," *International Journal of Refugee Law, Special Supplementary Issue* 12 (1) (2000), 11–45.

[10] Jane McAdam, "Convention Refugee Status and Subsidiary Protection Working Party, First Report," in James C. Simeon (ed.) *Forced Migration and the Advancement of International Protection*, 7th World Conference, November 6–9, 2006, International Association of Refugee Law Judges, (MultiCopy, Haarlem, 2008), pp. 225–237.

[11] For a detailed study of these issues see Michelle Foster, *International Refugee Law and Socio-Economic Rights: Refuge from Deprivation* (Cambridge University Press, 2007). See also Kate Jastram's chapter in this volume.

the legal and evidentiary issues in the refugee status and asylum cases that they hear on a daily basis.

Accordingly, the research workshop sought to bring together a number of leading high court and superior court judges, academics, senior government officials, and graduate and undergraduate students to address a limited number of "critical" legal issues in international refugee law.[12] One of the primary objectives of the research workshop was not only to explore and clarify, from a variety of theoretical and conceptual perspectives, a number of critical issues in international refugee law but also to identify the key points or areas of international refugee law that require further development and/or research.[13]

This present volume is a further product of the Research Workshop on Critical Issues in International Refugee Law. It not only consists of the substantially revised academic papers that were presented at the research workshop but also a number of new contributions that were not presented at the research workshop.[14]

1.1 What are the "critical issues" in international refugee law?

Among the many pressing legal issues and concerns in the field of international refugee law today, which of these can be identified as being the "critical issues?" The phrase "critical issues" can be broken

[12] For a complete overview of the Research Workshop on Critical Issues in International Refugee Law held at York University in Toronto, Canada, on May 1 and 2, 2008, see the Critical Issues in International Refugee Law (CIIRL) website at www.yorku.ca/ciirl/index.html.

[13] For a thorough review of the legal issues addressed in the Research Workshop on Critical Issues in International Refugee Law see James C. Simeon, "Research Workshop on Critical Issues in International Refugee Law, May 1 and 2, 2008, York University," *Refuge: Canadian Periodical on Refugees*, vol. 25, Issue 2, 2008, pp. 202–11.

[14] Guy Goodwin-Gill's paper at the research workshop, "The One, True Way: National Courts, Refugee Law and the Interpretation of Treaties," is not included, unfortunately, in this collection but is available in Guy Goodwin-Gill and Hélène Lambert (eds.), *The Limits of Transnational Law: Refugee Law, Policy Harmonization and Judicial Dialogue in the European Union*, (Cambridge University Press, 2010). Elspeth Guild's and Nergis Canefe's contributions to the collection were not delivered at the research workshop although they both played significant roles at the research workshop as well as the pre- and post-research workshop meetings that were held to discuss the possibility of developing wider ongoing international collaborative research projects. This introductory chapter, of course, was not presented at the research workshop and is also an original contribution to this volume.

down in to its two principal components and meanings; that is to say, *critical* in the sense of being, of course, decisive or crucial,[15] and *issue* in the sense of a "point in question, important subject of debate or litigation."[16] What are then the decisive or crucial subjects of debate or litigation within the field of international refugee law today?

The method that was used to determine these "critical issues" was, in essence, a process of informal informed discussion and consensus among a wide group of leading jurists and academics in the field of international refugee law. Canvassing a wide group of persons working directly in the field, including, those who participated in the research workshop, led to the identification of four legal issues and concerns that formed the basis for the four sessions that were held at the research workshop. The "critical issues" that emerged from this process were: the role of national courts in the interpretation and application of international refugee law, and specifically the *1951 Convention* and its *1967 Protocol*; the standard of proof in complementary protection cases in Europe and North America; the manner in which states have implemented more restrictive measures on refugees following 9/11, particularly, with respect to Articles 1F and 33.2, and the response of national courts and human rights treaty bodies; and, economic harm as a basis for refugee protection in five common law jurisdictions: Australia, New Zealand, Canada, the United States, and the United Kingdom.

The four "critical issues" in international refugee law identified were in large part a reflection of those who participated in the research workshop. Conspicuously absent from these proceedings were representatives from the UNHCR. This was neither deliberate nor by design but rather due to the unavailability of UNHCR officials to be able to attend and to participate in the research workshop. Presumably, if representatives of the UNHCR and, indeed, if other noted academics and jurists in the field, who were invited, had been able to participate in the deliberations at the research workshop, the list of "critical issues" examined, as well as the outcomes of the research workshop itself, may have been substantially different. However, from the very outset it was decided that a highly interactive

15 Della Thompson (ed.), *The Oxford Dictionary of Current English* 2nd edn, (University of Oxford, 1992), p. 200.

16 *Ibid.*, pp. 470–471.

research workshop would be best suited for this type of international gathering of leading academics and high court and superior court jurists rather than a symposium or conference. Accordingly, the number of research workshop participants was limited to ensure that everyone in attendance would have a full opportunity to participate in each of the sessions. It was assumed that a small group of participants would allow for a greater discussion and exchange of views on the legal issues under deliberation. Hence, the number of participants was held to about thirty people.[17]

Nevertheless, the research workshop organizers were satisfied that an authoritative list of "critical issues" confronting international refugee law today had been identified and that the format of the research workshop was particularly well suited for eliciting a fruitful dialogue and exchange on the substantive national refugee law and international refugee law issues under consideration.

1.2 Bridging the theorist/researcher – jurist/ practitioner divide

The structure and format of the Research Workshop on Critical Issues in International Refugee Law was unique and innovative. Each session of the research workshop was structured on the following basis. A leading academic in the field of international refugee law presented an academic paper outlining in some detail the legal issues on a substantive area of concern. This was followed by one or more judicial commentary or commentaries by leading senior jurists on the academic paper presented. Immediately following the academic and judicial exchange there was a round-table discussion on the legal issues raised in the academic paper and the judicial commentaries on the substantive legal issues under examination.

Each session concluded with an academic legal commentator's remarks on the academic-judicial exchange and the round-table discussion for that session. The role of the academic legal commentator was to highlight the key points of convergence and divergence that arose from the academic theorist-researcher and jurist-practitioner

[17] In fact, it was extremely difficult to keep the number of participants to thirty people and in the end, the number of persons who participated actually exceeded forty people over the two days of the research workshop.

exchange and the subsequent round-table discussions. The academic legal commentators were also asked to identify the most promising areas of further research that might help to resolve any obvious impasse or diverging and/or opposing views or approaches on the legal issues under examination during the session.

In the opinion of the organizers and participants, this structure for each of the sessions of the research workshop was effective in stimulating a thorough review, dialogue and debate on the substantive legal issues under examination for each session. This sentiment was expressed by the participants to the research workshop organizers informally during the research workshop or in their responses to the evaluation forms that were provided to the organizers at the end of each day of the research workshop.[18]

The structure and format of the research workshop helped to bring together the oft times opposing perspectives of the researcher and decision-maker in the examination of the substantive national refugee law and international refugee law issues under consideration. The perspective of the practicing or working jurist, who has to manage a heavy and, typically, a broad ranging and difficult case load, is tempered by the specialized knowledge and experience of having to deal with the practical realities of conducting refugee hearings and having to address "real life" situations within the hearing room and in the law, while, at the same time, having to decide the legal issues and the merits of the applications for asylum before them. On the other hand, the perspective of the researcher is premised on theoretical and conceptual assumptions, data collection and analysis, and logical and evidence based conclusions. Frequently, this is based on assumptions of how things work, or at least ought to work, in practice. Accordingly, there can often be a wide gulf between how things are intended to be and how things actually are, in short, the difference between theory and practice. Hence, the assumptions of the theorist-researcher may be very different from the experience of the jurist-practitioner.

Accordingly, the design of the research workshop was intended to diminish, if not overcome, this divide between the theorist-researcher

[18] Helen Wong (Legal Research Assistant), "Critical Issues in International Refugee Law, Research Workshop Evaluation Results Summary," (Research Workshop on Critical Issues in International Refugee Law, York University, Toronto, Canada, May 26, 2008).

and the jurist-practitioner or, more simply, as noted above, the gap between theory and practice. It was also anticipated that by bringing together distinguished legal academics and jurists in the field, in this particular structural setting or format, at the research workshop that it could lead participants to a fuller and deeper appreciation and understanding of the legal issues under examination during each of the four research workshop sessions. It was also hoped that this, in turn, could lead possibly to greater insights into the legal issues under consideration while, at the same time, stimulating the emergence and development of viable solutions as well as avenues for further constructive research on the legal issues and concerns under examination. The research workshop sought to generate new ideas for the resolution of the legal issues presently confronting international refugee law.

2 THE RESEARCH WORKSHOP ACADEMIC PAPERS, JUDICIAL RESPONSE AND ROUND-TABLE DISCUSSIONS

2.1 Panel Session 1: "[A]nd there can only be one true meaning."Adan [2001] 2 AC 477, p. 517.

The official opening address of the 2008 Research Workshop on Critical Issues in International Refugee Law was presented by perhaps the world's foremost authority in international refugee law, Professor Guy Goodwin-Gill, Senior Research Fellow, All Souls College, University of Oxford. The title of Professor Goodwin-Gill's opening address was the "The One, True Way: National Courts, Refugee Law and the Interpretation of Treatises." The judicial commentary for Professor Goodwin-Gill's opening address was provided by the Honourable Allan Lutfy, Chief Justice of the Federal Court (Canada).

In essence, Professor Goodwin-Gill argued that there could only be but one "critical issue" in international refugee law and that is the "progressive development" of the *1951 Convention* and *1967 Protocol.* Professor Goodwin-Gill concluded his opening address by arguing that the international refugee regime is premised on individual state responsibility, with the national courts serving on the front lines and playing an important formative role in the application and interpretation of the *1951 Convention*. Professor Goodwin-Gill asserted:

> The bottom line, though, is that I do not believe in uniformity. I believe in consistency with principle, and that the 1951 Convention, its object and purpose, and good faith provide the sufficient principled basis for protecting new categories of refugees.
>
> And, I believe, that the lack of uniformity is simply the price we pay for progressive development, and *that* is the one, true way.[19]

Chief Justice Allan Lutfy pointed out that from a judicial point of view in Canada the "critical issues" in international refugee law are return to a substantial risk of torture, including, diplomatic assurances and/or memoranda of understanding and the Safe Third Country Agreement with the United States. Chief Justice Lutfy noted that on the issue of the substantial risk of torture the Canadian courts are being informed by their judicial colleagues in the European courts. There is the further matter of diplomatic assurances and/or memoranda of understanding between first and third countries concerning returning a person to a risk of torture. In this regard, there is also the European Court of Human Rights decision in *Saadi*[20] that deals with the risk of keeping the person within a state's borders balanced against the risk of returning the person back to their country of nationality or country of former habitual residence where they could be possibly tortured.

As noted, a further critical issue in Canada is the Safe Third Country Agreement with the United States. Chief Justice Lutfy raised the question, is the Safe Third Country Agreement between Canada and the United States a question, more generally, of governance or a question of the respective Executive Branches of government making decisions? Chief Justice Lutfy further noted that Professor Goodwin-Gill stated that judicial decisions are not a source of law because they do not directly bind the state. Nonetheless, the judiciary does force the Executive Branch to move on issues. He requested that Professor Goodwin-Gill elaborate on his remarks on this point.

[19] Guy S. Goodwin-Gill, "The One, True Way," p. 15 [emphasis as in the original].

[20] *Saadi* v. *Italy*, App. No. 37201/06, European Court of Human Rights (Grand Chamber), 28 February 2008. Concurring opinion of Judge Myjer, joined by Judge Zagredbelsky.

Professor Goodwin-Gill responded by stating that in the United Kingdom, the House of Lords, in *Adan*, decided that the United Kingdom was unable, in view of its international obligations, to send a person back to a country that does not have the same degree of protection from a risk of torture as in the United Kingdom. Professor Goodwin-Gill also stated that *Saadi* is an important case because it notes, in a clear and unambiguous way, that there are no exceptions, in particular, no national security exceptions, to returning a person to a country where they face a real risk of torture.

These questions and issues were further joined in the round-table discussion that took place during this session. It was further noted that *Saadi* will prove to be an important case because it clearly outlines the absolute requirement of the state to protect a person against the possible risk of torture. The *Saadi* decision raises issues of how trustworthy are diplomatic assurances and how much monitoring is required to ensure the protection of a person upon their return to a state where there may be a possible risk of torture.

A further issue joined in the round-table discussions was the auto-interpretation of the *1951 Convention* or the role and responsibilities of national courts in the application and interpretation of the *1951 Convention*.[21] Professor Goodwin-Gill argued that there are two perspectives to auto-interpretation: (1) non-opposability; and, (2) creative discourse. The former recognizes the right of states to interpret international law and treaties for the purposes of determining their own conduct.[22] And, the latter, for the application and interpretation of Conventions "in good faith and in accordance with the ordinary meaning to be given to the terms of the treaty in their context and in the light of its object and purpose."[23] Professor Goodwin-Gill argued that auto-interpretation of the *1951 Convention* provides for the progressive development of international refugee law.

Another issue that came to the fore in the round-table discussions for this session was consistency in national and international refugee law adjudication. This was a common concern among all the participants at the research workshop and, indeed, is a critical issue that cuts across all jurisdictions that are state parties to the

[21] Guy S. Goodwin-Gill, "The One, True Way," p. 8.

[22] *Ibid.*, p. 9.

[23] *Ibid.*, p. 13, Article 31(1) 1969 *Vienna Convention on the Law of Treaties* 1155 UNTS 331.

1951 Convention and/or *1967 Protocol*, and including the UNHCR. Indeed, as one participant at the research workshop observed, it is a problem that is "cataclysmic to the EU asylum system." It was noted emphatically that the wide divergence of acceptance rates on asylum applications from the same source country is an "attack on the legitimacy of the asylum system."

Various explanations were tendered for the wide variations in asylum acceptance rates, including, the variation in the type of asylum system in place from country to country; the differences in credibility assessment; the necessity for initial judicial training and ongoing professional development; whether a situation involving armed conflict is deemed to be an international or internal armed conflict or not; whether the judiciary within a particular state is open to the judgments of the judiciaries in other states; the degree of independence the refugee law adjudicators have for rendering their decisions; and so on.

The session concluded with Professor Obiora Okafor, Osgoode Hall Law School, York University, providing his academic review commentary. He observed that there were a number of tensions, disagreements and agreements that were evident during this session. Professor Okafor noted that one of the tensions that was evident in the session was that between the independence of the refugee law decision-maker and the search for a reduction of the conceptual incoherence of decisions at the first instance. He also noted that there was general agreement amongst the participants at the research workshop that independence should not be equated with "maverick" judgements that can be a shelter for "politics." Professor Okafor also pointed to the tension between uniformity of the international refugee protection regime and its fragmentation that was highlighted in Professor Goodwin-Gill's opening address. He posed the question, "How does one balance creativity and uniformity in international refugee law?" Furthermore, he noted that there was no disagreement on the absolute bar against the use of torture. Professor Okafor also referred to the Supreme Court of Canada's judgment in *Suresh*[24] that has made the point, in *obiter* that diplomatic assurances are not to be trusted. Professor Okafor also remarked that there was general agreement among the research workshop participants that there are

[24] *Suresh* v. *Canada (Minister of Citizenship and Immigration)*, [2002] 1 SCR 3.

intimate linkages between international refugee law and other areas of international law such as international human rights law, international criminal law and international humanitarian law.

2.2 Panel session 2: International refugee protection – The 1951 Convention and subsidiary protection

Professor Jane McAdam, Associate Professor and Director of the International Law Programmes, Faculty of Law, University of New South Wales, Sydney, Australia, presented the academic paper for the second panel session. Professor McAdam's academic paper was entitled, "The Standard of Proof in Complementary Protection Cases: Comparative Approaches in North America and Europe." Professor McAdam stated that her "paper focuses on the legal impediments to obtaining subsidiary protection in the EU [European Union] that have manifested themselves in the eighteen months since the Qualification Directive entered into force for the EU Member States."[25] However, the particular issue that Professor McAdam addressed in her paper was Article 15(c) of the Qualification Directive.[26] Chapter V, Qualification for Subsidiary Protection, Article 15, of the EU Qualification Directive states as follows:

Article 15, Serious harm
Serious harm consists of:

(a) death penalty or execution; or
(b) torture or inhuman or degrading treatment or punishment of an applicant in the country of origin; or
(c) serious and individual threat to a civilian's life or person by reason of indiscriminate violence in situations of international or internal armed conflict.[27]

In essence, Professor McAdam argues that Article 15(c) is "poorly understood, inconsistently applied across the Member States, and

[25] Jane McAdam, "The Standard of Proof in Complementary Protection Cases: Comparative Approaches in North America and Europe," Research Workshop on Critical Issues in International Refugee Law, York University, May 1, 2008, p. 1.

[26] *Ibid.*

[27] Council Directive 2004/83/EC of 29 April 2004 on minimum standards for the qualification and status of third country nationals or stateless persons as refugees or as persons who otherwise need international protection and the content of the protection granted, OJ L. 304, 30/09/2004 P. 0012 – 0023, Chapter V, Article 15.http://eur-lex.europa.eu/LexUriServ/LexUriServ.do?uri=CELEX:32004L0083:EN:HTML (accessed August 17, 2009).

in some jurisdictions is the only subsidiary protection category given full consideration when a Convention claim fails."[28] Indeed, Professor McAdam states that Article 15(c) does not even function as a form of subsidiary protection.[29]

Professor McAdam points out that the EU states follow independent analyses of the meaning of Article 15(c), without regard for either the jurisprudential trends of the European Court of Human Rights or the interpretations adopted in other EU states and that this has led to a wide variation in acceptance rates from those persons who are fleeing from Iraq, Chechnya and Somalia.[30] Part of the difficulty, she notes, is that Article 15(c) has not been transposed in a uniform manner into the national law of EU states. Moreover, EU states are applying higher evidentary burdens for those who are claiming subsidiary protection under Article 15(c), than either Articles 15(a) or 15(b) or for Convention refugee claims.

Professor McAdam also points out that it appears that the words "serious and individual threat," in Article 15(c), are being interpreted as requiring a higher threshold and, consequently, a heavier burden of proof.[31] The reference to "international or internal armed conflict" is also leading to divergence in interpretation among EU states.[32] Professor McAdam states that because there is "no singular meaning of 'international or internal armed conflict' in international humanitarian law, determining whether or not one exists for the purposes of a determination under Article 15(c) imposes a further layer of analysis which is neither straightforward nor clear-cut."[33]

The standard of proof established under the Qualification Directive for Article 15 is found in Article 2(e) that states:

> "person eligible for subsidiary protection" means a third country national or a stateless person who does not qualify as a refugee but in respect of whom *substantial grounds have been shown for believing* that the person concerned, if returned to his or her country of origin, or in the case of a stateless person, to his or her country of former habitual residence, would face a real risk of suffering serious harm as defined in Article 15 ...[34]

[28] Jane McAdam, "The Standard of Proof in Complementary Protection Cases," p. 1.
[29] *Ibid.*, p. 2. [30] *Ibid.*, p. 6. [31] *Ibid.*
[32] *Ibid.*, p. 11. [33] *Ibid.*
[34] Council Directive 2004/83/EC of 29 April 2004 [emphasis added].

"Substantial grounds" has been interpreted in EU states as being the same standard of proof as the "well-founded fear" standard for Convention refugee applications, that falls below the civil standard of a "balance of probabilities."[35] In Canada the standard of proof for complementary protection claims under section 97 of the *Immigration and Refugee Protection Act* (IRPA), is the higher standard of the "balance of probabilities" or "more likely than not," that the Federal Court of Appeal has ruled is a higher standard of proof than a well-founded fear of persecution for Convention refugee status.[36] A higher standard of proof for subsidiary protection is also applied in the United States. Consequently, the standards of proof followed in Europe and in North America are generally different, with the higher standard of proof for complementary and subsidiary protection found in North America. The exception here, as Professor McAdam argues, is Article 15(c) of the Qualification Directive that de facto requires a higher standard of proof.

There were two judicial commentaries for Professor McAdam's academic paper. The first was presented by Justice Professor Harald Dorig, Vice-President of the Senate for Asylum and Migration Law, Federal Administrative Court of Germany (Bundesverwaltungsgericht), and the other was presented by Justice Caroline Layden-Stevenson, now with the Federal Court of Appeal, but who was with the Federal Court (Canada) at the time of the research workshop.

2.2.1 Justice Professor Harald Dorig's commentary

Justice Professor Dorig began by noting that the Federal Republic of Germany implemented the EU Qualification Directive in two stages, in 2005 and in 2007. He stated that the *German Residence Act 2005* implemented important elements of the Qualification Directive, particularly concerning persecution by non-state agents for the purposes of recognizing nexus to the ground of membership in a particular social group for asylum claims involving gender related persecution.[37]

[35] Jane McAdam, "The Standard of Proof in Complementary Protection Cases," p. 14.

[36] *Ibid.*, p. 17. See *Li* v. *Canada (Minister of Citizenship and Immigration)* [2003] FCJ No. 1934; 2003 FC 1514; aff'd in *Li* v. *Canada (Minister of Citizenship and Immigration)* [2005] FCJ No. 1; 2005 FCA 1, paras. 18–28.

[37] Harald Dorig, "Refugee Protection and Subsidiary Protection under the EU Directive 2004/83/EC and its transformation in Germany," Research Workshop on Critical Issues in International Refugee Law, York University, Toronto, May 2008, p. 1.

Justice Professor Dorig indicated that there are three protection categories in Europe and within German law: (1) Refugee Protection; (2) International or European Subsidiary Protection; and, (3) Additional National Subsidiary Protection.[38] He further noted that with respect to Article 15(c), the phrase "by reason of indiscriminate violence" has not been transposed in German law.[39]

Justice Professor Dorig further noted that the standard of proof for subsidiary protection is the same as for refugee protection. He noted that standard of proof in the Federal Republic of Germany is a "significant probability" of being persecuted or suffering serious harm upon return to the applicant's country of nationality.[40] Justice Professor Dorig cited the European Court of Human Right's judgment in *Salah Sheekh,* 11 January 2007, as consistent with the German law that "serious and individual threat to a civilian's life or person," as found in Article 15(c), requires that the applicant "show that you belong to a group which is persecuted generally (for example, Christians in Iraq), then you need not show anything more that 'singles you out.'"[41]

With respect to the issue of "international or internal armed conflict," Justice Professor Dorig states that these terms should be interpreted by means of international humanitarian law.[42] He made the point that it is important to keep in mind that the *1949 Geneva Conventions* and the *1977 Protocols* are intended to protect civilians within their countries of origin while Article 15(c) of the Qualification Directive is intended to protect civilians outside their countries of origin from being returned to a situation where their life or person are threatened due to international or internal armed conflict.[43] Justice Professor Dorig concluded his commentary by stating that the EU has widened subsidiary protection "remarkably" under the Qualification Directive.[44]

[38] *Ibid.*

[39] *Ibid.*, p. 3. See *German Residence Act 2005*, section 60, Prohibition of Deportation, Article 60(7), sentence 2.

[40] *Ibid.*, p. 4. This standard of proof was set by the Federal Administrative Court of Germany (Judgment of 18 July 2001 – BVerwG 1 B 71.01).

[41] *Ibid.*, p. 5.

[42] *Ibid.* Specific reference is made to the *1949 Geneva Conventions* and the *1977 Additional Protocols I and II.*

[43] *Ibid.*, p. 6. [44] *Ibid.*, p. 7.

2.2.2 Justice Caroline Layden-Stevenson's commentary

Justice Caroline Layden-Stevenson began her commentary by noting that the Federal Court (Canada) only grants about 15 to 20 percent of the leave application for judicial review that it receives on the decisions of the Immigration and Refugee Board of Canada (IRB). She also noted that there are no appeals of the decisions of the Federal Court (Canada) rulings, unless the judge hearing the judicial review certifies a legal question of general importance to the Federal Court of Appeal.

Justice Layden-Stevenson stated that under IRPA, section 97, those applicants who do not fall under the five grounds of the *1951 Convention* can seek complementary protection rather than subsidiary protection under the EU Qualification Directive. Complementary protection in Canada affords the applicant the same rights and protection, unlike the EU Qualification Directive, as those who are determined to be Convention refugees. For the applicant to succeed under section 97 of IRPA, the applicant must establish that their removal from Canada to their country of nationality or former country of habitual residence would subject them to personal injury or a risk to life or cruel and unusual treatment or punishment. The risk faced by the applicant must be personal and it cannot be one that is generally faced by others in the country.[45]

Justice Layden-Stevenson stated that initially the standard of proof for section 97, complementary protection, was the same as section 96, Convention refugee status, that is, below the civil standard of

[45] Section 97 of the Immigration and Refugee Protection Act 2001 (c. 27) states as follows:

(1) A person in need of protection is a person in Canada whose removal to their country or countries of nationality or, if they do not have a country of nationality, their country of former habitual residence, would subject them personally–
  (a) to a danger, believed on substantial grounds to exist, of torture within the meaning of Article 1 of the Convention Against Torture; or
  (b) to a risk to their life or to a risk of cruel and unusual treatment or punishment if
    (i) the person is unable or, because of that risk, unwilling to avail themself of the protection of that country,
    (ii) the risk would be faced by the person in every part of that country and is not faced generally by other individuals in or from that country,
    (iii) the risk is not inherent or incidental to lawful sanctions, unless imposed in disregard of accepted international standards, and
    (iv) the risk is not caused by the inability of that country to provide adequate health or medical care.

proof, balance of probability, or what is termed "reasonable chance (or good grounds)," "serious possibility," or "more than a mere possibility."[46] The matter went to the Federal Court of Appeal, she said, and it was determined that the standard of proof for section 97 should be the "balance of probabilities" or the "more likely than not" standard.[47] The leave to appeal the Federal Court of Appeal decision to the Supreme Court of Canada was denied.

Justice Layden-Stevenson stated that the higher standard of proof under section 97 does require a separate analysis to determine whether the applicant is a "person in need of protection." However, if the applicant is not found to be a person in need of protection or a Convention refugee, Justice Layden-Stevenson noted, that there are other alternatives available for the applicant such as an application under humanitarian and compassionate grounds.

2.2.3 The round-table discussion

During the round-table discussion for this session it was noted that international criminal law could provide a fruitful avenue for defining what constitutes "armed conflict," whether international or internal. There was some agreement on taking this general approach and applying the legal definitions and concepts that have been worked out in other branches of public international law for international refugee law and, in particular, for subsidiary protection under Article 15(c) of the Qualification Directive.

The point was made that subsidiary protection did not simply emerge with the *2004 EU Qualification Directive*. Rather, it is evident under the *1950 European Convention of Human Rights and Fundamental Freedoms*.[48] The tradition of protection of international human rights is at least as strong as protecting the rights of refugees under the *1951 Convention*.

A further issue was raised with respect to subsidiary and complementary protection and the enlargement, seemingly, of the circle of protection beyond those who meet the legal definition of Convention

[46] *Adjei* v. *M .E .I.*, [1989] 2 F.C. 680, 7 Imm. L.R. (2d) 169, 57 D.L.R. (4th) 153, 132 N.R. 24 (F.C.A.). *Ponniah* v. *M. E. I.* (1991), 13 Imm.L.R. (2d) 241, 132 N.R. 32 (F.C.A.).

[47] Jane McAdam, "The Standard of Proof in Complementary Protection Cases," p. 14.

[48] *Convention for the Protection of Human Rights and Fundamental Freedoms*, Rome, 4.XI.1950, http://conventions.coe.int/treaty/en/Treaties/Html/005.htm (accessed August 17, 2009).

refugee. However, at the same time, there is a fluctuating standard of proof for subsidiary protection. The question was asked, "Is this merely another way of confining subsidiary protection which should be available to other vulnerable persons who do not fit the definition of refugee in the *1951 Convention* and its *1967 Protocol*?"

The point was also made that out of the 20,000 to 25,000 asylum applications in Canada each year a maximum of about 250 people, if that, benefited from section 97 of IRPA. It was also noted that fewer people are receiving subsidiary protection in the Federal Republic of Germany than one would expect or might think.

2.2.4 The academic review commentator's remarks – Professor Elspeth Guild

Professor Elspeth Guild, Faculty of Law, Radboud University, The Netherlands, and Partner, Kingsley Napley, London, UK, presented the academic review commentator's remarks for this session. She said that she would focus her remarks on the three "big picture" points that were raised in this session: (1) sovereignty: international obligations versus national sovereignty; (2) the individual versus the collective; (3) the "rolling power" of the administration versus the judiciary. Professor Guild noted that these three sets of tensions are inherent in the world that we live in and how the role of law is played out on the body of individuals who are seeking asylum.

With respect to the issue of sovereignty, Professor Guild, stated, it is the Geneva Convention versus other types of protection. The point was also made that the world is becoming a more complex place to live in and to understand. On the second tension, the individual versus the collective, Professor Guild stated that, "Law likes the individual not the collective." Under EU law, the legal system becomes quite nervous when dealing with collective rights. She also observed that if the judiciary escapes national law through the interpretation of international or supranational law, the power of the administration to control sovereignty is weakened.

2.3 Panel session 3: Exclusion under Article 1F and prosecution

Professor Geoff Gilbert, School of Law and the Human Rights Centre, University of Essex, United Kingdom, delivered the academic paper for the third panel session on "Exclusion Under Article 1F and Prosecution." The title of Professor Gilbert's research workshop academic paper was "Running Scared Since 9/11: Refugees, UNHCR and the Purposive Approach to Treaty Interpretation."[49] The thesis of his paper is, as the title implies, that refugee receiving states, principally in the Global North, have implemented more restrictive measures on refugees since 9/11. Moreover, he argues that judges have applied more liberal interpretations of Articles 1F and 33.2 of the *1951 Convention* and have thereby excluded more asylum applicants since 9/11. However, this trend has not been evident, he notes, in the international human rights treaty bodies that have responded to those asylum seekers excluded from Convention refugee status by protecting their fundamental human rights.

Professor Gilbert began his presentation by noting that the United Nations Security Council linked the threat of international terrorism to those who are seeking Convention refugee status both immediately before and after 9/11. He makes specific reference to UN Security Council Resolutions 1269 (19 October 1999), Resolution 1368 (12 September 2001), Resolution 1373 (28 September 2001), and Resolution 1377 (12 November 2001).[50] He notes that it is important to emphasis that Resolution 1377 clearly states, in no uncertain terms, that:

> acts of international terrorism are contrary to the purposes and principles of the Charter of the United Nations, and that the financing, planning and preparation of as well as any other form of support for acts of international terrorism are similarly contrary to the purposes and principles of the Charter of the United Nations.[51]

This leads Professor Gilbert to argue that by the end of 2001 those seeking Convention refugee status were being seen in a completely different light. He indicates that states were now looking at asylum applicants as potential security risks and, possibly, even as security threats.[52]

[49] Geoff Gilbert, "Running Scared Since 9/11: Refugees, UNHCR, and the Purposive Approach to Treaty Interpretation," Research Workshop on Critical Issues in International Refugee Law, York University, Toronto, May 2008.

[50] *Ibid.*, pp. 1–2. [51] *Ibid.*, p. 2. [52] *Ibid.*, p. 3.

Professor Gilbert further notes that to be excluded under Article 1F(a), crimes against peace, war crimes, or crimes against humanity; (b), serious non-political crimes; or (c) guilty of acts contrary to the purposes and principles of the United Nations, only requires "serious reasons for considering." This standard of proof for Article 1F has been interpreted by the courts as not an onerous or very high standard to meet.[53] It is certainly far less than the criminal standard of proof of "beyond a reasonable doubt." Further, whereas Article 1F excludes those who are undeserving of Convention refugee status and its attendant benefits, Article 33.2 requires the state to show "reasonable grounds" that the person is a danger to the security of the country of refuge or if convicted of a particularly serious crime constitutes a danger to the community of that state.[54] Professor Gilbert further notes that following September 11, 2001, states passed new legislation that emphasized exclusion from asylum. The examples presented by Professor Gilbert in this regard include the United Kingdom, the United States, and Australia.[55]

Likewise, Professor Gilbert is also quite critical of the UNHCR for issuing its November 2001 document, "Addressing Security Concerns Without Undermining Refugee Protection," that he describes as "something of a curate's egg."[56]

The courts in the Global North, in a number of important judgments, Professor Gilbert argues, took an expansive interpretation of Articles 1F and 33.2. Specifically, he cites the New Zealand Supreme Court decision in *Zaoui*,[57] the Federal Court of Appeal of Canada decision in *Zrig*,[58] and the United Kingdom Immigration Appeal Tribunal decision in *The Secretary of State for the Home Department, re AA (Palestine)*.[59] On the other hand, Professor Gilbert points to

[53] *Ibid.*

[54] *Ibid.*, Article 33.2 reads as follows: "The benefits of the present provision [*non-refoulement*] may not, however, be claimed by a refugee who there are reasonable grounds for regarding as a danger to the security of the country in which he is, or who, having been convicted by a final judgement of a particularly serious crime, constitutes a danger to the community of that country."

[55] *Ibid.*, pp. 5–7.

[56] *Ibid.*, p. 8., *Addressing Security Concerns without Undermining Refugee Protection: UNHCR's Perspective*, UNHCR Geneva (29 November 2001).

[57] *Zaoui* [2002] UKIAT04870 HX34452–2001.

[58] *Zrig* v. *Canada (Minister of Citizenship and Immigration)* (CA) [2003] FCA 178.

[59] *The Secretary of State for the Home Department, re AA (Palestine)* [2005] UKIAT 00104 Appellant AA (Palestine).

the human rights treaty monitoring bodies as providing "a degree of protection to those excluded where they have jurisdiction."[60] In this regard, Professor Gilbert presents the Committee Against Torture's decision in *Agiza v. Sweden,*[61] and the Human Rights Committee decision in *Alzery v. Sweden.*[62] Both exemplifying situations where asylum applicants who were excluded from Convention refugee status were immediately returned to their country of nationality, Egypt, and incarcerated and who were likely tortured. In both instances, the Swedish authorities had received diplomatic assurances from the Egyptian authorities that the two men's personal and human rights would be respected fully, according to the Egyptian constitution and law.[63] Professor Gilbert observes that the adequacy of such diplomatic assurances or Memoranda of Understanding must be subject to review by a court, according to *Turkish National Extradition Case (Case No. 4, ARs 22/86)* 106 *International Law Reports*, 298 at 301.[64] This did not happen in either the case of Mr. Agiza or Mr. Alzery.

Professor Gilbert concludes his analysis by stating that judges have been "prepared to hide behind the 'plain meaning' smokescreen to limit refugee rights" and that the "only bright light shining through this gloom has been the decisions of the human rights treaty bodies."[65]

2.3.1 Justice Geoffrey Care's judicial commentary

Justice Geoffrey Care provided the judicial commentary for Professor Geoff Gilbert's academic paper by asking the pertinent question, "Is Geoff Gilbert right to suggest that anyone is running scared? If so who exactly and why – and did it start on 9/11?"[66] Justice Care points out that Professor Gilbert's survey of the legislative amendments and

[60] Geoff Gilbert, "Running Scared Since 9/11," p. 13.

[61] *Agiza* v. *Sweden*, Comm. No. 233/2003, U.N. Doc. CAT/C/34/D/233/2003(2005).

[62] *Alzery* v. *Sweden*, CCPR/C/88/D/1416/2005, 10 November 2006.

[63] Both of these cases are fully addressed in Professor Elspeth Guild's chapter in this volume, "Asymmetrical Sovereignty and the Refugee: Diplomatic Assurances and the Failure of Due Process in *Agiza* v. *Sweden* and *Alzery* v. *Sweden*."

[64] Geoff Gilbert, "Running Scared Since 9/11," p. 17, at footnote 58.

[65] *Ibid.*, p. 18.

[66] Geoffrey Care, "Commentary on the Paper by Geoff Gilbert, 'Running scared since 9/11: Refugees, UNHCR and the purposive approach to treaty interpretation,'" Research Workshop on Critical Issues in International Refugee Law, York University, Toronto, Canada, May 1–2, 2008, p. 1.

the court rulings is almost entirely drawn from the EU, USA and other Pacific Rim countries (Australia, New Zealand and Canada). In this regard, he takes issue with Professor Gilbert for not "casting [his] research more widely"[67] and, consequently, any general conclusions that could be drawn from this sampling of states would, therefore, be necessarily limited. Nonetheless, Justice Care praises Professor Gilbert's academic paper because the,

> focus [of] his approach to treaty interpretation in this manner stimulates our enquiry into the general fragility of democracy when it is perceived to be under threat and concentrates our minds on just what guarantees human rights treaties should, and do, give when under this sort of pressure.[68]

Justice Care prefaces his remarks by making two observations. The first with respect to the ineluctable relationship between disparities among, between and within states and security: the greater the disparities among, between and within states the greater the likelihood of insecurity. And, in the second, he makes the following prescient point, with respect to diplomatic assurances and Memoranda of Understanding, that is well worth repeating:

> In most states if some assurance of fair trial or absence of torture is thought to be needed, the assurance is by definition likely to be valueless. The same goes for expecting a "*rogue state*" to be able to provide a safe haven.[69]

As the founding President of the International Association of Refugee Law Judges, (IARLJ), Justice Care states that one of the principal reasons for establishing the IARLJ was the harmonization of refugee jurisprudence globally, and not just regionally, as well as to promote a common interpretation of the *1951 Convention* and knowledge of, at the very least, each country's approach to procedural matters.[70] He notes that in the case of the EU it is the European Court of Human Rights that "has to some extent been a harmonizing instrument."[71]

Justice Care notes further that, at least in the United Kingdom, the courts have played an important role in overturning the attempts of the Executive to erode the fundamental rights that underpin a democratic state. Here he points to the example of the UK Court of Appeal overturning the decision of the Special Immigration Appeal

[67] *Ibid.* [68] *Ibid.*, p. 2. [69] *Ibid.*
[70] *Ibid.*, p. 5. [71] *Ibid.*

Commission (SIAC) in *Abu Qatada*.[72] On the other hand, Justice Care takes issue with Professor Gilbert for his position in favour of an international court or tribunal as the "only sure bulwark" for the protection of human rights.[73] He notes that the European Court of Human Rights, a supranational court, thus far has refused to accept that it has jurisdiction in relation to allegations of a lack of fair trial. Citing *Maaouia v. France*,[74] Justice Care points out that the European Court of Human Rights "continues to hold that refugee status determinations are not determinations of civil rights or obligations."[75] In short, the European Court of Human Rights is opposed to applying Article 6, the fair trial provisions, of the *European Convention of Human Rights and Fundamental Freedoms*, for asylum applications, thus, implying that supranational and international courts may not be the entire answer to the steadfast protection of human rights as outlined in the international instruments.

2.3.2 The round-table discussion on exclusion under Article 1F and prosecution

During the round table on this panel session it was noted that the courts have now brought under control some of the excesses that occurred post-9/11. It was also pointed out that in Canada Article 1F(c) of the *1951 Convention* has all but been abandoned since 2001. It was further observed that there has been cross-pollination of jurisprudence across jurisdictions on Article 1F and that Canadian case law on Article 1F(a) has been cited widely in the UK and New Zealand. It was also noted that Article 1F(a) has a much more direct connection to the international legal jurisprudence.

There was also some discussion regarding the manner in which complicity and membership in or association with various organizations are construed and the manner in which organizations have

[72] *Abu Qatada* v. *Secretary of State for the Home Department* [2007] UKSIAC 15/2005 (26 February 2007), www.bailii.org/uk/cases/SIAC/2007/15_2005.html. *Omar Othman* v. *The United Kingdom* – 8139/09 [2009] ECHR 855 (26 May 2009) www.bailii.org/eu/cases/ECHR/2009/855.html. "Abu Qatada Court of Appeal ruling: time for UK to abandon deportation with assurances," Posted: 9 April 2008, amnesty.org.uk, www.amnesty.org.uk/news_details.asp?NewsID=17718.

[73] Geoffrey Care, "Commentary on the Paper by Geoff Gilbert," p. 10.

[74] *Maaouia* v. *France* – 39652/98 [2000] ECHR 455 (5 October 2000). www.bailii.org/eu/cases/ECHR/2000/455.html.

[75] Geoffrey Care, "Commentary on the Paper by Geoff Gilbert," p. 10.

been defined as terrorist organizations since 9/11. The observation was made that prior to 9/11 there was a greater willingness to distinguish between organizations that had a single brutal purpose and multi-faceted organizations. Following 9/11, the point was made that there is a far greater reluctance on the part of the judiciary to make these kinds of distinctions.

It was noted that outside Canada and The Netherlands, the use of the exclusion clauses has changed considerably following 9/11. Some of the questions that have been raised with the increased application of Article 1F, were the following: How should association with a particular group be used in cases where the issue of Article 1F is raised? If the association involves a terrorist group is mere membership sufficient for the applicant to be excluded from Convention refugee status? How should you deal with those applicants who have truly changed their ways? Or, is exclusion permanent? Another concern with respect to Articles 1F and 33.2 is what implications does exclusion have for those who are sent back to their alleged countries of nationality? If there are substantial reasons for considering that these persons will be tortured or suffer cruel and unusual treatment or punishment or the death penalty should these persons be returned to their countries of nationalty or former habitual residence?

The difference between Article 1F and Article 33.2 is that the first deals with the asylum applicant's past actions and the second deals with the asylum applicant's potential future actions. It was also noted that some jurisdictions are limiting the influence of the judiciary by limiting judicial review. For example, in the United States, the sweeping legislative changes with respect to the "material support for terrorism" provisions are so widely defined that judges have limited discretion.[76] The definition that the U.S. Congress enacted for "material support" is so broad that anyone who provided any kind of support to a terrorist group would be excluded from Convention refugee status. The sweeping statute leaves judges with little to no discretion.

[76] See *In the Matter of S-K* 24, I&N Dec. 475 (BIA 2008) Decided March 11, 2008. US Department of Justice Executive Office for Immigration Review, Board of Immigration Appeals (BIA).

2.3.3 Professor Audrey Macklin's review commentary

Professor Audrey Macklin, Faculty of Law, University of Toronto, provided the review commentary for this session and began by stating that terrorism in the post-9/11 era is the subject of at least three domains: migration law; law of war; and criminal law. She noted that all of these domains outline the scope of Article 1F. Professor Macklin observed that while there is a migration dimension to terrorism, it is not necessarily true that terrorism is a problem that migration law can resolve.

Professor Macklin also argued that refugee law is nested within migration law, the subject of which is predicated on the citizen/non-citizen distinction. The subject of human rights law, on the other hand, addresses the rights of people irrespective of their citizenship status. Consequently, there is a tension between migration law and the universality of human rights law where the distinction between the citizen and the non-citizen is irrelevant. Under human rights law, she stated, a person cannot be excluded from humanity.

Professor Macklin pointed out that one of the features of terrorism, as it is defined in the criminal law in some jurisdictions, is how to distinguish terrorism from ordinary crime. An element of risk prevention is reflected, Professor Macklin observed, in the efforts to deal with the root causes of terrorism at a much earlier stage than other crimes.

Professor Macklin also underscored that the significance of the fair trial provisions under the *European Convention of Human Rights and Fundamental Freedoms*. She further stated that one way of understanding the issues related to the exclusion clauses is to note that a human rights perspective is being superimposed on migration law and criminal law and that all have a direct bearing on exclusion issues.

2.4 Panel session 4: Economic, Social and cultural rights as grounds for a claim for refugee status

Professor Kate Jastram, Berkeley Law, University of California at Berkeley, presented the academic paper for this session. Professor Jastram began by stating that socio-economic persecution is a problematic area of international refugee law. She stated that people can be persecuted when they are deprived of their livelihood or when they are denied employment commensurate with their qualifications. She also noted that economic harm is problematic for at least the following four reasons: (1) economic disadvantage or harm can be part of other types of harm that can cumulatively amount to persecution; (2) economic refugees can look like economic migrants and, thus, evidence of economic disadvantage can serve to undermine their claim rather than to support it; (3) some human rights approaches are skewed in favour of civil and political rights and, thus, view violations of economic, social or cultural rights as less worthy of refugee protection; (4) economic, social and cultural rights law is underdeveloped. Professor Jastram also pointed out that the vagueness of such concepts as "progressive realization," that is central to the interpretation of the *International Convention on Economic, Social and Cultural Rights,* has led to the belief that socio-economic rights are merely aspirational. She noted further that there has been a great deal of work done on justiciability issues in this field of international law and, in particular, states parties' obligations with respect to socio-economic rights.

Professor Jastram observed that there are generally two approaches to dealing with refugee status claims involving economic harm and they tend to result in similar outcomes. The first approach is to use the same standard of proof that is used for any claim for refugee status, that is, a reasonable chance of suffering a sustained or systemic violation of core human rights. The second approach is to use a higher standard of proof for refugee claims based on economic harm, that is, the hardship or denial of core human rights must affect the applicant's ability to subsist. Interestingly, despite the different standards of proof, the outcomes tend to be the same. Professor Jastram argues that this is so because, irrespective of the approach taken, the de facto standard of proof applied to refugee claims based on economic harm tends to be rigorous. Hence, notwithstanding the approach adopted, the applicant would have to show a complete inability to earn a livelihood to have their claim to refugee status succeed.

Professor Jastram made the salient point that there is no distinction on the basis of the nature of the persecutory treatment or the types of harm in the *1951 Convention* or *1967 Protocol*. Yet, what has emerged in practice is a clear distinction between socio-economic harm and other types of harm or persecutory treatment. This may stem from a cautionary and restrictive approach that is taken by the judiciary and officials in some states to the application and interpretation of the *1951 Convention* and its *1967 Protocol*. It has been argued that with the international refugee protection regime presently in such a weakened state that Convention refugee status should be reserved only for the most severe cases of persecution. Accordingly, a higher standard of proof should be used for the determination of Convention refugee status when socio-economic forms of human rights are being violated. Professor Jastram indicates that this type of approach is further justified by the argument that those who are facing these types of human rights abuses in their countries of nationality should stay in their countries to bring about meaningful reforms to end these forms of human rights violations and harm.

Professor Jastram also draws on the work of Michelle Foster, in her book, *International Refugee Law and Socio-Economic Rights: Refuge from Deprivation*,[77] who calls for consistency between human rights law and refugee law and the need to address the divergences in these two areas of the law. Professor Jastram notes that Michelle Foster advocates that refugee law judges should use a "minimum core obligation" approach in deciding what level of violation of socio-economic human rights constitutes persecutory treatment for determining Convention refugee status.[78] This requires judges to make a distinction between core and periphery human rights. However, this approach to the determination of refugee status and asylum claims based on socio-economic human rights violations is not, Professor Jastram notes, without its critics.

Those who are critical of adopting the "minimum core obligation" approach to refugee status determination point out that the human rights enunciated in the international conventions and covenants are outlined in vague and indeterminate ways. It is also argued that human rights law is expanding and diversifying, but that this also carries its own risk of fragmented norms and authorities. The

[77] Michelle Foster, *International Refugee Law and Socio-Economic Rights: Refuge from Deprivation* (Cambridge University Press, 2007).

[78] Kate Jastram, "Economic Harm as a Basis for Refugee Status," Research Workshop on Critical Issues in International Refugee Law, York University, Toronto, Canada, May 1–2, 2008, p. 15.

point was also made that consistency in refugee status and asylum adjudication is difficult to achieve when judges are applying human rights law without understanding fully the norms and the authorities on which these are based. Professor Jastram stated that this helps to explain why this is such a vexing and confusing area for not only refugee status and asylum applicants but for refugee law adjudicators and judges as well.

2.4.1 The judicial commentary on economic, social and cultural rights' violations as a basis for refugee status

Three judicial commentaries were presented on Professor Jastram's academic paper. Juan Osuna, at that time the Acting Chairman of the United States Board of Immigration Appeals (BIA), presented the first, Justice Esme Chombo, High Court of Malawi, presented the second, and Justice Anna Mactavish, Federal Court (Canada), presented the third.

Juan Osuna began by noting that the issue of the violation of economic, social and cultural rights as a basis for a claim to refugee status is tied to a number of other issues. The threshold that the applicant for asylum must meet to be determined a Convention refugee is high when economic, social and cultural rights violations are the basis of the well-founded fear of persecution. He noted that daily life in the applicant's country of nationality must be intolerable. Juan Osuna said that this is undoubtedly a high test to meet.

Juan Osuna noted that in the United States this is complicated further by the fact that the Asylum Officers, the first instance decision-makers for asylum applications, are situated in the U.S. Department of Homeland Security. This has raised questions whether the first instance decision-makers are part of the enforcement arm of the U.S. government as opposed to independent adjudicators. Asylum and immigration in the United States, as in other countries, are highly sensitive public policy concerns. Juan Osuna observed that this makes it difficult for those seeking asylum on the basis of violations of economic, social and cultural harm amounting to persecution. The violation of these socio-economic rights is not seen as equivalent to violations of political and civil rights. In cases where the asylum applicant can make a connection between an ethnic group and economic harm, Juan Osuna pointed out, there is a greater chance that the asylum applicant would be accepted than if the application relied solely on economic, social and cultural rights violations. In these instances, he stated, the basis of harm is harder to prove and, consequently, there is a lower chance of success.

Justice Esme Chombo stated that her remarks would be focused specifically on Southern Africa. She noted that there is clearly a well-established human right for refugees to survive when they face persecution in their own countries. However, there are limitations, she stated, for those who claim asylum on the basis of a right to work or a right to health care. Justice Chombo pointed out that the Republic of South Africa has the largest number of asylum seekers in Africa and even though asylum seekers have a right to work in the Republic of South Africa there has been expressed opposition from many South Africans about the opportunities given to asylum seekers to work there.[79]

Justice Chombo noted that many countries in Africa that host refugees have scarce resources. The citizens within these countries are struggling to make do with the limited resources available to them. Accordingly, when asylum seekers come into these countries, she asked, should they be given a right to work? She stated that in Malawi the government tightened the rules for asylum seekers to seek employment because Malawi citizens were asking why asylum seekers should be given the right to work when there are insufficient resources available for their own citizens.

Justice Chombo also noted that the allowances that are given to refugees in camps are sometimes higher than the basic pay for citizens in host countries. For instance, the United Nations High Commissioner for Refugees (UNHCR) gives refugees within camps capital to start their own businesses, an advantage denied to nationals of the host country. This results in nationals within their own country not having the same spending power as the refugees within the camps and citizens can, consequently, end up feeling like refugees within their own countries.

[79] See Human Rights Watch, "South Africa: Protect Victims of Xenophobic Violence: Provide Basics of Food, Water, Shelter, and Safety to Displaced," June 5, 2008. www.hrw.org/en/news/2008/06/05/south-africa-protect-victims-xenophobic-violence (accessed August 30, 2009). Human Rights Watch, "South Africa, Events of 2008," *World Report 2009*, www.hrw.org/en/world-report/2009/south-africa (accessed August 30, 2009).

Justice Chombo stated that the Global North has more resources than the Global South. The states in the Global North may be able to accommodate asylum seekers with welfare policies. The reality, she stated, is that refugee law may be perceived differently in the Global North than the Global South because of the availability or the lack thereof of resources. The right of asylum seekers to obtain jobs in hosting countries is creating tensions between nationals and asylum seekers. Do states that host refugees, she asked, have an obligation to provide work for everyone or for their own citizens? Justice Chombo stated that before we consider the right to work, it may be appropriate, to create an enabling environment for everyone within the country.

Justice Chombo also noted that in some jurisdictions, states are imposing laws that are excluding the courts from refugee cases. In these jurisdictions, she observed, once the Minister makes a decision on a refugee claim, it cannot be appealed to the courts.

Justice Anne Mactavish, Federal Court (Canada), began her judicial commentary by noting that in Canada asylum claims that are based on economic, social or cultural persecution are assessed the same way as asylum claims on the basis of a violation of any other human rights. She also stated that the *Canadian Charter of Rights and Freedoms*, unlike the *Constitution of the Republic of South Africa*, does not guarantee economic rights. Justice Mactavish stated that there are a number of factors that complicate the analysis of asylum claims that are based on economic, social or cultural persecution. She noted that these types of claims to asylum may see a number of intersecting grounds that may complicate the analysis. She further observed that it has been argued that some judges may see asylum applications based on economic, social or cultural harm as opening the "floodgates," that is, allowing for large numbers of asylum applicants to make claims for Convention refugee status.

Justice Mactavish also referred to the Federal Court of Appeal of Canada decision in *Sanchez*,[80] which ruled that the asylum applicant would have to give up his sideline business. Chief Justice John D. Richard ruled in *Sanchez* that,

[80] *Sanchez* v. *Canada (Citizenship and Immigration)* 2007 FCA 99 (March 8, 2007).

In this case, Mr. Sanchez was being targeted by FARC for what he was doing, i.e. reporting violators of the city's by-laws to the authorities, "not for what he was in an immutable or fundamental way." Denial of his side business interest would therefore not affect a fundamental principle of human rights.[81]

Mr. Sanchez was an engineer, who's full-time job was with the Columbian Ministry of Agriculture, with a specialty in environmental clean-up, and his sideline business was reporting signage violations to the local authorities.[82] On the certified question before the Federal Court of Appeal, the ruling was,

> persons claiming to be in need of protection solely because of the nature of the occupation or business in which they are engaged in their own country generally will not be found to be in need of protection unless they can establish that there is no alternative occupation or business reasonably open to them in their own country that would eliminate the risk of harm.[83]

Justice Mactavish concluded her judicial commentary by stating that economic, social and cultural rights are a bit amorphous and hard to define.

2.4.2 The round-table discussion on economic, social and cultural rights as a basis for claiming convention refugee status

During the round-table discussion for this session a number of important points were made. For instance, it was noted that the explanation that there is a reluctance on the part of the judiciary to apply economic, social and cultural rights because of their alleged vagueness or ambiguity is nothing more than an excuse. It was argued that civil and political rights can often be just as vague or amorphous as economic, social and cultural rights. The point was made that the obscurity of human rights norms often has to do with the context. The vagueness or difficulty in appreciating human rights has less to do with how these human rights are categorized.

It was further noted that the high courts have acknowledged that economic desires should not preclude anyone from obtaining Convention refugee status.

The following question was also posed during the round-table discussions for this session. If an asylum applicant is making a claim

[81] *Ibid.*, paragraph 19. [82] *Ibid.*, paragraph 3. [83] *Ibid.*, paragraph 20.

to refugee status in a country that does not impose discriminatory policies against the asylum applicant's group but, nonetheless, the asylum applicant suffers economic hardship because of the social norms of his/her country of nationality could this still be interpreted as persecution? In this situation, it was suggesting that the state in question would have an obligation to remedy the situation in favour of the asylum applicant.

It was also pointed out that for the last five or six years that severe economic human rights violations have been seen as crimes against humanity. Consequently, it was argued that if international criminal law could hold a person responsible for deprivation of livelihood, then, surely refugee law should certainly be able to do the same.

2.4.3 Professor Sharryn J. Aiken's review commentary

Professor Sharryn Aiken, Faculty of Law, Queen's University, Kingston, Canada, began by stating that Roger Zetter, Director of the Refugee Studies Centre, University of Oxford, has observed that even though there are now far more labels for refugees there are actually fewer refugees. She noted that it is extremely important to keep in mind the context when considering questions of socio-economic persecution. She also pointed out that this is not, of course, a new phenomenon. Socio-economic forms of persecution are among the first repressive measures introduced by totalitarian regimes such as Nazi Germany. She emphasized that socio-economic persecution should not be treated differently than other forms of persecutory treatment such as political persecution. Professor Aiken further underscored the point that it is important not to conflate what persecution means in relation to an asylum applicant's economic status and the Convention grounds.

Professor Aiken observed that refugee law requires an analysis of the issues on the periphery and including issues facing non-refugees in host countries. She also stated that in the context of scarcity, we would not be getting support for refugee studies unless we also study the situation in the Global South.

Professor Aiken also suggested that the broad definition of persecution in the *Rome Statute of the International Criminal Court* goes some considerable way in incorporating socio-economic harm as part of its definition. Article 7(2)(g), Crimes against humanity, of the *Rome Statute* states:

> "Persecution" means the intentional and severe deprivation of fundamental rights contrary to international law by reason of the identity of the group or collectivity;[84]

Professor Aiken also alluded to the case of the Sri Lankan refugees who were trying to come to Canada and who were discovered on the West Coast of Africa. She said that the Canadian authorities chartered a plane to return the asylum seekers who were trying to reach Canada back to Sri Lanka. Professor Aiken stated that the Canadian immigration officials involved in this interdiction acknowledged that mixed migratory flows always present difficulties. At that time, she noted, Sri Lanka was Canada's chief refugee source country. Professor Aiken stated that at least one of the refugees from this group who was returned to Sri Lanka was detained and tortured by the Sri Lankan authorities upon their return.[85]

3 THE HONOURABLE JUSTICE ALBIE SACHS'S KEYNOTE ADDRESS: "ONCE A REFUGEE, NOW A JUDGE, HEARS A CASE ABOUT THE RIGHTS OF REFUGEES."

The Honourable Justice Albie Sachs, Constitutional Court of the Republic of South Africa, gave a moving and personal keynote address on a topic that drove to the very heart of the central themes

[84] *Rome Statute of the International Criminal Court*, Article 7(2)(g), Crimes against Humanity, Adopted on 17 July 1998 and entered into force on 1 July 2002. http://untreaty.un.org/cod/icc/statute/99_corr/cstatute.htm. (accessed August 31, 2009.)

[85] Sharryn J. Aiken, "National Security and Canadian Immigration: Deconstructing the Disclosure of Trade-Offs," http://cc.bingj.com/cache.aspx?q=sri+lankan+refugees+intercepted+in+senegal+1998&d=76582065107821&mkt=en-CA&setlang=en-CA&w=ea3b845f,738d0d46. (accessed August31, 2009). See also "In Search of The African Queen: A People-Smuggling Operation" (2000) Documentary by Katerina Cizek, This documentary follows the events surrounding the Canadian government's interception of 190 Sri Lankan Tamils on the West Coast of Africa, in Senegal, in 1998. With the assistance of the United States, the International Organization of Migration (IOM), the Canadian government returned the men to Sri Lanka before they could arrive in Canada and make claims to refugee status. Some of the young Sri Lankan Tamils were arrested on their arrival in Sri Lanka and possibly tortured. See http://translate.google.ca/translate?hl=en&sl=fr&u=http://www.cerium.ca/In-search-of-the-African-Queen-II&ei=c2usSvrOMJTllQexsMTaBg&sa (accessed September 12, 2009).

of the Research Workshop on Critical Issues in International Refugee Law. He began his remarks by noting how as a young lawyer he was arrested and incarcerated for defending his clients against the discriminatory laws of the apartheid government of South Africa. When he was released from detention, he went to the United Kingdom to seek refuge. He said that he was a refugee on two occasions in his life. The first occasion was when he went to the United Kingdom to seek asylum and the second was when he went to Mozambique.

In speaking about being a refugee, Justice Sachs noted that one's sense of dependence is heightened when one must go to bureaucrats to ask for their right to *be*, for the right to work, to live, and so on. In terms of the criteria for categorizing someone as a refugee, Justice Sachs said that the de-contextualized and de-personalized criteria can be good and useful for fair analysis; however, it does not feel good to be categorized in such a way. He preferred to be called (and considered himself to be) a "freedom fighter" or a "displaced person," but not a refugee. He also observed that the threat of being called a terrorist is grave.

Justice Sachs noted that states are, by far, responsible for the use of torture against their own citizens. He also pointed out that states have created more torture victims than any other entities, whether in Europe, Africa, Asia, or the Americas. When the African National Congress (ANC) was in the midst of its struggle against apartheid it considered whether it could legitimately use torture and decided overwhelming against it for the reason that it was against the very thing that the ANC was struggling to achieve, "respect for human dignity and life."

Justice Sachs remarked that a person's own life experience cannot help but affect their values and judgments. Likewise, a judge's own personal experience cannot help but influence their judgments on the cases that they hear and decide. He mentioned that he had just completed a manuscript for a book titled, *The Strange Alchemy of Life and Law*,[86] where he explores this subject at some length. Justice Sachs stated that he did not seek judicial office, but it was something that history had thrust upon him. Indeed, he noted that he was not

[86] Albie Sachs, *The Strange Alchemy of Life and Law* (Oxford University Press, 2009). http://ukcatalogue.oup.com/product/9780199571796.do. (accessed August 23,2009).

inclined to judicial decision-making and that this was something that did not come naturally to him.

Justice Sachs also briefly outlined a number of cases that he had decided on the Constitutional Court of South Africa, including, his dissenting judgment in the case of the *Union of Refugee Women and Others*.[87] Justice Sachs said that refugee law brings together interesting areas in the world of law such as what it means to be a human being, why people move from one place to another, and what is going on in the world today. Refugee law is, he observed, value laden and procedural and brings to light the importance of fairness.

Justice Sachs made the point that when a judge decides a case that the importance of values cannot be under estimated. He stated that there is a duty to intervene, in an appropriate way, if torture is present. What concerns South Africans the most, he said, include the following: torture, fair trial, and capital punishment.

4 STRATEGIES TOWARDS INTERPRETATIVE HARMONY

Common themes emerged from the panel sessions at the Research Workshop on Critical Issues in International Refugee Law that point in the direction of strategies towards interpretative harmony in international refugee law. These were also the explicit or implicit focus of the round-table discussions in each of the four panel sessions at the research workshop.

Professor Goodwin-Gill suggested that there was but one overriding critical issue in international refugee law and that was the "progressive development" of the *1951 Convention* and its *1967 Protocol*. Indeed, Professor Goodwin-Gill argued that the crux of the creative future development of the *1951 Convention* and *1967 Protocol* rested with the judicial pronouncements that emerge from the state parties' national courts and that auto-interpretation is the means for achieving this ultimate goal and at the cost, unfortunately, of a lack of consistency.

[87] *Union of Refugee Women and Others* v. *Director, Private Security Industry Regulatory Authority and Others* (CCT 39/06) [2006] ZACC 23; 2007 (4) BCLR 339 (CC) (12 December 2006) www.saflii.org.za/za/cases/ZACC/2006/23.html (accessed August23, 2009).

Another common central theme that emerged in all of the panel sessions was "consistency" in the application and interpretation of the *1951 Convention* and *1967 Protocol* and regional instruments such as the EU's Qualification Directive that is intended to develop a common asylum system across EU Member States. Consistency, or deciding like refugee status and asylum applications in the same way, is not only a fundamental tenet of any legal system and the administration of justice but also a key indicator of the integrity of any refugee status determination system. Professor McAdam argued that the application and interpretation of the EU Qualification Directive has led to inconsistent outcomes across EU Member States. Rather than creating a common asylum system, the EU Qualification Directive has, so far, managed to create a fractured one. Inconsistent asylum grant or acceptance rates or outcomes on like claims among EU States have been due, it has been suggested, to the variations in evidentiary burdens, the higher standards of proof that are applied to claims for subsidiary protection under Article 15(c), the lack of common definition for what constitutes "international or internal armed conflict," and the variation in interpretation of the "substantial grounds" standard for deciding applications for subsidiary protection, among others. Similar factors have been advanced for the lack of consistency in refugee status and asylum applications in other jurisdictions, including, within the UNHCR.[88]

The situation in the EU and North America can be described as both similar and different. Canada's system of complementary

[88] Brian Gorlick, "Common Burdens and Standards: Legal Elements in Assessing Claims to Refugee Status," *International Journal of Refugee Law*, 15 (3) (2003), 357–376. Brian Gorlick, "(Mis)perception of Refugees, State Sovereignty, and the Continuing Challenge of International Protection," in Anne F. Bayefsky (ed.) *Human Rights and Refugees, Internally Displaced Persons and Migrant Workers: Essays in Memory of Joan Fitzpatrick and Arthur Helton* (Boston: Martinus Nijhoff Publishers, 2006), pp. 79–81. Cecile Rousseau, Francois Crepeau, Patricia Foxen, France Houle, "The Complexity of Determining Refugeehood: A Multidisciplinary Analysis of the Decision-Making Process of the Canadian Immigration and Refugee Board," *Journal of Refugee Studies*, 15 (1) (2002), 43–70; Sean Rehaag, "The Troubling Patterns in Canadian Refugee Adjudication," *Ottawa Law Review*, 39 (2) (2007–2008), 335–365. Jaya Ramji-Nogales, Andrew I. Schoenholtz, and Philip G. Schrag, "Refugee Roulette: Disparities in Asylum Adjudication," *Stanford Law Review*. 60 (2) (2007), 295–412. James C. Simeon, "A Comparative Analysis of the Response of the UNHCR and Industrialised States to Rapidly Fluctuating Asylum Applications: Lessons and Best Practices for RSD Design and Administration," *International Journal of Refugee Law*, vol. 22, No. 1 (March 2010), 72–103.

protection, unlike the EU's subsidiary protection, provides equivalent benefits to persons found to be in need of international protection to the persons who are determined to be Convention refugees. In the EU, a person who is granted subsidiary protection will not obtain the same benefits as the person who is determined to be a Convention refugee. In North America, the standard of proof for complementary protection is higher than for Convention refugee status, but the benefits are equivalent. In the EU, the standard of proof for subsidiary protection is the same as for Convention refugee status, save for Article 15(c) which is higher, Professor McAdam has argued. It is also important to note that those who are granted subsidiary protection in the EU receive fewer benefits than those who are determined to be Convention refugees. Hence, one can conclude that in North America it is harder to obtain complementary protection but once it is received the benefits are equivalent to those who are determined to be Convention refugees. In the EU, obtaining subsidiary protection is as difficult as obtaining Convention refugee status, with the one notable exception under Article 15(c), but the benefits are not the same. The two key variables with respect to subsidiary and complementary protection in these regions are: (1) where the bar is set as the standard of proof; and, (2) the level of benefits that accrue to those who are determined to require international protection, that is, whether it is the same level of benefits or less than those who are determined to be Convention refugees. The variance between the EU and North America is both with the standard of proof and the provision of benefits for those who are deemed to be persons in need of international protection.

Following the traumatic events of September 11, 2001, in the United States, there has been an overriding concentration on security concerns by states and intergovernmental organizations. This has been fueled by ongoing terrorists attacks worldwide and/or threats of attacks since 9/11. Professor Geoff Gilbert argues that the standard of proof for the exclusion clause under Articles 1F of the *1951 Convention*, "serious reasons for considering," is not an onerous test and can easily be used to capture and exclude more refugee status and asylum applicants than heretofore.

A common underlying theme across all sessions at the research workshop was security, in the light of the seemingly ever-growing phenomenon of terrorism. Nonetheless, the standard of proof was, yet again, a predominant theme within this panel session of the research workshop as well.

The key concept for socio-economic human rights claims for refugee status and asylum is the phrase, "progressive realization." This is the key obligation of states parties in the implementation of the *International Covenant on Economic, Social and Cultural Rights*. However, as Professor Kate Jastram notes, in some jurisdictions there is a higher standard of proof for asylum claims based on violations to socio-economic rights than for civil or political rights.

Within each of these panel sessions, what emerged was the necessity for state parties to have a common standard of proof when deciding who is a refugee or person who requires subsidiary or complementary protection. The "progressive realization" of the *International Covenant of Economic, Social and Cultural Rights* and the "progressive development" of the *1951 Convention* and *1967 Protocol*, as well as other international human rights instruments, are also key considerations in moving toward interpretative harmony. As Michelle Foster and others have argued, there must be congruence between international human rights law and international refugee law through the consistent application of international human rights law to the adjudication and appeal of refugee status and asylum applications. In this regard, the current United Nations High Commissioner of Human Rights, Navanethem Pillay, has called on refugee law judges to employ the Universal Human Rights Index, developed by the Office of the UN High Commissioner of Human Rights, for the adjudication of claims to asylum and refugee status.[89]

Promoting consistency in international refugee law is not a call for mindless, unexamined or unchallenged uniformity, but rather a tool for advancing the integrity of the refugee status determination systems across all jurisdictions as well as just outcomes for all those who are seeking Convention refugee status and/or subsidiary

[89] Navanethem Pillay, United Nations High Commissioner for Human Rights, "Promoting a Broader Understanding of Refugee Law: The Jurisprudence of the Human Rights Treaty Bodies as a Source of Interpretation," Keynote Address delivered at the 8th World Conference of the International Association of Refugee Law Judges (IARLJ), Cape Town, South Africa, January 28–30, 2009. The Universal Human Rights Index is found at the following website, www.universalhumanrightsindex.org/.

or complementary protection, and other forms of international protection.

5 CONCLUSION

The Research Workshop on Critical Issues in International Refugee Law undertook a unique and innovative approach to addressing a limited number of critical issues in international refugee law today. It brought together some of the leading high court and superior court justices and academics in the field of international refugee law to analyze, to debate and to discuss a limited number of the critical legal issues and concerns with the objectives of trying to find the most promising solutions and avenues for further research on these problematic areas of international refugee law.

What emerged from the research workshop were the common themes of the "progressive development" of the *1951 Convention* and its *1967 Protocol*, the necessity of achieving broad-based consistency for maintaining fundamental justice and the integrity of refugee status and asylum adjudication and appeal, the importance of common evidentiary burdens and standards of proof, the significance of the "progressive realization" of the *International Covenant of Economic, Social and Cultural Rights* for adjudicating refugee status and asylum claims based on socio-economic human rights violations, and the achievement of a progressive human rights approach to the adjudication of claims to Convention refugee status and subsidiary and complementary forms of international protection through the congruence of international human rights law, international humanitarian law, international criminal law and international refugee law.

CHAPTER I

From refugee to judge of refugee law: a tentative introduction to some off-the-cuff remarks

Justice Albie Sachs

Who is the enemy? In May last year, I knew exactly who the enemy was. It was someone who sought to entice me away from completing a manuscript on which I was working relentlessly. I was on long leave, a Ford Foundation Scholar in Residence, trying to complete a book about the connections between my life experiences, on the one hand, and my decision-making processes as a judge, on the other. The more attractive the seduction, the greater the danger. I succumbed, but not completely. The invitation was to participate in a research workshop in Toronto on Critical Issues in International Refugee Law. And since I was actually going to be in Toronto at the time, I gave way a little … could I prepare a few notes at the last minute, and then make an impromptu presentation? The organisers agreed. The theme I promised came to me from the book I was writing – *The Strange Alchemy of Life and Law*. Hence the title of the proposed talk: *From Refugee to Judge of Refugee Law*.

I made a point of getting to the workshop an hour before my presentation was due. The plan was to give myself enough time to pull a few thoughts together. But the paper I heard on my arrival was so interesting that I decided to postpone any note jotting till discussion-time. Then the debate turned out to be even more fascinating than the paper! So I ended up without a single note, nor any thought-through concepts. The only option was to embark on a stream of legal consciousness presentation and hope for the best. Impromptu ramblings are extremely risky; occasionally they allow the speaker to stumble into unexpectedly interesting terrain. But more often what results is a mish-mash that might possibly be of interest to a psychoanalyst but does nothing but bore the audience. Anyhow, I just started chatting, with one idea following the other, until suddenly the allotted time was over. I felt rather embarrassed at having given a totally ad hoc and inconsequential presentation. To my total surprise, some months later the editor of this book asked for a copy of my paper. 'I didn't have one', I answered. 'Can't you reconstruct it from your notes?' 'I didn't have any notes.' 'What about from memory?' 'I don't remember what I said – did anyone make a record?' It appeared that some cryptic soundbites had been scribbled down, so I had to be thankful for small mercies.

What follows, then, are not the actual words spoken by me, but a stream-of-consciousness re-fabrication of some vague memories prompted by a few disparate notes of an ad hoc presentation. There is, however, one solid and incontrovertible part. It consists of extracts from a judgment I wrote concerning a constitutional challenge to a statute that excluded refugees in blanket fashion from working in the private security industry. So, with these words in mind, let the consciousness stream …

A RELUCTANT 'REFUGEE'

The first time I arrived in England as a refugee I was something of an emotional and psychological wreck. While practising at the Bar in Cape Town I had been locked up in solitary confinement for 168 days. The isolation was punishing, unbelievably so. It was so strict that I might possibly have been the only person in the world who did not know for quite a while that Kennedy had been assassinated. But I held out, and on my release ran eight miles from the detention centre in the heart of the City, and flung myself fully clothed into the sea. Outwardly, I was strong, even triumphant, but in reality I was crushed. Two years later I was again detained in solitary confinement, this time for three months in an awaiting-trial jail where I had frequently interviewed clients. The authorities referred to me as a terrorist, and I was subjected to torture by sleep deprivation. On this occasion, when I was released I did not run to the sea, or even climb Table Mountain. I slouched home.

The resistance to apartheid was being severely battered. It was difficult to escape from Cape Town, which was a thousand kilometres from the nearest land border. My clients expected me to keep them out of jail, not to go to jail myself. So it was either go full-time underground, or leave the country. We didn't have the structures, and I didn't have the courage, to go underground. So sick at heart, I became a partner in my own humiliation, and applied for what was called an 'exit permit'. After a long delay I was allowed to leave with a document that said I was stripping myself forever of my citizenship, and would be committing a criminal offence under South African law if ever I returned.

At that time I was subjected to a 'banning order' that restricted me from leaving the portion of Cape Town reserved for white occupation only, and forbade me on pain of imprisonment from entering the harbour area. So I had to suffer the further indignity of entreating the authorities to give me written permission to board the ship that was to take me from the country of my soul and deposit me, perhaps for the rest of my life, into a stateless limbo. When I got to my cabin, there was one farewell phone call I needed to make. Knowing that the phone would be bugged, I spoke carefully to a lawyer friend: 'Dullah, I am on the Cape Town Castle (ocean liner), this is my last phone call before I go into exile … I just wanted to say goodbye … I will be back one day.' As the ship steamed out and passengers joyously threw streamers to friends at the dockside, I just stared numbly at the disappearing quayside. Part of me was jubilant; I was safe, safe, safe. And a week later when we were in the middle of the Atlantic and England scored a goal in overtime and won the World Cup, and a below-deck roar seemed to lift the boat out of the ocean, I smiled with delight like everybody else on board. How most forced migrants would love to depart from their countries in an ocean liner! Yet each refugee makes his or her own journey, and while I happily played ping pong, tennequoits and bridge, and dressed up for the fancy-dress ball, the spikes of my pain and humiliation never stopped tearing at my insides.

Just as a diver must rise slowly from the ocean depths, so do victims of repression need to emerge gradually into freedom. It is not just the need to come to terms with the separation anxiety that most people feel when they move from their customary habitat to a place where everything is unfamiliar. There is the trauma that proceeded that compelled the departure; the loss of autonomy and sense of defeat at having been overwhelmed by irresistible forces beyond your control; and finally there is the emotion of doom at not being able to return. Asylum may save you from continued persecution. It may even possibly permit your courage to resurge. But it does not in itself repair the damage that accompanied being extruded against your will from the land of your birth.

Two weeks cruising through the waves did allow some of the trauma to abate. Yet when I arrived in England I was still in turmoil. Day after day, almost obsessively, I would lie on my back on Hampstead Heath and stare up at the kites flying peacefully, this way and that, overhead. I became addicted to serenity. Yet I felt existentially de-centred. There was a total disjuncture between the over-turbulent character of life in South Africa, and the over-stolid way in which people seemed to get on with their lives in England. The very placidity that gave me a sense of security there, seemed to mock all our passionate endeavour in South Africa. As a child I had read in weekly 'comics' about the brave exploits of pilots in the Battle of Britain. The war was far away, something 'in the news'. Then, as the war neared its end, we were told to eat up all our food and remember the poor starving children of Europe. Now all was reversed. I was in Britain, a country that shook its head in disbelief at the violence, suffering and hunger in far-away South Africa.

Although I could control my movements, I could not regulate my emotions. At the simplest level, the sense of trust that I would survive through the day, and the night, and the next day, without being locked up, was ineffable. Yet, however marvellous it was to be living far away from terror, I could not subdue a degree of wild anger against the country to whose shores I had come. An irrational rage, flowing from my helplessness, projected itself onto my hosts. Had it not been Britain that had finally subjugated indigenous African resistance in Southern Africa, and gone on to 'unite the white races' to create the Union of South Africa in 1910? And who, if not British investors, had been the greatest beneficiaries of the exploitation of cheap black labour? Feelings of grievance went forth and multiplied … who was now using a veto to prevent sanctions from being applied to bring apartheid to an end, and who were calling Nelson Mandela a 'terrorist' … ? I particularly hated us being called 'terrorists'. We were fighting for freedom, and only after all other avenues to get the vote had firmly been closed, had we reluctantly included armed struggle as part of our campaign for liberation. Yet we had specifically refused to use terrorism directed at civilians, just as we had decided resolutely against employing torture to get information from people sent to kill our leadership and destroy our organisation. A deep sense of morality and respect for human life lay at the core of all our endeavours … how dare they call us terrorists … how dare they!

It was all so confusing. There were many people and organisations in the UK who received us with understanding and love. I was able to complete a doctorate at Sussex University, have three books published and even to take part in an interview on the first night that colour television was broadcast in London. I spent many productive years as a law lecturer at Southhampton University (having been taken on, I suspected, on the basis that because I was reasonably articulate and came from overseas, I should be able to teach International Law).

Many people who migrate feel uncertain about the extent to which they should immerse themselves in the culture of their new country and risk giving up the identity they had developed in their country of origin. In my case, the process went the other way. I engaged as much as I could with British society, always intending to take home with me whatever could enrich the new democracy we were going to build one day. So the more I plunged into British life, the more South African did I feel. Similarly, I always had the idea that I was not only receiving opportunities but also giving something to the society I was now in. Today, I think of the strange experience of being at the Donmar Theatre, with an American tourist at my side, watching the Royal Shakespeare Company putting on a beautifully modulated version of the *Jail Diary of Albie Sachs*, and being too timid to nudge him and say: 'You know something … ?' Then the Law Faculty allowed me to put on the first full academic course in the UK on Law and Discrimination. Later, I was able to get a book on sexism and the law published. As ANC choirs always sang so beautifully throughout the world: *When freedom comes along … we shall ever remember … the things you've done for us.*

In 1977 I moved to Maputo in newly independent Mozambique, where I took up a position as Professor of Law at the recently established law faculty [Faculdade de Direito] at the University of Eduardo

Mondlane. By now I had learned something about International Law, but I did not teach refugee law because it simply did not exist as an area of academic study, not there, nor anywhere else in the world. Refugee law in fact came to me in a purely practical form. The United Nations High Commission for Refugees in Mozambique required people like myself to complete application forms to enable us to be classified as refugees. Although the objective was primarily to provide us with protection against cross-border raids by South African commandos, I was reluctant to fill in the forms. I wondered why I felt uncomfortable being called a refugee, and came to the conclusion that, as so much in law, the significance of the term depended on the context in which it was used. In some circumstances receiving the label 'refugee' could literally save your life. In others it consigned you to being a disempowered member of an anonymous mass, whose existence would be determined by classification and controlled by the will of others. I believed that I and others, who had been displaced from our country because of our actions in compliance with United Nations calls to end apartheid, should be treated as freedom fighters, and not as refugees. Yet, out of respect for my hosts, I signed the forms and identified myself as a refugee, without for a moment feeling I was one. (As it turned out, this 'status' did not protect me from an assassination attempt).

The second time I arrived in England as a refugee, I came as a physical wreck on a stretcher. In 1988, as I was about to go to a beach on the outskirts of Maputo, a bomb placed in my car by South African agents exploded, and I lost my right arm and the sight of an eye, and had my right heel shattered. Ten days later, to protect me from a further attempt on my life, I was flown to London. For the first time in my life I travelled first class, but sadly I was virtually unconscious the whole way. Then I was taken semi-comatose by ambulance to the London Hospital, where my brother was a doctor. The National Health Service had changed, and I had to pay a full fee for the ambulance and partial fees for my stay at the hospital. But I did not feel aggrieved. To this day I recall the touch of the hands of my nurses as they removed my bloodstained bandages, cleaned my body and put fresh bandages on again. I remember with continued amazement and gratitude the way in which the physiotherapists encouraged me to find strength in myself, first, to wriggle my backside from my bed to the commode, later, to stand, quite literally, on my own two feet, then, to walk, and finally, go up and down stairs leading with the correct foot ('good foot up to heaven, bad foot down to hell'). Somehow the organised love of the hospital staff bound me more directly, intimately and unambiguously to my host country than all the multifarious forms of support and solidarity had done on my previous sojourn. And, to complete the transformation, I had the unexpected experience of being visited from time to time by a Special Branch officer from Scotland Yard, who kept me under surveillance not to report on my activities, but to ensure that no harm came to me.

In the public mind I was always regarded as a refugee from apartheid violence. Yet in purely technical terms that status disqualified. After polite but very intensive questioning by a security official, and a long delay during which there was an opportune change of government, I received British citizenship and a UK passport. During seven lean years of statelessness, I had travelled with some difficulty on a 'Travel Document'. But now I could move around the world freely until one day, I was sure, I would recover my South African passport.

Of all the journeys I was to make, undoubtedly the most wonderful was the one I undertook twenty-three years, eight months, two weeks and a day after the day I sailed from Cape Town. It took me to Johannesburg International Airport, where I arrived joyously as a free person bursting with knowledge to be used in transforming the land of apartheid into a non-racial democracy. When I got off the plane an Afrikaans-speaking airport security official took me aside and said: 'Welcome home, Albie.' This unexpected greeting somehow helped me become aware of a thread that had connected up all the different experiences of exile over nearly a quarter of a century. The connecting element was my participation in the freedom struggle. My expulsion from the country had been brought about not by some malign, irrational and irresistible calamity, but as a consequence of voluntary adherence to certain beliefs. The years of displacement that followed were tied in with these beliefs. My immersion in British and Mozambican life served to re-enforce rather than undermine my South African identity. I would tell people that I never considered myself to be 'an exile', but rather to be a person 'living in exile'. Living in exile located one but did not determine who I was; exile was as much a presence as an absence.

So all the way through I was able to be both an intensely patriotic South African, and, like Tom Paine, a proud citizen of the world. Thus, 'the reason for everything' that many people believe in, was not for me some occult force beyond human understanding. It was a core choice in my life, which provided significance and continuity to the long years of my comity lost and my country regained.

One of the key experiences that I took home with me, of particular relevance to this book, was speaking at the Centre for Refugee Studies at Oxford University, newly founded by Dr. Barbara Harrell-Bond. For the first time, refugee law was being developed as an independent, multi-disciplinary area of study. I had just come out of hospital, and had been asked to talk about the way the law impacted on my life as a refugee. Still physically frail, my leg gave way while I was giving my presentation and I collapsed to the ground. Consternation! But my mind was still robust. I was rapidly learning some of the key characteristics of refugee law. At its heart lay not systems of classification and structures of administration, important though these were. The core binding elements were respect for human dignity and insistence on fairness, of procedure and respectfulness of outcome. I discovered that dignified dialogue was the key to the relationship between those offering help and those receiving it and central to ensuring that people displaced by persecution could be allowed to speak in their own voices. I learnt about the role that law could play in encouraging self-reliance rather than dependence, and integration rather than segregation.

Perhaps it was our experience as South Africans that had made my generation particularly averse to seeing refugees in prototypical terms. We certainly did not regard ourselves as constituting forlorn families huddled in camps waiting for handouts from benefactors. We had no doubt that host countries benefited from the skills, song, business acumen, political ideas, music and cuisine we brought with us. Similarly, we constantly envisaged one day taking back home with us some of the multitude of riches we had found in our host countries. Properly configured and applied, then, the law could transform refugees from being objects of pity into participants in processes of humane good-neighbourliness.

Finally, I discovered that refugee law focused on the creation of legal and other mechanisms to anticipate and prevent forced migrations if possible, and to repair and heal, or at least to mitigate, their effects, if not. As the African proverb puts it: 'the foot has no nose', that is, we must look after each other because we never know where our own life journeys could one day lead us to.

B UNION OF REFUGEE WOMEN CASE[1]

Background

I had been a member of the Constitutional Court for ten years when the first case dealing with refugee law came before us. Brought by a body called Union of Refugee Women, which had the support of civil society organisations, it concerned the treatment of refugees in South Africa, more especially in the area of employment. Literature presented to the Court asserted that while the provisions of the Refugees Act were notably progressive, their implementation left much to be desired. This particular matter had in fact started off simply as a complaint about implementation. It concerned the rights of refugees to work in the private security industry, and was triggered by a suddenly imposed blanket exclusion in the Private Security Industry Regulation Act[2] (Private Security Act) of all refugees from working in that industry. Refugees who had previously been given permits to work in private security, had their permits suddenly withdrawn. During the course of the litigation the applicants broadened their challenge and sought a declaration that the relevant section in the Private Security Act was unconstitutional. It stated broadly that non-nationals who were not permanent residents could not enter the security industry, unless they were given special exemption.[3] At

[1] What follow are extracts from a judgment I wrote, introduced by remarks prepared for this paper. The judgment is *Union of Refugee Women* v. *Director: Security Industry Authority* [2006] ZACC; 2007 (4) SA 395 (CC); 2007 (4) BCLR 339.(CC), www.constitutionalcourt.co.za, which contains the full text of my judgment as of well as two other judgments in the case, all with full citations.

[2] Act 56 of 2001.

[3] Section 23(1) of the Private Security Industry Regulation Act provides:

> Any natural person applying for registration … may be registered as a security service provider if the applicant is a fit and proper person to render a security service, and –
> (a) is a citizen or has permanent resident status in South Africa.
> …
>
> (6) Despite the provisions of subsections (1) … the Authority may on good cause shown and on grounds which are not in conflict with the purpose of this Act and the objects of the Authority, register any applicant as a security service provider.

the same time, the Refugees Act[4] declared in an unqualified way that accredited refugees could seek employment.[5] How could these provisions be reconciled?

All ten judges who sat in the matter agreed that the blanket exclusion was unlawful, and that each applicant should have had his or her case reviewed on an individual basis. The three judgments also emphasised that refugees should be assisted so as to be able to understand the processes involved. A costs award was made in favour of the applicants. The Court divided, however, on the question of the constitutionality of section 23(1) of the Private Security Act.

Four of the members of the Court stated that refugees were a group vulnerable to discrimination. Though the exclusionary provision in the section had a legitimate and laudable purpose, its terms were not narrowly tailored to that purpose. They accordingly held that, taking account of South Africa's international obligations, the overbroad exclusion was unfairly discriminatory and inconsistent with the Constitution. Six judges, however, felt that unconstitutionality could be avoided if the provisions of the Private Security Act were applied in a way that was consistent with South Africa's international obligations. In particular, the authority concerned should be required to apply the exemption powers in an individualised manner which gave due recognition to the status and entitlements of refugees.

It should be noted that after five years' residence in South Africa, refugees were entitled to become permanent residents. So the exclusion applied only to refugees who had been in the country for less than five years.

Which group did I belong to?

The reader would correctly assume that life experiences sharpen and intensify judicial instincts. But sitting on the Bench one realises that these experiences are strongly mediated by the legal culture within which we operate. Our Constitution is overtly value-laden. The matters that reach us are rarely solved simply by textual analysis. We spend much time balancing competing interests, relying heavily

[4] Act 130 of 1998.

[5] Section 27 of the Refugees Act provides, in relevant part, that:
A refugee –
(f) is entitled to seek employment.

on the principle of proportionality. For this very reason we aim as much as possible to achieve principled and fully articulated solutions to problems. Analysts have battled without success to find discernable ideological blocs in our Court. None of us could simply be categorised as pro-or anti- either refugees or the Executive. In one way or another, all of us had taken part in the struggle against apartheid. We all shared the view stated in the preamble to the Constitution that we came from a past of great injustice, and that our Constitution was aimed at transforming our country rather than protecting an unfair status quo. Yet, as in this case, we often disagreed on precisely how the Constitution should be applied in a particular set of circumstances. And as this case also demonstrated, sometimes the tenor of the language used and the socio-juridical vision emanating from a judgment can be as meaningful as its technical outcome.

Thus, although the remedies we proposed were different, in practice the divergence was small. All the members of the Court agreed on the importance of applying relevant international law principles, and ensuring that the Refugees Act be implemented in a humane and supportive way. And all of us, I believe, adopted an approach that emphasised the human dimension of what was at stake. Where we differed was over the most appropriate technical ways of achieving respect for the dignity of those affected. In formal terms, the issue was whether the constitutionality of the exclusionary provision could be saved by requiring the exemption clause to be applied in a manner that fully acknowledged the rights of refugees, without completely destroying legitimate legislative objectives concerning regulation of the private security industry. The reader will see from extracts from a judgment I wrote, on which side I came out in this case, and possibly be surprised.

Judgment of Sachs J, in Union of Refugee Women case

In my view, special emphasis has to be given to four considerations, all of which bear on the status given by law to refugees. Taken together, they strongly favour the notion that being an accredited refugee in itself goes a long way to establishing good cause for exemption.

The first factor to take into account is the set of obligations undertaken by South Africa in terms of international law. The second is the significance of the provisions of the Refugees Act. The third is the historical and social setting in which the rights and entitlements of refugees have to be determined. And the fourth is the constitutionally mandated obligation to counteract xenophobia.

Obligations under international law

After achieving democracy in 1994, South Africa for the first time adhered to a number of international instruments dealing with refugees. Refugees are legally entitled to a standard of treatment in host countries that encompasses both fundamental human rights and refugee-specific rights. The former are enshrined in international human rights law; for the latter, the 1951 UN Convention Relating to the Status of Refugees (the Convention), which predates most human rights treaties, remains the main instrument and contains a relatively detailed enumeration of rights. In some cases the Convention requires state parties to extend to refugees the same standard of treatment as for nationals; in others it obliges states to accord refugees as favourable a treatment as possible, and not less favourable than that accorded to non-nationals generally in the same circumstances. In devising these two main yardsticks, those who drafted the Convention clearly sought to ensure that refugees would not end up as pariahs at the margins of host societies.

Thus the Convention obliges state parties to issue refugees with identity papers and with documentation required for international travel (the Convention travel document), prerequisites for many people to the rebuilding of their social lives and re-establishing means of livelihood. It forbids discrimination on the grounds of race, religion, or country of origin. And, of special importance, it protects refugees from being returned to the place where their lives and freedoms would be at risk (the principle of *non-refoulement*). Taken together, these obligations constitute a coherent and enforceable legal regime for refugees that are markedly more favourable than the discretionary regime generally applicable to immigrants.

The rationale for this regime and its binding element comes from the very circumstances that caused the refugees to abandon their homeland in the first place. In general terms, international refugee law, and the asylum built upon that regime, are designed to extend protection to refugees in an international context so as to substitute the national protection they have lost and cannot claim at home.

> They have been forced out of their country as a result of persecution or danger, and now must receive legal protection and the opportunity to realise the most fulsome life possible in a foreign country.
>
> ...
>
> In recreating as closely as possible the national protection lost or not claimable by a refugee, the refugee regime seeks to put the refugee in a situation as close as possible to that of the national of the country of asylum.

The positive obligation to admit refugees, provide them with asylum and treat them in accordance with specific standards, thus contrasts sharply with the absence of a mandatory obligation to admit foreigners to the state's territory. It would accordingly be inappropriate for the state to act towards refugees in a manner that is consonant with the general discretionary provisions of the regime constructed upon immigration, security, and other municipal priorities, while ignoring the specific obligations that flow from the refugee regime.

It is important therefore that the progressive legal construct for refugees not be dominated by and held hostage to priorities drawn from immigration control or protection of the local labour force. As Okoth-Obbo has pointed out:

> the refugee protection system has, and should have, a validity all of its own. It should not be viewed as only the balance from requirements established at the level of immigration control and national penal and criminal law enforcement. It is possible to secure and even expand refugee space without this being seen as a constriction of the ability of states to pursue legitimate influx control and law and order objectives.

The Convention devotes considerable attention to the question directly raised in the present matter, namely, the obligation to respect the right of a refugee to engage in wage-earning employment. This obligation requires acknowledgement of the right to receive at least the most favourable treatment accorded to nationals of a foreign country in the same circumstances; and in any case not to be subjected to restrictive measures for the protection of the national labour market after three years of residence. Furthermore, the Contracting States are expressly required to give sympathetic consideration to assimilating the rights of all refugees with regard to wage-earning employment to those of nationals. These provisions should not be read in a begrudging, technical way so as to limit work opportunities and to guarantee only the bare minimum. On the contrary, they should be viewed conjunctively and purposively as being designed to encourage self-reliance on the part of refugees and to promote the possibility of their being able to lead valuable, dignified and independent lives; the quality of asylum, like the quality of mercy, should not be strained.

Refugees Act

The preamble to the Refugees Act notes that:

> the Republic of South Africa has acceded to the 1951 Convention Relating to the Status of Refugees, the 1967 Protocol Relating to the Status of Refugees and the 1969 Organization of African Unity Convention Governing the Specific Aspects of Refugee Problems in Africa as well as other human rights instruments, and has in so doing, assumed certain obligations to receive and treat in its territory refugees in accordance with the standards and principles established in international law.

Section 6 goes on to state that the Act must be applied with due regard to the above-mentioned legal instruments as well as the Universal Declaration of Human Rights and any other international agreement to which the Republic is a party. The statutory matrix in which the right to seek employment is embedded is notably facilitative and rights-based. A refugee is: accorded full legal protection, including the rights set out in the Bill of Rights; entitled to identity and travel status documents; given an unrestricted right to seek employment; and able to apply for permanent residence after five years' continuous residence. Taken together, these provisions reflect acknowledgment by the legislature of the need to create a progressive and humane refugee regime in keeping with South Africa's international legal obligations. It is in this manifestly broad and supportive legislative setting that any question about the right to seek employment must be resolved.

The social and historical context

The context, which led to the adoption of the Refugees Act, was set out by the then Deputy Minister of Home Affairs in the following striking terms:

> Because of our history and our struggle we have increasingly had to bear the mantle of champions of the oppressed. Furthermore, because of the political and economic stability in our country, and the fact that thousands of us have experienced the pain of destitution and homelessness, South Africa is in a unique position to chart a humane policy as far as refugees are concerned. This has meant that South Africa has had to put into practice the concept of international solidarity and burden sharing, allowing the victims of international conflicts and human violations to seek a safe haven within our borders. Although in comparison we host a relatively small number of refugees, we are hoping that we could lead the way in the development of progressive refugee policies … South Africa had no experience of hosting refugees – instead we produced refugees. South African society has not been sufficiently educated on issues of refugees, the causes of refugees and particularly the government's responsibilities towards refugees.

These factors provide the stark background against which determinations must be made of what is 'good cause' in relation to access of refugees to employment in the security industry. It is not all that long ago that, during the late period of minority racist rule, tens of thousands of South Africans fled across our borders into neighbouring states. Few had documents or anything more than a change of clothing, if even that. They were well received and sheltered, and treated with humanity by many African states, who frequently paid a heavy price in lives and blood for fulfilling their international responsibilities. Thousands more South Africans were given shelter and enabled to lead productive lives in countries right across the globe. Many have returned and now occupy important positions in our country. These moral debts are paid off not through direct reciprocity, but by means of voluntary acceptance of international treaty obligations.

The preamble to the Constitution speaks of building 'a united and democratic South Africa able to take its rightful place as a sovereign state in the family of nations'. This acknowledges two things: the international support, based upon the principles of the Universal Declaration of Human Rights and the United Nations, that enabled our country to overcome division and achieve constitutional democracy, and the humanitarian obligations that go with achieving a dignified place as a democratic member of the international community.

Xenophobia

The Braamfontein Declaration has pointed out that:

> [x]enophobia is the deep dislike of non-nationals by nationals of a recipient state. Its manifestation is a violation of human rights. South Africa needs to send out a strong message that an irrational prejudice and hostility towards non-nationals is not acceptable under any circumstances.

This prejudice is strong in South Africa. It strikes at the heart of our Bill of Rights. Special care accordingly needs to be taken to prevent it from even unconsciously tainting the manner in which laws are interpreted and applied. If refugees are treated as intrinsically untrustworthy, with their capacity to perform honestly and reliably being placed presumptively in doubt, then xenophobia is given a boost and constitutional values are undermined. As the then Deputy Minister of Home Affairs pointed out at a conference on forced migration, because of the historic isolation of South Africa, our people's perceptions are unfortunately insular, thus making them very susceptible to xenophobia. She observed that this situation is further exacerbated by the fact that there is often a problematic confusion in the minds of people between foreigners who are here illegally and refugees. This confusion is created because these two groups often occupy the lowest economic stratum in our society. She observed that they are invariably black and do not speak any local languages.

The constitutional response to xenophobia need not, of course, involve exaggerated xenophilia. Just as refugees should be protected from irrational prejudice, so they should not be able to lay claim to irrational privilege. The law – in this case section 23(6) – must be applied in a manner that is fair, objective, appropriately focused and in keeping with the letter and the spirit of our international and national legal obligations. Exercises of power that purport to have a neutral foundation but track stereotypes are often seen as flowing from and reinforcing negative presuppositions. Indeed, the routinised way in which power is exercised can readily become entangled in the public mind with existing prejudicial assumptions, reinforcing prejudice and establishing a downward spiral of disempowerment. One of the purposes of refugee law is precisely to overcome the experience of trauma and displacement and make the refugee feel at home and welcome. Disproportionate and uncalled-for adverse treatment would defeat that objective and induce an unacceptable and avoidable experience of alienation and helplessness. It would be most unfortunate if the left hand of government, that supervises the security industry, took away what the right hand of government, that accords to accredited refugees a special status, gives.

Conclusion

The culture of providing hospitality to bereft strangers seeking a fresh and secure life for themselves is not something new in our country. As Professor Hammond-Tooke has pointed out, in traditional society–

> the hospitality universally enjoined towards strangers, [is] captured in the Xhosa proverb *Unyawo alunompumlo* ('The foot has no nose'). Strangers, being isolated from their kin, and thus defenceless, were particularly under the protection of the chief and were accorded special privileges.

Today the concept of human interdependence and burden sharing in relation to catastrophe is associated with the spirit of ubuntu-botho. As this Court said in *Port Elizabeth Municipality* v. *Various Occupiers*:

> The Constitution and PIE confirm that we are not islands unto ourselves. The spirit of *ubuntu*, part of the deep cultural heritage of the majority of the population, suffuses the whole constitutional order. It combines individual rights with a communitarian philosophy. It is a unifying motif of the Bill of Rights, which is nothing if not a structured, institutionalised and operational declaration in our evolving new society of the need for human interdependence, respect and concern.

These words were used in relation to homeless South Africans. The reminder that we are not islands unto ourselves, however, must be applied to our relationship with the rest of the continent.

The applicants in this matter all come from African countries. They have been granted refugee status because instability and bloodshed in their home countries has rendered life there intolerable. Their states of origin have either set out to persecute them or else been unable to provide them with the protection that citizens should be able to demand from their government. Two examples illustrate this. The tenth applicant, whose father was a schoolteacher, states that:

> It was alleged by the [Rwandan Patriotic Front] that all Hutu's were involved in the genocide, which occurred in my country during 1994. During the period

1994 to 1998 all my husband's family members were killed and two of my sisters, one of my brothers and a host of other family members were killed.

The twelfth applicant tells a similarly tragic story:

I have been a resident and citizen of the Democratic Republic of the Congo ... My father was a king in Bukavu, South Kivu. He was killed by rebel soldiers who were in the process of fighting a civil war against the government on or about April 2001. At the time of my father's death I was a student. The rebel soldiers killed my father because he refused to sign a proposition document.

One was the child of a schoolteacher, the other of a king. Both were students when forced to flee to South Africa. They do not seek handouts from the state, but simply the opportunity to work and earn a living. They have organised themselves into groups and received training as security guards. This capacitates them to do relatively humble tasks such as guarding parked cars or patrolling shopping malls.

I see no reason why access to employment in the security industry by persons in their situation should not be permitted in relation to sectors such as these, where no high security interests are at stake. To bar them would be to discriminate against them unfairly. At the same time I would not regard it as unfair to keep them from guarding installations and persons where particularly high security considerations come into play.

The greater power of officials to grant unqualified exemptions to enter the industry should not exclude a lesser power to grant a restricted exemption, the only proviso being that the basis for the qualification be fair and reasonable in the circumstances. Indeed, it would be dangerous and self-defeating for the public administration to function on the basis that if officials cannot grant everything an applicant might seek, they cannot grant anything at all. The converse should also apply: officials should not be required to accede to everything refugees may ask for on the basis that in fairness the applicants are entitled at least to something. The principle of 'all-or-nothing' is frequently dangerous in administrative law. It disregards the notion of proportionality that lies at the heart of fairness of treatment. Experience warns that because cautious administrators might be fearful of being regarded as unduly generous, in practice this principle will usually lead to nothing.

In summary: the applicants were correct in their initial approach to Court when they challenged the criteria used by officials who had excluded them in blanket fashion from the security industry, in some cases withdrawing permits already granted. For the reasons I have given, however, I believe that the applicants' subsequent challenge to the constitutionality of section 23(1) was over-ambitious. The mere fact of being refugees does not entitle them to be admitted as of right to all spheres of the private security industry. The key factor is that being an accredited refugee goes a long way in itself to establish that there is 'good cause' for exempting an applicant from the prohibition against non-nationals and non-permanent residents entering the security industry.

It is to be hoped that, bearing in mind the special status that accredited refugees enjoy under our law, the clarifications given by this Court will assist both refugees and officials in streamlining the processes involved, engaging with each other in a mutually respectful manner, and achieving outcomes that are objectively grounded, fair and reasonable.

C POSTSCRIPT

When I came back from exile I was welcomed to the home of Abdullah and Farieda Omar. Dullah was the person to whom I had made my last phone-call on departure. In 1994 President Nelson Mandela appointed him first Minister of Justice in democratic South Africa. During my interview, later that year, by the Judicial Services Commission for an appointment to South Africa's first Constitutional Court, I was asked what special contribution I thought I could make. I answered that I had benefited from studying and teaching law in England and the USA, and especially from teaching, examining and doing research in various independent African countries. And the man from Scotland Yard whose responsibility it was to ensure that no further harm came to me at the London Hospital, wrote to me recently, saying he had retired from his position in the security services, and would I consider addressing a training establishment which he now headed? I said I would.

CHAPTER 2

Individual risk, armed conflict and the standard of proof in complementary protection claims: the European Union and Canada compared

Jane McAdam

INTRODUCTION

Though the title of this chapter implies a technical and comparative legal analysis of the standard of proof in complementary protection claims vis-à-vis Convention refugee claims, this is only part of its substance. Indeed, while the standard of proof has become a central distinguishing feature in the Canadian context between attaining protection as a 'refugee' or as a 'person in need of protection',[1] this debate has been largely absent from the EU arena. Nevertheless, high evidentiary burdens, combined with a haphazard consideration of the three possible grounds for subsidiary protection in the EU, mean that as in Canada, subsidiary protection status is not simply a residual status for people who would be Convention refugees but for the absence of a nexus with one of the five Convention grounds.[2] Accordingly, this chapter focuses on the legal impediments to obtaining subsidiary protection in the EU that have manifested themselves since the Qualification Directive entered into force for

The law is current as at July 2009.

[1] Similarly, in the United States, the standard of proof – 'more likely than not' – is higher than the 'reasonable possibility' standard in asylum claims: 8 CFR §§ 208.16(c)(2), 208.13(b)(2).

[2] In Canada, both a 'refugee' and a 'person in need of protection' receive the same domestic legal status, whereas in the EU, beneficiaries of subsidiary protection receive a lesser status than Convention refugees: see Qualification Directive, arts. 19–34. The issue of status is not examined here, but has been dealt with comprehensively in J. McAdam, *Complementary Protection in International Refugee Law* (Oxford University Press, 2007), pp. 90–110; G.S. Goodwin-Gill and J. McAdam, *The Refugee in International Law*, 3rd edn. (Oxford University Press, 2007), pp. 330–35.

the EU Member States in October 2006.[3] Its particular focus is article 15(c), which extends protection to civilians facing 'a serious and individual threat to their life or person by reason of indiscriminate violence in situations of international or internal armed conflict'. This provision has been poorly understood, inconsistently applied across the Member States, and in some jurisdictions is the only subsidiary protection category given full consideration when a Convention claim fails. Its recent examination by the European Court of Justice ('ECJ') in *Elgafaji* has highlighted the interpretative difficulties that national courts have had in applying the provision, such as whether the standard of proof in article 15(c) is identical to article 15(b) – requiring the applicant to demonstrate specific individual exposure to the risk of harm – or whether, as the court held, it covers a more general risk of harm that does not require the applicant to show that he or she is specifically targeted by reason of factors particular to his or her personal circumstances.[4] That finding is also important for considering the evidentiary relationship between the subsidiary protection categories and Convention refugee status. This chapter examines how article 15(c) has been interpreted in the jurisprudence of a number of EU Member States and demonstrates why it is not presently functioning as a complementary form of protection. The chapter concludes by comparing the EU position with Canada.

BACKGROUND

On April 29, 2004, the Member States of the European Union adopted the Directive on Minimum Standards for the Qualification and Status of Third Country Nationals or Stateless Persons as Refugees or as Persons Who Otherwise Need International Protection and the Content of the Protection Granted, known as the Qualification

[3] Council Directive 2004/83/EC of 29 April 2004 on Minimum Standards for the Qualification and Status of Third Country Nationals or Stateless Persons as Refugees or as Persons Who Otherwise Need International Protection and the Content of the Protection Granted [2004] OJ L.304/12 ('Qualification Directive').

[4] *Elgafaji* v. *Staatssecretaris van Justitie*, Case C-465/07, Judgment of the European Court of Justice (Grand Chamber), 17 February 2009. The Netherlands sought a preliminary ruling from the European Court of Justice to clarify the meaning and purpose of article 15(c): see OJ C. 8/5 of January 12, 2008; Decision 200702174/1 (12 October 2007) of Dutch Council of State; *Elgafaji* v. *Staatssecretaris van Justitie*, Case C-465/07, Opinion of Advocate General Poiares Madura, 9 September 2008.

Directive. This Directive represented the fourth building block in the first phase of the Common European Asylum System,[5] intended to harmonize and streamline legal standards relating to asylum in the Member States of the EU.[6]

Described as 'unquestionably the most important instrument in the new legal order in European asylum because it goes to the heart of the 1951 Convention Relating to the Status of Refugees',[7] the Directive sought to clarify the constitutive elements of the Convention refugee definition and the rights flowing from refugee status, and establish a harmonized approach towards people with an international protection need falling outside the scope of the Refugee Convention, known as 'beneficiaries of subsidiary protection'. The Directive therefore has two components: clarifying the eligibility criteria for international protection, and setting out the resultant status for those who qualify. It is the first supranational instrument to elaborate a separate and distinct status for people who are not Convention refugees but are otherwise in need of protection.[8]

[5] The other instruments were: Council Directive 2001/55/EC of 20 July 2001 on Minimum Standards for Giving Temporary Protection in the Event of a Mass Influx of Displaced Persons and on Measures Promoting a Balance of Efforts between Member States in Receiving Such Persons and Bearing the Consequences thereof [2001] OJ L.212/12 (Temporary Protection Directive); Council Directive 2003/9/EC of 27 January 2003 laying down Minimum Standards for the Reception of Asylum Seekers [2003] OJ L.31/18; Council Regulation (EC) No 343/2003 of 18 February 2003 Establishing the Criteria and Mechanisms for Determining the Member State Responsible for Examining an Asylum Application Lodged in One of the Member States by a Third-Country National [2003] OJ L.50/1; Council Directive 2005/85/EC of 1 December 2005 on Minimum Standards on Procedures in Member States for Granting and Withdrawing Refugee Status [2005] OJ L.326/13. For the second phase of the Common European Asylum System, see the Hague Programme (adopted 5 November 2004).

[6] Under the Protocol on the Position of the United Kingdom and Ireland, and the Protocol on the Position of Denmark, annexed to the Treaty on European Union [2002] OJ C.325/5, those countries may elect not to adopt the asylum Directives. The UK and Ireland have, however, elected to adopt the Qualification Directive.

[7] H. Lambert, 'The EU Asylum Qualification Directive, Its Impact on the Jurisprudence of the United Kingdom and International Law', *International and Comparative Law Quarterly*, 55 (2006), p.161, referring to the Convention relating to the Status of Refugees (adopted 28 July 1951, entered into force 22 April 1954) 189 UNTS 137, read in conjunction with the Protocol relating to the Status of Refugees (adopted 31 January 1967, entered into force 4 October 1967) 606 UNTS 267.

[8] Note that the regional OAU Convention and the Cartagena Declaration apply Convention refugee status rather than a separate status: Organization of African Unity Convention Governing the Specific Aspects of Refugee Problems in Africa (adopted 10 September 1969, entered into force 20 June 1974) 1001 UNTS 45; Cartagena Declaration on Refugees (November 22, 1984) in Annual Report of the Inter-American Commission on Human Rights OAS Doc. OEA/Ser.L/V/II.66/doc.10, rev.1, 190–93 (1984–85).

It is important to recall that the Qualification Directive was based on pre-existing Member State practice, and aimed simply to harmonize existing concepts by drawing on the 'best' elements of the Member States' national systems.[9] It was therefore not intended as a comprehensive overhaul of protection, but rather as a partial codification of existing State practice that sought to balance the divergent political views of the various Member States.

Each Member State was supposed to have transposed the Qualification Directive into national law by October 10, 2006,[10] although as of August 2007, twelve Member States had still not transposed it in full, four had only partially transposed it,[11] and Greece had not transposed it at all.[12] Although an absence of implementing legislation should mean that the Directive's provisions apply directly where they are clear and unconditional,[13] there remain striking inconsistencies in whether, and how, the Directive is actually being applied (not least because some key provisions are not 'clear').[14] This necessarily undermines the process of harmonization that the Directive was intended to bring about.

Between March and July 2007, UNHCR undertook a comprehensive study of the implementation of the Qualification Directive in five Member States – France, Germany, Greece, the Slovak Republic and Sweden – which were selected as a geographical cross-section of

[9] 'Explanatory Memorandum' in Commission of the European Communities Proposal for a Council Directive on Minimum Standards for the Qualification and Status of Third Country Nationals and Stateless Persons as Refugees or as Persons Who Otherwise Need International Protection COM (2001) 510 final (12 September 2001) 5. Note that it was drafted prior to 1 May 2004 enlargement of the EU and hence relied on the State practice of the fifteen Member States at that time.

[10] Qualification Directive, art. 38. In accordance with articles 1 and 2 of the Protocol on the Position of Denmark annexed to the Treaty on European Union [2002] OJ C.325/5 and the Treaty establishing the European Community [2002] OJ C.325/33, the Qualification Directive does not apply to Denmark (see Qualification Directive, recital 40).

[11] 'Non-Transposition of two Directives in the Field of Immigration and Asylum: Commission Delivers Reasoned Opinions,' Press release, IP/07/1015, Brussels, 7 July 2007, p. 2.

[12] UNHCR, *Asylum in the European Union: A Study of the Implementation of the Qualification Directive*, (UNHCR, Brussels, 2007), p. 9 ('UNHCR Study'). Greece did so in July 2008: Presidential Decree 96/2008, Official Gazette A 152, 30 July 2008. See also European Council on Refugees and Exiles (ECRE) and European Legal Network on Asylum (ELENA), 'The Impact of the EU Qualification Directive on International Protection', October 2008, pp. 48–49 ('ECRE Study').

[13] *Internationale Handelsgesellschaft* [1970] ECR 1125, pp. 1213ff.

[14] See OJ C.8/5 of 12 January 2008; see also Decision 200702174/1 (12 October 2007) of the Dutch Council of State.

the EU, with a variety of legal systems and institutional frameworks, and which together received almost half of all asylum applications lodged in the EU in 2006.[15] The study's purpose was to highlight whether the Member States were adopting a consistent approach to interpreting the Directive, whether national law and practice was consistent with international standards, and whether good practices could be identified.[16] Its release in November 2007 coincided with the one-year anniversary of the deadline for transposition and the lead-up to the Commission's report to the European Parliament and the Council (by April 10, 2008) as to whether any amendments to the Directive were required.[17] Of particular relevance to the present chapter is UNHCR's analysis of the application of article 15 on subsidiary protection, and whether the threshold for establishing a need for subsidiary protection differs in substance to claims for Convention refugee status. In October 2008, the European Council on Refugees and Exiles released a study to complement that of UNHCR, which extended the focus of the inquiry to twenty EU Member States. Results of that study are also incorporated where relevant.

ARTICLE 15: MEMBER STATE PRACTICE PRE-*ELGAFAJI*

In legal terms, the inclusion of article 15 in the Qualification Directive expanded the scope of protection formally offered throughout the EU. In practice, however, narrow interpretations and procedural flaws mean that subsidiary protection is not, on the whole, increasing the numbers of people receiving protection in the Member States.[18] In Greece, for example, accelerated asylum procedures mean that subsidiary protection is not being systematically considered for asylum applicants, by contrast to France, Germany, Sweden and the UK, where a single procedure requires decision-makers first to assess an applicant's claim in accordance with the Convention grounds,

[15] UNHCR Study, p. 8. [16] *Ibid.*

[17] Qualification Directive, art. 37. See 'Communication from the Commission to the European Parliament, the Council, the European Economic and Social Committee and the Committee of Regions: Policy Plan on Asylum', (Brussels, June 2008).

[18] UNHCR Study, p. 11. Although Sweden grants subsidiary protection to very large numbers of people, this has not greatly affected numbers overall, given that this continues Sweden's historical practice of favouring subsidiary protection categories over Convention status, and Sweden's recognition rate for Convention refugees remains comparatively very low: p. 81.

before turning to the subsidiary protection criteria if that person is found not to be a Convention refugee.[19]

Perhaps the more fundamental problem, however, is the divergent interpretations being employed across the Member States in the assessment of refugee and subsidiary protection status. On the one hand, these interpretations reflect long-standing idiosyncracies of particular States; on the other, they highlight the problems created by poorly drafted, hastily adopted and decontextualized subsidiary protection provisions in the Qualification Directive. In the Member States' wily attempts to confine the categories of people to whom protection should be extended, they have in fact created a new area for divergence and inconsistency which undermines the very harmonization process.[20]

As anticipated by a number of commentators prior to the Directive's entry into force,[21] the particular problem is article 15(c). This provision extends subsidiary protection to civilians who face a 'real risk'[22] of a 'serious and individual threat' to their 'life or person by reason of indiscriminate violence in situations of international or internal armed conflict'.[23] Recital 26 provides further that: 'Risks

[19] UNHCR Study, pp. 80, 82. According to the ECRE Study, a single procedure is used in all Member States examined there: pp. 200–01.

[20] On the drafting history, see McAdam, *Complementary Protection in International Refugee Law*, ch. 2.

[21] See e.g. J. McAdam, 'The European Union Qualification Directive: The Creation of a Subsidiary Protection Regime,' *International Journal of Refugee Law*, 17 (2005), 461; UNHCR, 'UNHCR Annotated Comments on the EC Council Directive 2004/83/EC of 29 April 2004 on Minimum Standards for the Qualification and Status of Third Country Nationals or Stateless Persons as Refugees or as Persons Who Otherwise Need International Protection and the Content of the Protection Granted (OJ L 304/12 of 30.9.2004)', January 2005, p. 32; A. Klug, 'Harmonization of Asylum in the European Union – Emergence of an EU Refugee System?', *German Yearbook of International Law*, 47 (2004), p. 616–19; see also M.-T. Gil-Bazo, 'Refugee Status and Subsidiary Protection under EC Law: The Qualification Directive and the Right to be Granted Asylum' in A. Baldaccini, E. Guild and H. Toner, (eds.) *Whose Freedom, Security and Justice?: EU Immigration and Asylum Law and Policy* (Oxford: Hart Publishing, 2007), pp. 229–64; K. Zwaan (ed.), *The Qualification Directive: Central Themes, Problem Issues, and Implementation in Selected Member States* (Nijmegen: Wolf Legal Publishers, 2007), especially M. Garlick, 'UNHCR and the Implementation of Council Directive 2004/83/EC on Minimum Standards for the Qualification and Status of Third Country Nationals or Stateless Persons as Refugees or as Persons Who Otherwise Need International Protection and the Content of the Protection Granted (The EC "Qualification Directive"),' pp. 62–64. For the drafting history of the provision, see McAdam, *Complementary Protection*, ch. 2.

[22] Qualification Directive, art. 2(e).

[23] The standard is 'substantial grounds for believing': art. 2(e).

to which a population of a country or a section of the population is generally exposed do normally not create in themselves an individual threat which would qualify as serious harm.'

Member States' independent analysis of article 15(c), frequently without regard to the interpretations being adopted in other Member States, the jurisprudential trends in the European Court of Human Rights,[24] or the guidance of UNHCR,[25] has led to vastly different recognition rates across the EU of people fleeing violence in Iraq, Chechnya and Somalia,[26] and has created legal uncertainty about the meaning of a provision that is supposed to give rise to a uniform approach.[27]

The provision has caused difficulties in three main ways. First, does it provide protection only when article 3 of the European Convention on Human Rights ('ECHR') 'also has a bearing', or does it instead offer 'supplementary or other protection'?[28] If the latter, what criteria should be applied 'for determining whether a person … runs a real risk of serious and individual threat by reason of indiscriminate violence within the terms of Article 15(c)'?[29] Thirdly, how is the existence of an 'international or internal armed conflict' to be interpreted? Seeking clarification of the first two questions, the Dutch Council of State sought a preliminary ruling from the ECJ which was handed down in February 2009.[30] The third question has not been considered at a supranational level, but some guidance may be sought from national jurisprudence. Before examining these decisions, however,

[24] e g *Salah Sheekh* v. *The Netherlands* App. No. 1948/04 (January 11, 2007).

[25] UNHCR Study, p. 14 (referring, for example, to UNHCR's Annotated Comments of January 2005).

[26] For example, the percentage of Iraqi asylum applicants granted Convention refugee status at first instance in the first quarter of 2007 was as follows: 16.3 per cent (Germany), 1.7 per cent (Sweden), 0 per cent (Greece, Slovak Republic). The percentage granted subsidiary protection status was: 1.1 per cent (Germany), 73.2 per cent (Sweden), 0 per cent (Greece, Slovak Republic). See UNHCR Study, p. 13.

[27] See one suggestion for an international judicial commission: A. M. North and J. Chia, 'Towards Convergence in the Interpretation of the Refugee Convention: A Proposal for the Establishment of an International Judicial Commission for Refugees', in J. McAdam (ed.), *Forced Migration, Human Rights and Security* (Hart Publishing, Oxford, 2008).

[28] Convention for the Protection of Human Rights and Fundamental Freedoms (European Convention on Human Rights, as amended) (4 November 1950).

[29] OJ C.8/5 of January 12, 2008; see also Decision 200702174/1 (12 October 2007) of the Dutch Council of State; and *Elgafaji* (Advocate General's opinion).

[30] See *Elgafaji* (Grand Chamber).

it is helpful first to set out the inconsistencies that had emerged in Member State practice.

First, article 15(c) has not been transposed in a uniform manner in the national law of the five Member States examined in the UNHCR study, and of the remaining Member States, at least six have adapted wording which differs from article 15(c).[31] France has added a requirement that the threat to the civilian is 'direct', and in the Slovak Republic and Sweden, the provision is not limited to 'civilians'. The Swedish provision initially appears broader than article 15(c) because it extends to people fearing harm in 'other severe conflicts', but Sweden's restrictive interpretation of 'internal armed conflict' means that 'other severe conflicts' is used to cover situations which, in other Member States, would be encapsulated by 'internal armed conflict'.[32] Furthermore, Swedish law requires applicants to demonstrate 'serious abuses' (which could include disproportionate punishment, arbitrary incarceration, physical abuse and assault, sexual abuse, social rejection, severe harassment, etc) rather than a 'serious threat' to life or person.[33] German law does not transpose the reference to 'indiscriminate violence' (although UNHCR notes that this reflects recital 26).[34]

Secondly, and related to the absence of a harmonized approach, the elements of article 15(c) – 'serious and individual threat' due to 'indiscriminate violence' in 'situations of international or internal armed conflict' – are creating higher evidentiary burdens for applicants compared to articles 15(a) and (b) and Convention-based claims. Even though the standard of proof – 'substantial grounds … for believing'

[31] Law on the Legal Status of Aliens (29 April 2004) No. IX-2206 (Official Gazette No. 73–2539, 3 April 2004) art. 87 (Lithuania); *Loi modifiant la loi du 15 décembre 1980 sur l'accès au territoire, le séjour, l'établissement et l'éloignement des étrangers* (September 15, 2006) art. 26 (Belgium), which omits the 'individual' requirement. The ECRE Study also points to different wording in Germany (p. 51), Slovenia (p. 52), Hungary (p. 55), the UK (p. 58) and Sweden (p. 207).

[32] UNHCR Study, pp. 67–68. This is despite drafting records which suggested that 'other severe conflicts' would extend to political instability in the home State and a consequent lack of safeguards for basic human rights, including where the State is not a party to the conflict.

[33] See *Ibid.*, p. 68.

[34] *Ibid.* Under the draft Greek law, protection from indiscriminate violence was not restricted to situations of 'international or internal armed conflict,' but in the final text it is limited to such situations: see UNCHR Study, p. 69, referring to the then draft Presidential Decree, art. 52(c); see now Presidential Decree 96/2008, Official Gazette A 152, 30 July 2008, art. 15.

that the applicant faces a 'real risk' of serious harm if removed[35] – is identical for articles 15(a), (b) and (c), and is supposed to be comparable to the 'well-founded fear of persecution' standard for Convention claims, in real terms it will generally be harder to for a applicant to establish the requisite elements of article 15(c).

The pre-*Elgafaji* position has been compounded by the fact that in a number of jurisdictions, articles 15(a) and (b) have not been given any (meaningful) consideration by decision-makers, with article 15(c) seemingly becoming the residual category for subsidiary protection claims.[36] UNHCR has queried whether the infrequent examination of article 15(b) in Swedish case law is simply 'a matter of expediency,' or a more fundamental problem of confusion about the distinction between 'inhuman and degrading treatment' and 'serious threat to life or person'.[37] If, indeed, an absence of clear doctrinal guidance is leading decision-makers to favour article 15(c),[38] then there is a risk that applicants who would otherwise fall within article 15(b), assessed in accordance with the jurisprudence of the European Court of Human Rights, which does not require singling out,[39] will have to prove their claims at a higher standard. The result is that subsidiary protection claims may not be properly assessed, and that far from being a fallback status for people with a need for international protection but who do not satisfy the Convention definition, it is a more difficult status to obtain.[40]

(a) The requirements of article 15(c): individual threat

As anticipated prior to the Qualification Directive's entry into force,[41] the 'individual' requirement in article 15(c), read in conjunction with recital 26,[42] has been used in some Member States to deny

35 Qualification Directive, art. 2(e).

36 UNHCR Study, pp. 12, 70 (Swedish practice). This is somewhat surprising, given the extensive (pre-existing and continuing) jurisprudence of the European Court of Human Rights on article 3 of the ECHR, which parallels article 15(b) of the Qualification Directive and which provides a rich basis for interpretation of cases under that head.

37 UNHCR Study, pp. 70–71. 38 *Ibid.*, pp. 12, 70–71.

39 *Salah Sheekh* v. *The Netherlands*.

40 There are parallels with the Canadian position (see analysis below).

41 J. McAdam, 'The European Union Qualification Directive', p. 481.

42 UNHCR has recommended the deletion of recital 26: UNHCR Study, p. 74. The ECJ (at para. 37) made the important point that while 'the objective finding alone of a risk linked to the general situation in a country is not, as a rule, sufficient to establish that the conditions

protection to people who are at risk of serious harm but cannot show that they are being singled out.[43] In an article published prior to the Directive's transposition,[44] I argued that the language of article 15(c) could support a restrictive interpretation that a person in an area of indiscriminate violence would need to show at least that he or she were *personally* at risk – a very problematic requirement, since indiscriminate violence is, by definition, random and haphazard. I noted that if it were interpreted even more strictly, it might require individuals to be singled out, which would establish a higher threshold than is required for either Convention-based protection or temporary protection.

These concerns have been borne out in state practice. The Swedish Migration Board requires applicants to show that they are 'personally at risk' because of a 'particular circumstance'.[45] In France, applicants have to show that a personal characteristic, such as their profession, religion or wealth, is putting them at particular risk.[46] In Germany, applicants have to show that they are at greater risk than the general population or a part thereof.[47] In Austria, applicants have to show that they are personally targeted.[48] In the UK, the Asylum and Immigration Tribunal ('AIT') recently observed that the word 'individual' requires the applicant to demonstrate a personal risk 'relating

set out in Article 15(c) of the Directive have been met in respect of a specific person, its wording nevertheless allows – by the use of the word "normally" – for the possibility of an exceptional situation which would be characterised by such a high degree of risk that substantial grounds would be shown for believing that that person would be subject individually to the risk in question.'

43 UNHCR Study, p. 71ff, citing the approach of authorities in France, Germany and Sweden. The vast majority of Member States supported the requirement on the grounds that it would avoid 'an undesired opening of the scope of this subparagraph:' 12382/02 ASILE 47 (30 September 2002) para. 4. Lithuania, Belgium, Finland, Austria, the Czech Republic and Hungary do not have an 'individual' requirement: see respectively Law on the Legal Status of Aliens (29 April 2004) No. IX-2206 (Official Gazette No 73–2539, 3 April 2004) art. 87 (Lithuania); *Loi modifiant la loi du 15 décembre 1980 sur l'accès au territoire, le séjour, l'établissement et l'éloignement des étrangers* (15 September 2006) art. 26 (Belgium); Aliens Act 2004, section 89 ; ECRE Study, pp. 27, 218.

44 J. McAdam, 'The European Union Qualification Directive', pp. 480–81.

45 See Lifos dokumentnr 16852, beslut 5 juli 2007 (2) (English version available at www.migrationsverket.se/include/lifos/dokument/www/07070582.pdf), as referred to in UNHCR Study, p. 72.

46 See decisions referred to in UNHCR Study, p. 73.

47 *Ibid.* This is due to the way recital 26 has been combined with art 15(c) in section 60(7) of the Residence Act 2004.

48 ECRE Study, p. 217.

to the person's specific characteristics or profile or circumstances', despite a previous ruling from the same body that held: 'It would be ridiculous to suggest that if there were a real risk of serious harm to members of the civilian population in general by reason of indiscriminate violence that an individual Appellant would have to show a risk to himself over and above that general risk.'[49]

As Hathaway has observed, to demand a 'singling out' of an applicant 'confuses the requirement to assess risk on the basis of the applicant's particular circumstances with some erroneous notion that refugee status must be based on a completely personalized set of facts'.[50]

In the context of claims derived from situations of generalized oppression, therefore, the issue is not whether the claimant is more at risk than anyone else in her country, but rather whether the broadly based harassment or abuse is sufficiently serious to substantiate a claim to refugee status. If persons like the applicant may face serious harm in her country, and if that risk is grounded in their civil or political status, then in the absence of effective national protection she is properly considered to be a Convention refugee.[51]

Similarly, as Goodwin-Gill and I have argued, where large groups are seriously affected 'by the outbreak of uncontrolled communal violence, it would appear wrong in principle to limit the concept of persecution to measures immediately identifiable as direct and individual'.[52] The US Asylum Regulations dispensed with the singling out requirement in 1990, instead requiring only that a applicant show 'a pattern or practice … of persecution of a group of persons *similarly situated* to the applicant', and his or her 'own inclusion in, and identification with, such group of persons such that his or her fear of persecution upon return is reasonable'.[53]

[49] *Lukman Hameed Mohamed* v. *Secretary of State for the Home Department* AA/14710/2006 (unreported, 16 August 2007), cited in UNHCR, 'UNHCR Statement: Subsidiary Protection under the EC Qualification Directive for People Threatened by Indiscriminate Violence' (January 2008), p. 6 ('UNHCR Statement'). See also ECRE Study, pp. 26–29.

[50] J.C. Hathaway, *The Law of Refugee Status* (Butterworths, Toronto, 1991), pp. 91–92 (citations omitted).

[51] *Ibid.*, p. 97 (citations omitted).

[52] Goodwin-Gill and McAdam, *The Refugee in International Law*, p. 129. See the reference there in fn 364 to *R* v. *Secretary of State for the Home Department, ex parte Jeyakumaran* (No. CO/290/84, QBD, unreported, 28 June 1985).

[53] 8 CFR §208.13(b)(2)(iii) – asylum (emphasis supplied); §208.16(b)(2) – withholding.

The relevant question, therefore, should be whether the applicant faces a reasonable chance of persecution or (in the case of subsidiary protection) serious harm. Over-emphasis of the word 'individual' in article 15(c) of the Qualification Directive places a burden on applicants which goes beyond that required under the Refugee Convention, and undermines the notion of subsidiary protection as a complementary form of human rights protection.[54] As the European Court of Human Rights has observed in the context of article 3 of the ECHR, the effect of such a stringent individual requirement 'might render the protection offered by that provision illusory if ... the applicant were required to show the existence of further special distinguishing features'.[55] This has been echoed by UNHCR in the specific context of the Qualification Directive.[56] It is not in line with comparable jurisprudence of the European Court of Human Rights on article 3 of the ECHR, where the court has expressly stated that to demonstrate a 'real risk' of inhuman or degrading treatment or punishment, a person does not have to establish 'further special distinguishing features concerning him personally in order to show that he was, and continues to be, personally at risk'.[57]

Clarification by the European Court of Justice: Elgafaji

The ECJ has now clarified that article 15(c) does not require an applicant to 'adduce evidence that he is specifically targeted by reason of factors particular to his personal circumstances',[58] tacitly endorsing UNHCR's view that article 15(c) provides 'added value' to articles 15(a) and (b) by offering protection from serious risks which are *situational*, rather than *individually* focused.[59]

[54] UNHCR has stressed the importance of a full and inclusive interpretation of the refugee definition in the Convention, including recognizing its applicability in situations of generalized violence and armed conflict where a nexus to at least one of the five Convention grounds can be demonstrated: UNHCR Study, p. 99; see also UNHCR Statement, p. 5.

[55] *Salah Sheekh* v. *The Netherlands*, para. 148.

[56] UNHCR Study, p. 74.

[57] *Salah Sheekh* v. *The Netherlands*, para. 148.

[58] *Elgafaji* (Grand Chamber), para. 45.

[59] UNHCR Statement, 5. UNHCR argued that the use of the word 'individual' simply indicates that a person must face a real, rather than a remote, risk, and accordingly should 'not lead to a higher threshold and heavier burden of proof' being imposed (at p. 6). See also the discussion of this standard of proof in Amnesty International (German section) and others, 'Joint Opinion on the Legislation to Implement EU Directives on Residence and

In his opinion of September 9, 2008, the Advocate General similarly found that article 15(c) is supplementary to articles 15(a) and (b).[60] The test under article 15(c) is met where the indiscriminate violence feared 'is so serious that it cannot fail to represent a likely and serious threat to that person'.[61] In terms of the standard of proof, the individual nature of the threat 'does not have to be established to such a high standard under Article 15(c) of the Directive as under Article 15(a) and (b) thereof,' but 'the seriousness of the violence will have to be clearly established so that no doubt remains as to both the indiscriminate and the serious nature of the violence of which the applicant for subsidiary protection is the target'.[62] The Advocate General stated:

> the more the person is individually affected (for example, by reason of his membership of a given social group), the less it will be necessary to show that he faces indiscriminate violence in his country or a part of the territory which is so serious that there is a serious risk that he will be a victim of it himself. Likewise, the less the person is able to show that he is individually affected, the more the violence must be serious and indiscriminate for him to be eligible for the subsidiary protection claimed.[63]

In its reasoning, the ECJ explained that the word 'individual':

> must be understood as covering harm to civilians irrespective of their identity, where the degree of indiscriminate violence characterising the armed conflict taking place – assessed by the competent national authorities before which an application for subsidiary protection is made, or by the courts of a Member State to which a decision refusing such an application is referred – reaches such a high level that substantial grounds are shown for believing that a civilian, returned to the relevant country or, as the case may be, to the relevant region, would, solely on account of his presence on the territory of that country or region, face a real risk of being subject to the serious threat referred in Article 15(c) of the Directive.[64]

Accordingly, 'the more the applicant is able to show that he is specifically affected by reason of factors particular to his personal

Asylum Law' (August 2007) www.proasyl.de/fileadmin/proasyl/fm_redakteure/Englisch/Joint_Opinion_Eu_directives.pdf (2 April 2008).

[60] *Elgafaji* (Advocate General's opinion), para. 32. The Advocate General's role is to provide a detailed analysis of the legal aspects of the case and present an impartial and independent opinion on the appropriate response.

[61] *Ibid.*, para. 42. [62] *Ibid.* See also para. 36.

[63] *Ibid.*, para. 37. See also the approach in *AM & AM (Armed Conflict: Risk Categories) Somalia CG* [2008] UKAIT 00091, para. 110.

[64] *Elgafaji* (Grand Chamber), para. 35.

circumstances, the lower the level of indiscriminate violence required for him to be eligible for subsidiary protection'.[65]

The UK AIT criticized the Advocate General's opinion for failing to explain the meaning of article 15(c) as a whole,[66] stating that its focus on two aspects of article 15(c) in relative isolation ('serious and individual [threat]' and 'indiscriminate violence') left unclear the scope of other key terms, such as 'threat,' 'civilian's life or person', 'international or internal armed conflict', and 'by reason of indiscriminate violence'. The ECJ similarly avoided any extensive discussion of these additional terms, although it did observe that a 'threat' was something inherent in the general situation of armed conflict and did not require evidence of 'specific acts of violence', and that 'indiscriminate violence' implies violence that 'may extend to people irrespective of their personal circumstances'.[67] On the nature of an 'international or internal armed conflict', the court simply stated that it was to be 'assessed by the competent national authorities before which an application for subsidiary protection is made, or by the courts of a Member State to which a decision refusing such an application is referred',[68] avoiding any discussion about whether such determination ought to be made in accordance with international humanitarian law or other standards. Thus, while the decision in *Elgafaji* addressed some aspects of article 15(c), it did not resolve all the interpretative difficulties raised by that provision.

(b) International or internal armed conflict

Given the considerable divergence in interpretation among Member States on the meaning of 'international or internal armed conflict', it is regrettable, although understandable given its terms of reference, that the ECJ did not provide guidance on this point. The main debate is whether the phrase should be interpreted in accordance with international humanitarian law, and whether this imposes a further layer of analysis that could, if interpreted too rigidly, divert the focus from the key inquiry, namely the risk to the applicant and his or her need for protection. Alternatively, the objective of subsidiary

[65] *Ibid.*, para. 39. [66] *AM & AM*, para. 113.

[67] *Elgafaji* (Grand Chamber), para. 34. [68] *Ibid.*, para. 35.

protection might be better realized by leaving aside the peculiarities of international humanitarian law and focusing on the risk to fundamental human rights occasioned by indiscriminate violence in situations of conflict.

The approach in Sweden, Germany and Belgium is that the phrase must be understood according to its meaning under international humanitarian law.[69] The Supreme Administrative Court of the Czech Republic has taken a slightly broader view by holding that an internal armed conflict exists if article 1(1) of Additional Protocol II is met (provided that the exclusionary conditions in article 1(2) are not satisfied), or if a conflict satisfies the criteria set out by the International Criminal Tribunal for the Former Yugoslavia in *Tadić* (protracted armed violence and organized armed groups).[70] At first blush, an international humanitarian law approach seems to inject a degree of harmony into the provision's interpretation since it requires evaluation of a particular conflict against accepted international standards and seems to embrace a holistic approach to international law. However, neither the Qualification Directive itself nor the records of its drafting reveal an intention to interpret 'international or internal armed conflict' in its international humanitarian law sense. Moreover, there is a risk that unless the analysis of the nature of the conflict remains secondary to the assessment of harm faced by the applicant – the key protection issue – this evidentiary threshold may lead to a protection gap. Since there is no single meaning of 'international or internal armed conflict' in international humanitarian law,[71] determining whether or not one exists for the purposes of a determination under article 15(c) may impose a layer of analysis which is neither straightforward nor clear-cut. The specialist nature of international humanitarian law means

69 UNHCR Study, p. 77; BVerwG 10 C 43.07, VGH 13a B 05.30833 (June 24, 2008) (unofficial translation released by the court), paras. 19, 22, 37; ECRE Study, p. 221. See also *KH (Article 15(c) Qualification Directive) Iraq CG* [2008] UKAIT 00023, para. 60, now overturned by *QD (Iraq)* v. *Secretary of State for the Home Department* [2009] EWCA Civ 620, paras. 18, 34–36.

70 Judgment of the Supreme Administrative Court of the Czech Republic, 13 March 2009, No. 5 Azs 28/2008, www.nssoud.cz. For the content of the *Tadić* criteria, see *Prosecutor* v. *Ramush Haradinaj, Idriz Balaj and Lahi Brahimaj*, Case No. IT-04–84-T, Trial Chamber, 3 April 2008, paras. 49, 60; *Prosecutor* v. *Ljube Boškoski and Johan Tarčulovski*, Case No. IT-04–82-T, Trial Chamber, 10 July 2008, paras. 177–78, 199–203.

71 See e.g. International Committee of the Red Cross, 'How is the Term "Armed Conflict" Defined in International Humanitarian Law?' (Opinion Paper, March 2008).

that considerations of 'armed conflict' in that context are necessarily confined to a construction within the framework of the Geneva Conventions and their Additional Protocols. The lack of clarity in this regime as to when an 'internal armed conflict' exists highlights the difficulty of a taking an international humanitarian law approach to article 15(c).[72] A strict insistence on that approach takes us no closer to a definitive 'answer' than if it were dispensed with altogether.[73] It both adds a complexity to the deliberation and confines the circumstances to which article 15(c) applies.[74] The English Court of Appeal has described it as an 'unarticulated gloss of a fundamental kind',[75] stating that the phrase 'situations of international or internal armed conflict' in article 15(c) 'has an autonomous meaning broad enough to capture any situation of indiscriminate violence, whether caused by one or more armed factions or by a state, which reaches the level described by the ECJ in *Elgafaji*'.[76]

Accordingly, there is an argument that in observing the object and purpose of the Qualification Directive, the focus is on the protection needs of the individual claimant, whereas the purpose for tightly construing the notion of 'armed conflict' in the international humanitarian law context is to determine prosecution and punishment of those accused of violating rules that may or may not apply, depending on

[72] In *Ibid.*, the International Committee of the Red Cross identifies three types of non-international armed conflicts: (a) those within the meaning of common article 3 of the 1949 Geneva Conventions (not formally defined); (b) those within the meaning of article 1 of Additional Protocol II; and (c) those encompassed by article 8(2)(f) of the Rome Statute, based on the jurisprudence of the International Criminal Tribunal for the Former Yugoslavia in *The Prosecutor* v. *Dusko Tadić*, Decision on the Defence Motion for Interlocutory Appeal on Jurisdiction, IT-94–1-A, October 2, 1995, para. 70. Which meaning is to apply in an assessment of an individual's protection need under article 15(c) of the Qualification Directive?

[73] Hugo Storey, an immigration judge in the *KH* decision of 2008, previously argued that a disadvantage of taking an international humanitarian law approach was that 'strictly applied, it would only cover armed conflicts that were conducted in violation of international humanitarian law norms': H. Storey and others, 'Complementary Protection: Should There Be a Common Approach to Providing Protection to Persons Who Are Not Covered by the 1951 Geneva Convention?' (Joint ILPA/IARLJ Symposium, December 6, 1999) (copy with author), p. 15. However, in *KH* he stated: 'Once one adopts a purposive approach, the reasons for giving as far as possible an IHL meaning to key terms in Article 15(c) are overwhelming' (para. 33), and: 'An IHL approach provides an objective framework for interpreting Article 15(c) – in the form of an identifiable set of legal rules which exist and are applied both EU-wide and internationally' (para. 39).

[74] There must be a minimum level of intensity, 'parties to the conflict' must have a certain command structure, etc.

[75] *QD (Iraq)*, para. 18. [76] *Ibid.*, para. 35.

the characterization of the conflict. In the same way that the international crime of 'persecution' in the Rome Statute embodies a more exacting test than 'persecution' in international refugee law, there is scope for different meanings in different international law contexts.

Given the object and purpose of article 15(c) – protecting individuals from the risk of indiscriminate violence – and the overall object and purpose of the Qualification Directive, framed by the express legal background of international refugee and human rights law, the focus for qualification should be the protection needs of the applicant in light of the human rights violations of which he or she is at risk. Indeed, it is in respect of individual risk that the intensity or duration of a conflict is relevant, rather than as indicia of the conflict's nature. As the ECJ stressed in *Elgafaji*, subsidiary protection is 'complementary and additional to' refugee protection, and 'should be drawn from international obligations under human rights instruments and practices existing in Member States'.[77] International humanitarian law is not mentioned in the Directive, and while it may be illustrative in understanding article 15(c), it cannot be determinative. Article 15(c) thus incorporates all forms of armed conflict.

The concerns raised above have been borne out in State practice. In France, Germany and Sweden, differing interpretations have resulted in particular conflicts being characterized as within the scope of 'international or internal armed conflict' in some of those Member States, but not in others. For example, the French, Bulgarian and Czech authorities regard the situation in Iraq as an 'internal armed conflict', while the Swedish and Romanian authorities do not, and within Germany, there is inconsistency across the various state jurisdictions.[78] Whereas some German courts have stated that an armed conflict only needs to be of an unpredictable duration and intensity that threatens life or limb,[79] others have required the conflict to be comparable to a country-wide civil war.[80] The upshot of these varied views is that applicants from Iraq, Chechnya and Somalia cannot be

[77] *Elgafaji* (Grand Chamber), para. 7, referring to Qualification Directive, recitals 24 and 25 respectively.
[78] UNHCR Study, p. 76; ECRE Study, p. 215.
[79] UNHCR Study, see p. 77, fn 317.
[80] *Ibid.*, cited, p. 77, fn 318.

assured a consistent assessment of their situation across the Member States.[81]

Although UNHCR has acknowledged that the interpretation of 'international or internal armed conflict' should be *informed by* international humanitarian law, it has also emphasized that '[i]nternational protection needs arising from indiscriminate violence are not limited to situations of declared war or internationally recognized conflicts', and that '[n]o formal determination by a State or an organization regarding the existence of an "international or internal armed conflict" should be required'.[82] This is the approach taken in the regional refugee instruments which extend protection to situations of generalized violence, such as the OAU Convention's extension of protection to people fleeing 'external aggression, occupation, foreign domination or events seriously disturbing the public order in either part or the whole' of their country, and the Cartagena Declaration's application to people whose 'lives, safety or freedom have been threatened by generalized violence, foreign aggression, internal conflicts' and so on.[83]

International humanitarian law is not irrelevant to the interpretation of article 15(c), but its use must be sensitive to the primary purpose of that provision – assessing a person's need for international protection, within the particular legal framework of the Qualification Directive. While ignoring international humanitarian law in interpreting terms that stem directly from it could lead to even greater inconsistency in the interpretation of article 15(c), as different Member States independently seek to define the meaning of terms within that provision,[84] there is also a risk that interpreting the 'armed conflict' too strictly may undermine the protection of fundamental human rights which subsidiary protection is intended to safeguard. The European Council on Refugees and Exiles recommends that Member States take 'a cautious approach' in determining whether or not an international or internal armed conflict exists, 'declaring when in doubt that such

[81] *Ibid.*, p. 78. [82] UNHCR Statement, p. 6. [83] UNHCR Study, p. 79.

[84] See Skeleton Argument on behalf of the Applicant in *Hamed* v. *Secretary of State for the Home Department*, AIT, January 25, 2008 (R. Husain and S. Knights), paras. 52–53 (copy on file with author). Storey, for example, describes international humanitarian law as 'a ready made international framework of reference for defining key terms': H. Storey, 'EU Refugee Qualification Directive: A Brave New World?' *International Journal of Refugee Law*, 20 (2008), p. 36.

a situation exists, and that people fleeing from it merit protection'.[85] The excellent international humanitarian law analysis of article 15(c) in the appellant's Skeleton Argument in *Hamed* v. *Secretary of State for the Home Department* shows how those principles can help to achieve a unified approach to article 15(c), provided that they are applied with regard to contemporary jurisprudence, guidance from the International Committee of the Red Cross and, most importantly, the object and purpose of the Qualification Directive. The key issue, as intimated by UNHCR,[86] is that they need to be understood within the protection context of the Qualification Directive and not to be construed in such a way as to create protection gaps.

It therefore seems more appropriate to turn to other refugee law tools that protect people fleeing armed conflict, such as the OAU Convention, the Cartagena Declaration and the Temporary Protection Directive, to ascertain the kinds of situations in which protection is forthcoming.

In the EU context, the Temporary Protection Directive is of particular relevance. This instrument, which in the event of a mass influx extends protection inter alia to people 'who have fled areas of armed conflict or endemic violence',[87] does not require the existence of an 'international or internal armed conflict' to be triggered. As I have argued previously, for legal and logical consistency, article 15(c) ought to protect people fleeing individually or in small groups from situations which, in a mass influx, would result in protection – especially since article 15(c) was originally intended to protect those who, but for the fact that they arrived individually rather than as part of a mass influx, would fall within the scope of the Temporary Protection Directive.[88] Indeed, the rationale behind the Temporary Protection Directive is that the *size* of the influx makes it inefficient or impossible to process claims in the normal way,[89] *not* that the nature of the threat is unique to mass influxes. To limit subsidiary protection in this way therefore seems both illogical and

[85] ECRE and ELENA, 'The Impact of the EU Qualification Directive on International Protection', p. 29.
[86] UNHCR Statement, p. 6.
[87] Temporary Protection Directive, art. 2(c).
[88] See Explanatory Memorandum; see also Skeleton Argument in *Hamed*, paras. 26–29; McAdam, *Complementary Protection in International Refugee Law*, p. 74; Goodwin-Gill and McAdam, *The Refugee in International Law*, p. 296, fn. 76.
[89] Temporary Protection Directive, art. 2(a).

inconsistent.[90] UNHCR has accordingly recommended the deletion of 'international or internal armed conflict' from article 15(c).[91]

As a postscript, it should be noted that in its first review of the Qualification Directive, the European Commission stated that despite stakeholders stressing the need for clarification of article 15(c),[92] 'in view of the interpretative guidance provided by this judgment [*Elgafaji*] and of the fact that the relevant provisions were found to be compatible with the ECHR, an amendment of Article 15(c) is not considered necessary'.[93]

STANDARD OF PROOF: ARTICLE 2(E)

The standard of proof for subsidiary protection is that 'substantial grounds have been shown for believing that the person concerned, if returned to his or her country of origin ... would face a real risk of suffering serious harm as defined in Article 15'.[94] The reference to 'substantial grounds' stems from the case law of the European Court of Human Rights on article 3 of the ECHR and the Committee against Torture on article 3 of the Convention against Torture,[95] and was deliberately selected in order to avoid divergence between international practice and that of the Member States themselves.[96] The Committee against Torture has consistently held that 'substantial

[90] As a comment by the French delegation during the drafting process shows, there is a deep-seated fear that whole populations will flee on the basis of generalized violence if subsidiary protection status does not require individual harm to be demonstrated. It was stated that the expression 'international or internal armed conflict' 'risks opening the possibility of obtaining subsidiary protection to the entire population of countries involved in conflicts': 12199/02 ASILE 45 (September 25, 2002), p. 20, fn 8.

[91] UNHCR Study, p. 79.

[92] Commission of the European Communities, 'Proposal for a Directive of the European Parliament and of the Council on Minimum Standards for the Qualification and Status of Third Country Nationals or Stateless Person a Beneficiaries of International Protection and the Content of the Protection Granted (Recast)' Brussels, COM(2009) 551 final/2, 2009/0164 (COD), p. 5.

[93] *Ibid.*, p. 6 (emphasis in the original).

[94] Qualification Directive, art. 2(e).

[95] Convention against Torture and Other Cruel, Inhuman or Degrading Treatment or Punishment (adopted 10 December 1984, entered into force 26 June 1987) 1465 UNTS 85 ('CAT').

[96] Council of the European Union Presidency Note to Strategic Committee on Immigration, Frontiers and Asylum on September 25, 2002, Doc. 12148/02 ASILE 43 (20 September 2002) p. 5. The Netherlands supported Sweden's argument that wording from decisions of the Committee against Torture should be taken into account to avoid different rulings from different courts of bodies concerning similar situations: 12199/02 ASILE 45 (25 September 2002), p. 3, fn. 3. See also *Kacaj* [2001] INLR 354.

grounds' involve a 'foreseeable, real and personal risk' of torture.[97] They are to be assessed on grounds that go 'beyond mere theory or suspicion' or 'a mere possibility of torture',[98] but the threat of torture does not have to be 'highly probable'[99] or 'highly likely to occur'.[100] The European Court of Human Rights has said that the relevant test is a 'real risk' of torture or inhuman or degrading treatment.[101] The UK AIT has interpreted this as simply meaning that the risk 'must be more than a mere possibility' – a standard which 'may be a relatively low one'.[102]

The UK takes the view that the 'substantial grounds' test in article 2(e) of the Qualification Directive is intended to replicate the 'well-founded fear' standard under the Refugee Convention. In *Sivakumaran*, the House of Lords said that that standard implies 'a reasonable degree of likelihood',[103] which generally falls somewhere lower than the 'balance of probabilities'.[104] As the AIT stated in *Kacaj*:

The link with the Refugee Convention is obvious. Persecution will normally involve the violation of a person's human rights and a finding that

[97] See e.g. *EA* v. *Switzerland* (Comm. No. 28/1995) UN Doc. CAT/C/19/D/28/1995 (November 10, 1997) para. 11.5; *X, Y and Z* v. *Sweden* (Comm. No. 61/1996) UN Doc. CAT/C/20/D/61/1996 (May 6, 1998) para. 11.5; *IAO* v. *Sweden* (Comm. No. 65/1997) UN Doc. CAT/C/20/D/65/1997 (May 6, 1998) para. 14.5; *KN* v. *Switzerland* (Comm. No. 94/1997) UN Doc. CAT/C/20/D/94/1997 (May 19, 1998) para. 10.5; *ALN* v. *Switzerland* (Comm. No. 90/1997) UN Doc. CAT/C/20/D/90/1997 (May 19, 1998) para. 8.7; *JUA* v. *Switzerland* (Comm. No. 100/1997) UN Doc. CAT/C/21/D/100/1997 (November 10, 1998) para. 6.6; *SMR and MMR* v. *Sweden* (Comm. No. 103/1998) UN Doc. CAT/C/22/D/103/1998 (May 5, 1999) para. 9.7; *MBB* v. *Sweden* (Comm. No. 104/1998) UN Doc. CAT/C/22/D/104/1998 (May 5, 1999) para. 6.8; *KT* v. *Switzerland* (Comm. No. 118/1998) UN Doc. CAT/C/23/D/118/1998 (November 19, 1999) para. 6.5; *NM* v. *Switzerland* (Comm. No. 116/1998) UN Doc. CAT/C/24/D/116/1998 (May 9, 2000) para. 6.7; *SC* v. *Denmark* (Comm. No. 143/1999) UN Doc. CAT/C/24/D/143/1999 (May 10, 2000) para. 6.6; *HAD* v. *Switzerland* (Comm. No. 126/1999) UN Doc. CAT/C/24/D/126/1999 (May 10, 2000) para. 4.10; *US* v. *Finland* (Comm. No. 197/2002) UN Doc. CAT/C/30/D/197/2002 (May 1, 2003) para. 7.8.

[98] *EA* v. *Switzerland*, para. 11.3.

[99] *Report of the Committee against Torture*, UN GAOR, 53rd Session, Supp. No. 44, UN Doc. A/53/44 (1998), Annex IX.

[100] *EA* v. *Switzerland*, para. 11.3.

[101] See *Cruz Varas* v. *Sweden* (1991) 14 EHRR 1; *Vilvarajah* v. *United Kingdom* (1991) 14 EHRR 248.

[102] *Kacaj*, para. 12. This threshold has also been used in Canada with respect to 'well-founded fear' in Convention refugee claims: *Ponniah* v. *Canada (Minister of Employment and Immigration)* (1991) 13 Imm. L.R. (2d) 241 (FCA), p. 245.

[103] *R* v. *Secretary of State for the Home Department, ex parte Sivakumaran* [1988] AC 958 (HL), p. 994 (Lord Keith); p. 996 (Lord Bridge, Lord Templeman); p. 997 (Lord Griffiths); p. 1000 (Lord Goff).

[104] Article 7(b) of the original proposal for the Qualification Directive stated that well-founded fear was to be 'objectively established' by considering whether there was 'a reasonable

there is real risk of persecution would be likely to involve a finding that there is a real risk of a breach of the European Convention on Human Rights. It would therefore be strange if different standards of proof applied ... Since the concern under each Convention is whether the risk of future ill-treatment will amount to a breach of an individual's human rights, a difference of approach would be surprising. If an adjudicator were persuaded that there was a well-founded fear of persecution but not for a reason which engaged the protection of the Refugee Convention, he would ... be required to reject a human rights claim if he was not satisfied that the underlying facts had been proved beyond reasonable doubt. Apart from the undesirable result of such a difference of approach when the effect on the individual who resists return is the same and may involve inhuman treatment or torture or even death, an adjudicator and the tribunal would need to indulge in mental gymnastics. Their task is difficult enough without such refinements.[105]

In that case, the AIT rejected the government's submission that a higher standard of proof was applicable to claims under article 3 of the ECHR on the basis that:

There is nothing in the jurisprudence of the human rights' Court or Commission which requires us to adopt a different approach to the standard applicable to the Refugee Convention; indeed, in our view, there is every reason why the same approach should be applied. Different standards would produce confusion and be likely to result in inconsistent decisions. We therefore reject the argument of the Secretary of State on this issue.[106]

While the AIT's reasoning highlights the substantial merits of this approach, both from a procedural and a protection perspective, it should be noted that the UK interpretation of the standard of proof does not automatically follow from the wording of the Qualification Directive itself.[107] Indeed, Battjes, Carlier and Piotrowicz and van

possibility that the applicant [would] be persecuted'. The Explanatory Memorandum (at p. 15) noted that a 'fear of being persecuted ... may be well-founded even if there is not a clear probability that the individual will be persecuted or suffer such harm but the mere chance or remote possibility of it is an insufficient basis for the recognition of the need for international protection'.

105 *Kacaj*, para. 10. 106 *Ibid.*, para. 15.

107 See my earlier discussion of this point: McAdam, *Complementary Protection in International Refugee Law*, pp. 61–64. While the AIT (at para. 143 of *KH*) criticized my assessment of this on the grounds that the standard of proof issue had been resolved by *Kacaj*, that decision does not bind other Member States, and the wording of the Directive (and its drafting history) leave room for alternative interpretations.

Eck have observed that the 'substantial grounds' threshold could be interpreted as setting a higher standard of proof than 'well-founded fear', as is the case in Canada and the US.[108] Indeed, during the drafting process, Sweden sought to replace 'substantial grounds' with 'well-founded fear' (as per an earlier draft) to ensure that the same proof entitlements were established for beneficiaries of subsidiary protection as for refugees. At the time, Germany also observed that the 'substantial grounds' terminology might create problems of proof assessment, although argued that these could be resolved by article 4.[109] These concerns are not merely academic. In Portugal, it is presently the case that the Aliens and Border Service requires applicants to prove 'beyond any doubt' that flight from a general situation of insecurity is caused by individual reasons directly linked to flight.[110]

In Canada, the expression 'substantial grounds for believing' has been interpreted as imposing a higher standard than 'well-founded fear'. In 2003, the Canadian Federal Court held that 'substantial grounds for believing' meant that the degree of risk for complementary protection claims under section 97 of the Immigration and Refugee Protection Act 2001[111] was to be determined 'on the balance

[108] H. Battjes, *European Asylum Law and International Law* (Martinus Nijhoff Publishers, Leiden, 2006), p. 225, referring also to J.-Y. Carlier, 'Réfugiés: Identification et statut des personnes à protéger. La direction "qualification"', in F. Julien-Laferrière, H. Labayle and Ö. Edström (eds.), *The European Immigration and Asylum Policy: Critical Assessment Five Years after the Amsterdam Treaty* (Bruylant, Brussels, 2005), text to fn. 34; R. Piotrowicz and C. van Eck, 'Subsidiary Protection and Primary Rights,' *International and Comparative Law Quarterly*, 53 (2004), p. 113. Battjes also suggests that the level of risk might be higher than under the Convention against Torture (p. 225; see also Carlier at p. 1B(2)), and that the test applied by the UN Human Rights Committee is stricter than that of the European Court of Human Rights.

[109] 12199/02 ASILE 45 (25 September 2002), p. 3, fn. 3. See further McAdam, *Complementary Protection in International Refugee Law*, pp. 62–63.

[110] UNHCR Statement, p. 20.

[111] Section 97(1) defines a 'person in need of protection' as someone falling outside the scope of the Refugee Convention who faces a personal danger of being tortured, as defined in article 1 of the CAT, or someone who faces a personal risk to life or a risk of cruel and unusual treatment or punishment where:

(i) the person is unable or, because of that risk, unwilling to avail themself of the protection of that country,
(ii) the risk would be faced by the person in every part of that country and is not faced generally by other individuals in or from that country,
(iii) the risk is not inherent or incidental to lawful sanctions, unless imposed in disregard of accepted international standards, and
(iv) the risk is not caused by the inability of that country to provide adequate health or medical care.

of probabilities',[112] by contrast to the 'well-founded fear' threshold for Convention refugee claims, meaning a 'reasonable chance or serious possibility'.[113]

This was affirmed by the Canadian Federal Court of Appeal. First, the court observed that section 97(1)(a) uses almost identical language to article 3 of the Convention against Torture, which means that the Committee against Torture's interpretation of article 3 is highly relevant. Accordingly, the court concluded that the relevant standard was 'on the balance of probabilities' or 'more likely than not', noting that 'the use of the word "would" requires a showing of probability'.[114] Secondly, the court indicated that the different nature of claims under section 96 compared to section 97(1)(a), such as the issue of nexus, meant that an identical standard of proof was not necessary (even though it recognized that there was 'no rational sense' in adopting a higher standard for the latter). The court extended the same threshold to section 97(1)(b) in the 'absence of some compelling reason' to the contrary.[115]

It has been suggested that an advantage of this dual-test approach is that it 'should encourage independent and separate analyses of the three different types of claims contained in the consolidated grounds of protection'.[116] While that is certainly important, there is no compelling reason why rigorous interpretation cannot occur even if the same standard of proof is applied. However, it has also been noted that in practice, the higher standard applied to section 97 can work to the advantage of applicants who are found not to

There is no statutory equivalent to article 15(c) of the Qualification Directive, but note the Immigration and Refugee Board Chairperson's Guidelines, 'Guideline 1: Civilian Non-Combatants Fearing Persecution in Civil War Situations', (March 7, 1996).

112 *Li* v. *Canada (Minister of Citizenship and Immigration)* [2003] FCJ No. 1934; 2003 FC 1514; affirmed in *Li* v. *Canada (Minister of Citizenship and Immigration*) [2005] FCJ No. 1; 2005 FCA 1, paras. 18–28.

113 This test derives from *Adjei* v. *Minister of Employment and Immigration* [1989] 2 FC 680.

114 *Li* v. *Canada (Minister of Citizenship and Immigration)* (2005), paras. 18–28. Since this was the interpretation which had been given in *Suresh* v. *Canada (Minister of Citizenship and Immigration)* [2000] FCJ No. 5 (FCA), Justice Rothstein said that Parliament could have enacted a lower test had it desired to depart from that interpretation.

115 *Li* v. *Canada (Minister of Citizenship and Immigration*) (2005), para. 38.

116 J. Reekie and C. Layden-Stevenson, 'Complementary Refugee Protection in Canada: The History and Application of section 97 of the Immigration and Refugee Protection Act (IRPA)', in International Association of Refugee Law Judges, *Forced Migration and the Advancement of International Protection* (2008), p. 282.

be credible, since objective factors, such as country of origin conditions, may trump the credibility issue and require that protection be granted.[117]

In the EU, where a single standard of proof means that the ultimate focus is supposed to be whether a real risk of serious harm exists,[118] it is in establishing *that* element that the burden under article 15(c) becomes particularly high. In addition to the requirements discussed above in relation to 'individual' threat and the meaning of an 'international or internal armed conflict,' the German authorities have imposed a very high threshold for risk under article 15(c): 'certain death or severest injuries'.[119] This goes far beyond what is required by article 2(e) – 'a real risk of suffering serious harm' – and is not in line with regional[120] or international interpretations of 'real risk'.[121] It also conflicts with the AIT's approach, namely that 'real risk' simply means that the risk 'must be more than a mere possibility'.[122] Thus, though the German courts have recognized that the situation in Iraq satisfies the 'armed conflict' criterion in article 15(c), they have held that 'there is no extreme danger which would necessitate the granting of subsidiary protection' on an individual basis.[123]

The result is that claims considered under article 15(c) of the Qualification Directive are subjected to additional evidentiary hurdles, making it more onerous for applicants to satisfy the test for subsidiary protection vis-à-vis Convention refugee status. Subsidiary protection is by no means an automatic safety net for people who do not meet the Convention definition of 'refugee' but whose fundamental human rights are at risk.

[117] Observations of Justice Carolyn Layden-Stevenson, Research Workshop on Critical Issues in International Refugee Law, York University, Toronto, May 1–2, 2008.

[118] *Kacaj*, para. 12. [119] UNHCR Study, p. 73.

[120] See *Ammari* v. *Sweden* App. No. 60959/00 (October 22, 2002); see also references in *KH*.

[121] *EA* v. *Switzerland*: risk must be foreseeable, real and personal. See UNHCR Study, p. 80.

[122] *Kacaj*, para. 12.

[123] UNHCR Study, p. 79, paraphrasing the German Federal Ministry of Interior Guidelines: Hinweise des Bundesministeriums des Inneren zur Anwendung der Richtlinie 2004/83/EG des Rates vom 29. April 2004 über Mindestnormen für die Anerkennung und den Status von Drittstaatsangehörigen oder Staatenlosen als Flüchtlinge oder als Personen, die anderweitig internationalen Schutz benötigen, und über den Inhalt des zu gewährenden Schutzes (ABl. EU L 304 vom 30. September 2004, S. 12 ff.) in der Bundesrepublik Deutschland vom 13. Oktober 2006.

CONCLUSION

The EU experience of harmonization in the field of asylum has not resulted in the interpretative consistency that some desired. The Qualification Directive is an instrument of compromise, and the political pressure to adopt it before ten new Member States joined the EU on 1 May 2004,[124] bringing with them their own views and legal heritages, partially explains the passage of some poorly drafted provisions and the subsequent confusion about their interpretation. The haste with which the Qualification Directive was ultimately adopted, combined with some Member States' attempts to pare back protection responsibilities to a bare minimum (for example, through the operation of article 15(c) and recital 26), means that far from simplifying the operation of asylum law in the EU, the Qualification Directive has in some areas created further inconsistencies and interpretative obstacles, thereby undermining the harmonization process. It is imperative that supranational instruments like the Qualification Directive are construed in a manner that safeguards the fundamental human rights they are intended to protect, rather than in a way that leads to protection gaps.

[124] J. van Selm and E. Tsolakis, 'The Enlargement of an "Area of Freedom, Security and Justice": Managing Migration in a European Union of 25 Members', Migration Policy Institute Policy Brief, May 2004, p. 2.

CHAPTER 3

Running scared since 9/11: refugees, UNHCR and the purposive approach to treaty interpretation

Geoff Gilbert

> States are not allowed to combat international terrorism at all costs. They must not resort to methods which undermine the very values they seek to protect. And this applies the more to those 'absolute' rights from which no derogation may be made even in times of emergency … Upholding human rights in the fight against terrorism is first and foremost a matter of upholding our values, even with regard to those who may seek to destroy them.[1]

INTRODUCTION

Even today, the events of 11 September 2001 in New York City, Washington DC and near Shanksville, Pennsylvania cast a long shadow. Heightened states of alert typify the daily experience of many, especially those engaging in international travel. It is an inconvenience that leads to more time being spent in airport queues than is good for anyone. Nevertheless, travellers put up with it because somehow it makes them feel safer. However, for those seeking refugee status, the events of that day in 2001 have had much more serious consequences. Specific refugee restricting provisions and the more general restrictions imposed on all travellers have made obtaining asylum more difficult since 11 September 2001; despite the fact that not a single refugee was involved in the attacks on the World Trade Centre or the Pentagon.[2] In spite of the fact that

[1] *Saadi* v. *Italy*, App. No. 37201/06, European Court of Human Rights (Grand Chamber), 28 February 2008. Concurring opinion of Judge Myjer, joined by Judge Zagrebelsky.

[2] On the other hand, it should be noted that some of those alleged to have been involved in the attacks on the United States embassies in Nairobi, Kenya, and in Dar es Salaam,

no refugee was involved, the international community, in the shape of the Security Council, immediately went on to link the threat of international terrorism with those seeking refugee status and intimated that the international protection of refugees could be used to facilitate terrorism.[3] United Nations Security Council Resolution 1368 (2001) of 12 September 2001 called in paragraph 4 for 'the international community to redouble their efforts to prevent and suppress terrorist acts … by … full implementation of … Security Council Resolutions, in particular resolution 1269 (1999)'. Resolution 1269 of 19 October 1999 had called upon states in paragraph 4 to:

> take appropriate measures in conformity with the relevant provisions of national and international law, including international standards of human rights, *before granting refugee status, for the purpose of ensuring that the asylum-seeker has not participated in terrorist acts*; (emphasis added).

Security Council Resolution 1373 (2001) of 28 September 2001 went further, directly and indirectly. Paragraph 2(g) decided that states should prevent the movement of terrorists by effective border controls: expanded constraints on all travellers adversely affect those seeking refugee status, too, and, in many cases, they are not in a position to readily obtain all the necessary documentation before fleeing a country where they have a well-founded fear of persecution on grounds of race, religion, nationality, membership of a particular social group or political opinion. Any such additional controls disproportionately increase their existing difficulties in seeking asylum. More directly, paragraph 3 called upon all states to:

> (f) Take appropriate measures in conformity with the relevant provisions of national and international law, including international standards of human rights, *before granting refugee status, for the purpose of ensuring that the asylum-seeker has not planned, facilitated or participated in the commission of terrorist acts*; (emphasis added)
> (g) Ensure, in conformity with international law, that refugee status is not abused by the perpetrators, organizers or facilitators of terrorist

Tanzania, had been granted asylum in the United Kingdom: see, *In re Al-Fawwaz (Appellant) (Application for a Writ of Habeas Corpus) (on Appeal from a Divisional Court of The Queen's Bench Division) et al.* [2001] 1 All ER 545, [2002] 1 AC 556, at paragraphs 1–5.

[3] See Mathew, 'Resolution 1373 – A Call to Pre-empt Asylum Seekers? (or 'Osama, the Asylum-Seeker')', in McAdam (ed.), *Forced Migration, Human Rights and Security* (Hart Publishing, Oxford, 2008), pp. 19–61.

acts, and that claims of political motivation are not recognized as grounds for refusing requests for the extradition of alleged terrorists;

While on its face the Resolution recognizes international law, including international human rights obligations, it juxtaposes seeking refugee status with facilitating the commission of terrorist acts.

Equating asylum with a safe haven for terrorists is not only legally wrong and thus far unsupported by the facts, but [*sic.*] it serves to vilify refugees in the public mind and promotes the singling out of persons of particular races or religions for discrimination and hate-based harassment.[4]

Reiterating language and ideas found in Resolutions 1269, 1368 and 1373, Security Council Resolution 1377 (2001) of 12 November 2001 dealt with a different aspect of refugee status in relation to terrorism. The Convention Relating to the Status of Refugees 1951[5] had included from its inception the capacity to exclude people from refugee status and to withdraw *non-refoulement* protection from recognized refugees in Articles 1F and 33.2, respectively.[6] Article 1F(c) excludes from refugee status those persons with respect to whom there are serious reasons for considering that s/he is guilty of acts contrary to the purposes and principles of the United Nations. In the fifth paragraph of the preamble to Resolution 1377, the Security Council provided as follows:

Stresses that acts of international terrorism are contrary to the purposes and principles of the Charter of the United Nations, and that the financing, planning and preparation of as well as any other form of support for acts of international terrorism are similarly contrary to the purposes and principles of the Charter of the United Nations.

Thus, by the end of 2001, those seeking to apply for refugee status were being looked at in a completely different light by states.

This chapter will address the way that states originally implemented more restrictive rules on refugees, supposedly in line with Articles 1F and 33.2, and how domestic courts and human rights treaty bodies responded. Domestic courts, to a very great extent,

[4] UNHCR, 'Addressing Security Concerns without Undermining Refugee Protection', Rev.1, November 2001, at para. 28.

[5] 189 UNTS 150, as amended by the 1967 Protocol, 606 UNTS 267. See also fn 18.

[6] See generally, the *International Journal of Refugee Law* (Special Issue), 'Exclusion from Protection', *IJRL* (Special Supp.) 12 (2000), 1–345.

initially hid behind the shadow of the 'ordinary meaning' of the text in these articles of the 1951 Convention, without setting the words in their context. The result was that decision-makers avoided any opportunity to find nuances in the text of Articles 1F and 33.2 that are readily found when interpreting Article 1A.2. On the other hand, supranational human rights treaty monitoring bodies protected from *refoulement* persons who had been excluded from refugee status under the 1951 Convention. More recently, however, domestic courts have adopted a more protection-orientated stance, although this is not uniform across, or even within, jurisdictions.

ARTICLES 1F AND 33.2 OF THE 1951 CONVENTION

While domestic law will form the basis for any individual claim to refugee status, that law will be founded on the 1951 Convention. As such, the appropriate starting point for any analysis of the scope of the exclusion clauses is the Vienna Convention on the Law of Treaties 1969,[7] in particular, Article 26 on good faith interpretation,[8] Article 27 on the inability to rely on domestic law for failure to perform international treaty obligations,[9] Article 31 on 'ordinary meaning … in context', and Article 32 on supplementary means of interpretation.[10] It is this context

[7] 1155 UNTS 331, 8 ILM 679, entered into force 27 January 1980. Although the VCLT only applies directly to treaties concluded by states after it came into force (Article 4), it is accepted that the VCLT reflects customary international law.

[8] 'Every treaty in force is binding upon the parties to it and must be performed by them in good faith'.

[9] 'A party may not invoke the provisions of its internal law as justification for its failure to perform a treaty'.

[10] Articles 31 and 32.

31. *General rule of interpretation*
   1. A treaty shall be interpreted in good faith in accordance with the ordinary meaning to be given to the terms of the treaty in their context and in the light of its object and purpose.
   2. The context for the purpose of the interpretation of a treaty shall comprise, in addition to the text, including its preamble and annexes:
      a. Any agreement relating to the treaty which was made between all the parties in connexion with the conclusion of the treaty;
      b. Any instrument which was made by one or more parties in connexion with the conclusion of the treaty and accepted by the other parties as an instrument related to the treaty.
   3. There shall be taken into account, together with the context:
      a. Any subsequent agreement between the parties regarding the interpretation of the treaty or the application of its provisions;
      b. Any subsequent practice in the application of the treaty which establishes the agreement of the parties regarding its interpretation;

that was increasingly being ignored when states interpreted Articles 1F and 33.2 of the 1951 Convention, although the position seems to be improving in some areas.[11] To paraphrase Philip Allott,[12] law is not like a motor car and not like a poem, but it is a bit like both. It is like a motor car in that it helps us get from A to B, the 'ordinary meaning' of Article 31 VCLT; it is like a poem, though, because poets have a certain meaning in mind when they composed it, but the reader/ listener puts their own interpretation on it later based on their own experience and subsequent events, the 'context' of Article 31.

Turning to the exclusion clauses of the 1951 Convention, despite the fact that some governments have fused Articles 1F and 33.2 into one provision when incorporating the Convention into domestic law, they are two different grounds on which someone who fled persecution might lose the protection of the state that would otherwise offer it. It almost goes without saying that these two articles are only relevant with respect to someone who would be or indeed is within the definition of a refugee found in Article 1A.2 – if someone is not a Convention refugee, they do not need to be excluded.[13] Article 1F, known as the exclusion clause, although the word exclude, or any derivative thereof, does not appear in the article, prevents someone even qualifying as a refugee.[14] To be

c. Any relevant rules of international law applicable in the relations between the parties.

4. A special meaning shall be given to a term if it is established that the parties so intended.

32. *Supplementary means of interpretation*

Recourse may be had to supplementary means of interpretation, including the preparatory work of the treaty and the circumstances of its conclusion, in order to confirm the meaning resulting from the application of article 31, or to determine the meaning when the interpretation according to article 31:

a. Leaves the meaning ambiguous or obscure; or

b. Leads to a result which is manifestly absurd or unreasonable.

[11] According to Article 32, one can have regard to the *travaux préparatoires* where there is ambiguity, even where that is to confirm the ordinary meaning in context. As is discussed below, the very idea that there is an ordinary meaning may be flawed and that context is always necessary. By way of illustration, the British comic Bob Monkhouse, now deceased, used to start his act in later years, when he was famous, with the lines that people used to laugh when he said that he wanted to be a comedian, but that they weren't laughing now – context is everything!

[12] 'New International Law', in British Institute of International and Comparative Law (BICCL), *Theory and International Law: An Introduction* (1991), p. 107 at p. 109.

[13] On the 'inclusion before exclusion' debate, see Gilbert, 'Current Issues in the Application of the Exclusion Clauses' in Feller, Türk and Nicholson, *Refugee Protection in International Law*,(2003), pp. 425–78, at pp. 464–66.

[14] Article 1F

excluded, only 'serious reasons' need to be proven that the applicant for refugee status falls within sub-paragraphs (a), (b) or (c), that is, that s/he committed a crime against peace, a war crime, a crime against humanity, a serious non-political crime or is guilty of acts contrary to the purposes and principles of the United Nations; the standard of proof for Article 1F that is ordinarily imposed on the state where the person is seeking refugee status is not very high.[15] Article 33.2, on the other hand, applies to persons who have refugee status in the state of refuge, but whose guarantee of *non-refoulement* is withdrawn; Article 33.2 does not challenge their refugee status.

33.2. The benefit of the present provision may not, however, be claimed by a refugee whom there are reasonable grounds for regarding as a danger to the security of the country in which he is, or who, having been convicted by a final judgement of a particularly serious crime, constitutes a danger to the community of that country.

Article 33.2 requires the state of refuge to show 'reasonable grounds' that the Article 1A.2 refugee is a danger to the security of the country of refuge or, having been convicted of a particularly serious crime, rather than there merely being serious reasons for considering that s/he committed a serious non-political crime for Article 1F(b), s/he constitutes a danger to the community of that country. It places a heavier burden on the state now wishing to be rid of the refugee. Furthermore, given that Article 33.2 simply removes the guarantee found in Article 33.1, customary *non-refoulement*, which some would

1F. The provisions of this Convention shall not apply to any person with respect to whom there are serious reasons for considering that.

(a) He has committed a crime against peace, a war crime, or a crime against humanity, as defined in the international instruments drawn up to make provision in respect of such crimes;
(b) He has committed a serious non-political crime outside the country of refuge prior to his admission to that country as a refugee;
(c) He has been guilty of acts contrary to the purposes and principles of the United Nations.

See Gilbert, 'Current Issues' at pp. 432ff.

[15] See UNHCR, 'Background Note to the 2003 Guidelines on the Exclusion Clauses,' HCR/GIP/03/05, 4 September 2003 (with Background Note), at para. 107, where it is opined that the 'balance of probabilities' is too low a threshold. See also, *Gurung* v. *Secretary of State for the Home Department* [2002] UKIAT 04870 HX34452–2001, 15 October 2002, at para. 95, holding that serious reasons 'implied something less than' the criminal or civil standards. As the United Kingdom Supreme Court said in *R (on the application of JS) (Sri*

deem, at least in some circumstances, to be a peremptory norm of international law, is not affected.[16]

While the consequence of the application of Articles 1F or 33.2 might appear to be very similar, there is a fundamental difference that explains in part some of the reaction of UNHCR to the events of 11 September 2001. Article 1F prevents a person qualifying as a refugee; the applicant does not obtain that status. Article 33.2 does not challenge refugee status, just its principal benefit. The *travaux préparatoires* to the 1951 Convention make clear that Article 1F was drafted to ensure that only the deserving were deemed to be refugees;[17]

Lanka) v. *Secretary of State for the Home Department* [2010] URSC 15. 39. It would not, I think, be helpful to expatiate upon article 1F's reference to there being 'serious reasons for considering' the asylum-seeker to have committed a war crime. Clearly, the Tribunal in *Gurung* (at the end of para 109) was right to highlight the 'lower standard of proof applicable in exclusion cases' – lower than that applicable in actual war crimes trials. That said, 'serious reasons for considering' obviously imports a higher test for exclusion than would, say, an expression like 'reasonable grounds for suspecting'. 'Considering' approximates rather to 'believing' than to 'suspecting'. Cf. *Oberlander* v. *A-G of Canada* [2009] FCA 330 at paragraph 20.

16 See Lauterpacht and Bethlehem, 'The scope and content of the principle of non-refoulement: Opinion' in Feller, Türk and Nicholson, *Refugee Protection*, at pp. 87–179.

17 For the *travaux*: see RefWorld www.unhcr.org/cgi-bin/texis/vtx/refworld/rwmain>. There is an intrinsic link 'between ideas of humanity, equity and the concept of refuge': see Standing Committee Note on the Exclusion Clauses, 8th Meeting, 30 May 1997, para. 3. The second aim of the drafters was to ensure that those who had committed grave crimes in World War II, other serious non-political crimes or who were guilty of acts contrary to the purposes and principles of the United Nations did not escape prosecution: Conference of Plenipotentiaries on the Status of Refugees and Stateless Persons, Summary Record of the Twenty-fourth Meeting, A/CONF.2/SR.24, 27 November 1951, statements of Herment, Belgium, and Hoare, United Kingdom. However, there was a degree of confusion between the fear that asylum might confer immunity upon serious international criminals and the issue of priority between extradition treaties and the 1951 Convention, although that was inevitable where extradition was the sole method of bringing perpetrators of such serious crimes before a court with jurisdiction to prosecute: see A/CONF.2/SR.24, SR.29 and SR.35, Item 5(a), 27 and 28 November and 3 December 1951, Conference of the Plenipotentiaries. See also, Weis, *The Refugee Convention, 1951: the Travaux Préparatoires Analysed with a Commentary* (1995) at p. 332.

Cf. The following paragraph from UNHCR SCIP Interim Report on Implementation of the 1951 Convention and the 1967 Protocol Relating to the Status of Refugees, EC/SCP/66, 22 July 1991.

54 Most States which have replied permit the extradition of refugees in accordance with relevant legislation and/or international arrangements if the refugee is alleged to have committed an extraditable offence in another country. A number of States, however, exclude the extradition of a refugee if, in the requesting State, he or she would be exposed to persecution on the grounds mentioned in Article 1 of the Convention, if he or she would not be given a fair trial (Article 6 of the European Human Rights Convention) or would be exposed to inhuman and degrading treatment (ibid, Article 3). One State generally prohibits the extradition of a refugee to his/her country of origin. In two States, the extradition

paragraph 7d of the 1950 Statute[18] had a similar purpose with respect to international protection by UNHCR. As will be discussed below, the question arises as to whether Article 1F can be used as a revocation clause for a refugee who ceases to be 'deserving'.

Despite the fact that Articles 1F and 33.2 had been part of the Convention since 1951 and that existing domestic legislation applying the Convention had included both forms of exclusion, after 11 September 2001 states brought in new legislation that emphasised exclusion from refugee status.

REFUGEES AND RESPONSES TO 11 SEPTEMBER 2001

Domestic law responses

As paragraph 189 of the UNHCR Handbook[19] provides:

> It is ... left to each Contracting State to establish the procedure that it considers the most appropriate, having regard to its particular constitutional and administrative structure.[20]

of a refugee is specifically excluded: in one because refugees, as regards extradition, are treated as nationals of the country and, therefore, by definition, cannot be extradited; in the other because refugees are protected against extradition by the constitution. Two States, on the other hand, permit the extradition of a refugee to a 'safe third country', *i.e.* a country other than the country of origin.

See also, Fitzpatrick, 'The Post-Exclusion Phase: Extradition, Prosecution and Expulsion', *IJRL (Supp)* 12 (2000), 272.

[18] Statute of the United Nations High Commissioner for Refugees, 14 December 1950, UNGA Res.428(V) Annex, UNGAOR Supp. (No.20) 46, UN Doc.A/1775 – exclusion is dealt with in para. 7:

> Provided that the competence of the High Commissioner as defined in paragraph 6 above shall not extend to a person:
>
> (d) In respect of whom there are serious reasons for considering that he has committed a crime covered by the provisions of treaties of extradition or a crime mentioned in article VI of the London Charter of the International Military Tribunal or by the provisions of article 14, paragraph 2, of the Universal Declaration of Human Rights.

The OAU Convention on the Specific Aspects of Refugee Problems in Africa 1969, 1000 *UNTS* 46, provides similarly in Article I.5 – the OAU Convention also includes serious non-political crimes as a ground for cessation in Article I.4(f).

[19] 1979 UNHCR Handbook on Procedures and Criteria for Determining Refugee Status, www.unhcr.org/publ/PUBL/3d58e13b4.pdf.

[20] See for example, *European Roma Rights Centre et al.* v. *Immigration Officer at Prague Airport and Secretary of State for the Home Department*, (Admin Ct) 8 October 2002, at para. 10. NB Article 32, dealing with expulsion, does provide some procedural guarantees.

While the 1951 Convention is international, its implementation is at the domestic level. There is no International Refugee Court or Tribunal to oversee treaty interpretation. This means that protection of refugees through the 1951 Convention is dependent on domestic legislation and national judges. In the wake of 11 September 2001, several states took the opportunity to make amendments to their legislation regarding those seeking refugee status. In the United Kingdom, the Anti-terrorism, Crime and Security Act 2001, the Nationality, Immigration and Asylum Act 2002, and the United Kingdom Borders Act 2007 were the principal statutes – section 34 of the first removed double balancing from the Article 1F determination process, the 2002 Act held that a crime punished by two years' imprisonment was particularly serious for the purposes of Article 33.2,[21] and section 32 of the 2007 Act allows for the deportation of foreign criminals unless that would breach the United Kingdom's obligations under human rights treaties or the 1951 Convention (s 33(1)). The United Kingdom also entered into Memoranda of Understanding with certain states to allow the return of persons who might otherwise fear torture, inhuman or degrading treatment.[22] In *MT, RB and U* v. *Secretary of State for the Home Department*, the Court of Appeal remitted three cases to the Special Immigration Appeals Committee (SIAC) for reconsideration concerning deportation to Algeria with

[21] See, however, *IH (section 72; 'Particularly Serious Crime') Eritrea* [2009] UKAIT 00012 (9 March 2009), where the AIT held that section 72 of the 2002 Act could not be read to create an irrebuttable presumption that a crime was particularly serious because that would be contrary to the Qualification Directive (Council Directive 2004/83/EC of 29 April 2004 on Minimum Standards for the Qualification and Status of Third Country Nationals or Stateless Persons as Refugees or as Persons who Otherwise Need International Protection and the Content of the Protection Granted, OJ L. 304/12. The Court of Appeal again addressed presumptions and 'particularly serious' in *EN and KC* v. *SSHD* [2009] EWCA Civ 630. It upheld *IH* and gave further thought to the nature of the presumption under s72.

[22] Deportation with Assurances pre-dates 11 September 2001 – see *Youssef* v. *Home Office* [2004] EWHC 1884 (QB), at paragraph 5.

On 14 January 1999, a submission was put to the Home Secretary by his advisers that since there was no safe third country to which Mr Youssef could be removed, the possibility of returning Mr Youssef to Egypt should be explored. It was appreciated from the outset that given the evidence that detainees were routinely tortured by the Egyptian Security Service it would not be possible to remove Mr Youssef to Egypt unless satisfactory assurances were obtained from the Egyptian Government that he would not be tortured or otherwise physically mistreated if he were sent back. 82. If the presumption that an offence described in a schedule to the 2004 Order is a particularly serious crime were irrebuttable, as indeed the Secretary of State contends, the Order would be manifestly irrational. However, even on the basis that the presumption is rebuttable, the 2004 Order is objectionable. The power

assurances – it accepted at paragraphs 125–127 that diplomatic assurances could be effective, but that some evidence in the closed portions of the hearings required reconsideration by SIAC: however, the House of Lords held that the assurances were adequate.[23]

In the United States, the central plank of the legislative response was the USA Patriot Act 2001.[24] Like the United Kingdom legislation, this Act covers a much broader range of matters than simply refugees.[25] Nevertheless, the impact on refugees was far-reaching, particularly with respect to removal and detention. Both powers

conferred by section 72(4)(a) may not be expressly qualified, but it is impliedly qualified by its context and purpose. It cannot be inferred that Parliament conferred on the Secretary of State the power to specify any offence she or he wanted as one giving rise to the statutory presumptions, irrespective of its seriousness. In my judgment, the power conferred by section 72(4)(a) is restricted to offences that the Secretary of State could reasonably consider as giving rise to the statutory presumptions. The Secretary of State could not reasonably or, I would add, rationally, have considered theft, unqualified as to the value or nature of what is stolen, as an offence that is a particularly serious crime or that gives rise to a presumption that the offender is a danger to the community. The same applies to a number of other offences in the Schedules to the 2004 Order, including those I have mentioned above. I conclude that the Secretary of State misunderstood the extend and purpose of the statutory power when formulating the schedules to the Order, and that in making the Order she exceeded the statutory power (I am grateful to Dr Paresh Kathrani for alerting me to this case. His full analysis of it can be found at www. refugeecaselaw.org/).

[23] [2007] EWCA Civ 808; [2009] UKHL 10. See Special Immigration Appeals Committee's (SIAC) acceptance of Jordanian assurances regarding Abu Qatada, *Abu Qatada* v. *Secretary of State for the Home Department* [2007] UKSIAC 15/2005, reversed by the Court of Appeal in *Othman (Jordan)* v. *Secretary of State for the Home Department* [2008] EWCA Civ 290, but reinstated by the House of Lords in *RB and U (Algeria) and Othman (Jordan)* v. *Secretary of State for the Home Department* [2009] UKHL 10. The House of Lords held that SIAC's decision regarding the sufficiency of assurances would have to be irrational before it could be challenged via judicial review, relying on the Federal Court of Canada's decision in *Sing* v. *Canada (Minister of Citizenship and Immigration)* 2007 FC 361 – [2009] UKHL 10 at paragraphs 116–117. Lawyers for RB, U and Othman have indicated that they will challenge the deportations in the European Court of Human Rights: *Guardian*, 19 February 2009, p. 4.

[24] Public Law 107–56, 26 October 2001. The term 'USA PATRIOT Act' means the Uniting and Strengthening America by Providing Appropriate Tools Required to Intercept and Obstruct Terrorism. See also, USA PATRIOT and Terrorism Prevention Reauthorization Act, 2005, and USA PATRIOT Act Additional Reauthorizing Amendments Act, 2006.

[25] For a short period starting in March 2003, the US Department of Homeland Security put in place Operation 'Liberty Shield'. One aspect of this related to indefinite detention of applicants for refugee status from thirty three countries and territories. According to Human Rights First's Asylum Protection News 15, 2003, applicants for refugee status from Afghanistan, Algeria, Bahrain, Bangladesh, Djibouti, Egypt, Eritrea, Indonesia, Iran, Iraq, Jordan, Kazakhstan, Kuwait, Lebanon, Libya, Malaysia, Morocco, Oman, Pakistan, Philippines, Qatar, Saudi Arabia, Somalia, Sudan, Syria, Thailand, Tajikistan, Tunisia, Turkey, Turkmenistan, United Arab Emirates, Uzbekistan and Yemen, as well as Gaza and the West Bank, were all to be detained. www.humanrightsfirst.org/asylum/torchlight/newsletter/newslet_15.htm. However, with little publicity, Operation 'Liberty Shield' was officially terminated at the end of April 2003 – see Human Rights First, 'In Liberty's Shadow',

predated 11 September 2001,[26] but their use has been increased since then and the fear is that this has been at the expense of human rights guarantees for those seeking refugee status. The Illegal Immigration Reform and Immigrant Responsibility Act (IIRIRA) 1996 provided for expedited removal with mandatory detention for persons arriving without proper documentation and, although there is an exception for refugees, it is difficult not to believe that the desire for speedy deportation provides for a greater risk of error.

> The government's authority to detain immigrants was expanded by regulation by [former] Attorney-General Ashcroft shortly after the attacks [of September 11]. In March 2003, this expanded authority was transferred to the new Department of Homeland Security. The Department of Justice and DHS have created nationality-based detention policies targeting Haitian asylum seekers and asylum seekers from thirty-three nations and two territories – mostly Middle Eastern and other Islamic countries and territories. Attorney-General Ashcroft has also initiated dramatic changes to the immigration appeal's process. These changes have undermined the fairness of the asylum adjudication system – leaving some asylum seekers detained for long periods of time as they appeal their asylum denials to the federal courts.[27]

More worryingly, in 2004 the Department of Homeland Security extended the power of expedited removal to Border Patrol Officers of persons found within 100 miles of the Canadian or Mexican border without proper documentation within fourteen days of entry. Ordinarily, such orders have to be issued by an immigration judge. The risk to those who would otherwise qualify for refugee status cannot be overestimated. In addition, United States Code Title 8 §1231(b)(3)(A) and (B), referring to §1227(a)(4)(B) and §1182(a)(3)(B)(iv) expanded the meaning of terrorist activities, so increasing the scope of Article 1F.[28]

In addition, Australia amended its Migration Act of 1958 to limit judicial discretion and expand the definition of 'character of concern'

2004 www.humanrightsfirst.org. Unfortunately, it is still possible to detain applicants for refugee status under other mechanisms.

[26] Illegal Immigration Reform and Immigrant Responsibility Act 1996, Public Law 104–208.

[27] In Liberty's Shadow, p. 17. See also *Demore* v. *Kim* 538 US 510 (2003).

[28] See, for instance

(iv) 'Engage in terrorist activity' defined:- As used in this chapter, the term 'engage in terrorist activity' means, in an individual capacity or as a member of an organization -

(I) to commit or to incite to commit, under circumstances indicating an intention to cause death or serious bodily injury, a terrorist activity;

for the purposes of visa applications,[29] although it should be noted that some Australian legislative changes stemmed from the *MV Tampa* incident that also took place in 2001[30] and it may be that the new Rudd government will reconsider such amendments.

It is undoubtedly the case in international law that states are entitled, indeed obliged, to take measures to protect themselves and

(II) to prepare or plan a terrorist activity;
(III) to gather information on potential targets for terrorist activity;
(IV) to solicit funds or other things of value for
  (aa) a terrorist activity;
  (bb) a terrorist organization described in clause (vi)(I) or (vi)(II); or
  (cc) a terrorist organization described in clause (vi)(III), unless the solicitor can demonstrate by clear and convincing evidence that he did not know, and should not reasonably have known, that the organization was a terrorist organization;
(V) to solicit any individual -
  (aa) to engage in conduct otherwise described in this subsection;
  (bb) for membership in a terrorist organization described in clause (vi)(I) or (vi)(II); or
  (cc) for membership in a terrorist organization described in clause (vi)(III) unless the solicitor can demonstrate by clear and convincing evidence that he did not know, and should not reasonably have known, that the organization was a terrorist organization; or
(VI) to commit an act that the actor knows, or reasonably should know, affords material support, including a safe house, transportation, communications, funds, transfer of funds or other material financial benefit, false documentation or identification, weapons (including chemical, biological, or radiological weapons), explosives, or training -
  (aa) for the commission of a terrorist activity;
  (bb) to any individual who the actor knows, or reasonably should know, has committed or plans to commit a terrorist activity;
  (cc) to a terrorist organization described in subclause (I) or (II) of clause (vi) or to any member of such an organization; or
  (dd) to a terrorist organization described in clause (vi)(III), or to any member of such an organization, unless the actor can demonstrate by clear and convincing evidence that the actor did not know, and should not reasonably have known, that the organization was a terrorist organization.

See the REAL ID Act 2005, Pub.L. 109–13, 119 Stat.231.

[29] See e.g. sections 5C and 91U.

[30] The *MV Tampa*, a Norwegian registered container ship, rescued several hundred persons from Asia, including Afghanistan and Sri Lanka, who were on board a small vessel between Indonesia and north Australia. They wanted to put them ashore on Christmas Island, but the Australian government refused. Eventually, after intensive negotiations, New Zealand and Nauru agreed to let them enter for processing. See Bostock, 'The International Legal Obligations owed to the Asylum Seekers on the *MV Tampa*', *IJRL* 14 (2002); 279 Schloenhardt, 'To Deter, Detain and Deny: Protection of Onshore Asylum Seekers in Australia', *IJRL* 14 (2002), 302; Pallis, 'Obligations of States towards Asylum Seekers at Sea: Interactions and Conflicts Between Legal Regimes', *IJRLv*14 (2002), 329; Willheim, '*MV Tampa*: The Australian Response', *IJRL* 15 (2003), 159; Edwards, 'Tampering with Refugee Protection: The Case of Australia', *IJRL* 15 (2003), 192; Magner, 'A Less than 'Pacific' Solution for Asylum Seekers in Australia', *IJRL* 16 (2004), 53.

their populations, but only those steps that can be deemed a necessity are justified. As the International Court of Justice held in the *Case Concerning Oil Platforms (Islamic Republic of Iran* v. *United States)*:[31]

On the basis of [Article XX of the 1955 Treaty of Amity, Economic Relations and Consular Rights between the United States and Iran], a party to the Treaty may be justified in taking certain measures which it considers to be 'necessary' for the protection of its essential security interests. As the Court emphasized, in relation to the comparable provision of the 1956 United States/Nicaragua Treaty in the case concerning Military and Paramilitary Activities in and against Nicaragua, 'the measures taken must not merely be such as tend to protect the essential security interests of the party taking them, but must be "necessary" for that purpose'; and whether a given measure is 'necessary' is 'not purely a question for the subjective judgment of the party' (ICJ Reports 1986, p. 141, para. 282), and may thus be assessed by the Court.

How much of the domestic legislation passed after 11 September 2001 that affected refugees was necessary to protect the essential interests of the United Kingdom, the United States and Australia is open to question. All three states have been the subject of attacks on their territory or population. It cannot be doubted that someone seeking to enter any state might try to utilize the refugee protection regime. However, the backgrounds of those responsible for the attacks have not been refugee-based. All three states had legislation in place prior to 2001 that allowed exclusion under Article 1F. To take one example, section 34 of the United Kingdom's Anti-terrorism, Crime and Security Act prohibited double balancing, a provision of ultimate futility, since even if the person is denied refugee status despite what would happen to her/him on surrender because s/he falls within Article 1F, the parallel obligations under the ECHR will not allow that person to be returned to a country where their human rights faced a real risk of violation. Gesture politics in the field of international protection in relation to a vulnerable population hardly seems to reflect 'measures … such as tend to protect the essential security interests' of the state and which are "necessary' for that purpose'.

[31] ICJ Reports 2003, p. 161 at paragraph 43. See generally, Goodwin-Gill, 'Forced Migration: Refugees, Rights and Security' in McAdam (ed.), *Forced Migration*, pp. 1–17, esp. pp.14–15.

UNHCR's responses

The plain language of Article 1F is that exclusion occurs where there are serious reasons for considering that the applicant for refugee status has 'committed' one of the crimes in sub-paragraphs (a) or (b) or that s/he 'is guilty of acts' contrary to the purposes and principles of the United Nations. Such language indicates direct participation by the applicant in the crime itself or its planning or concealment.[32] However, since 2001 there has been an increased tendency to exclude those associated with such crimes, sometimes on very tenuous grounds. Exclusion through association was dealt with in UNHCR's 2003 Guidelines on Exclusion,[33] discussed more fully below. UNHCR provides the following guidance.

> 26. Exclusion should not be based on membership of a particular organisation alone, although a presumption of individual responsibility may arise where the organisation is commonly known as notoriously violent and membership is voluntary. In such cases, it is necessary to examine the individual's role and position in the organisation, his or her own activities, as well as related issues as outlined … above.

Seniority in the organization may indicate complicity in its serious crimes that might justify exclusion, but regard must be had to 'the individual's position in it, and his or her ability to influence significantly its activities, as well as the possible fragmentation of the group' (para. 19). Equally, the voluntariness of membership of a notoriously violent organization also deserves careful scrutiny: is a farmer growing drugs for the FARC in Colombia acting freely, is a doctor who treats a member of a terrorist organization?[34] Courts in Canada and

[32] See *Suresh* v. *Canada (Minister of Citizenship and Immigration)* [2002] 1 SCR 3 at para 110, quoted below: see text at fn 44. See also, <reports.fja.gc.ca/fc/src/shtml/1996/pub/v2/1996fca0106.shtml>.

[33] See UNHCR, 'Background Note to the 2003 Guidelines', and *Gurung*.

[34] The English Court of Appeal was faced with such issues in *MH (Syria) and DS (Afghanistan)* v. *Secretary of State for the Home Department* [2009] EWCA Civ 226. The applicant for refugee status was denied under Article 1F(c) as a member of the PKK. However, in addition to the fact that she had joined at the age of thirteen and that she was seriously injured by a landmine before the age of majority, the Court held that the PKK was not at 'the extreme end of the continuum where mere membership may be sufficient to establish complicity in the acts of an organisation' (para 36(ii)) It then went on to look at her role in the PKK which had been 'minor in nature', first as a nurse in a refugee camp (although including nursing some combatants) and then as a language teacher in a primary school, such that she did not fall within Article 1F(c)(paragraphs 36(iii) and 37). In general, see Gottwald, 'Asylum Claims and Drug

the United States have found that the defence of duress might be available to counteract Article 1F.[35]

UNHCR's first response to 11 September 2001 was to emphasize that the 1951 Convention already permitted states to exclude terrorists. 'Addressing Security Concerns Without Undermining Refugee Protection'[36] of November 2001 set out the organization's primary concerns at paragraph 2: 'that bona fide asylum seekers may be victimized as a result of public prejudice and unduly restrictive legislative or administrative measures, and that carefully built refugee protection standards may be eroded'. Unfortunately, the document was something of a curate's egg: paragraph 4 provided that 'the terrorist threat in the context of asylum … should benefit from a review and *tightening* of procedural security measures where necessary' and paragraph 6 opined that the 'summary rejection of asylum-seekers at borders of points of entry *may* amount to refoulement' (emphasis added) where stronger assertions of refugee rights might have been expected. The 2003 Guidelines[37] were an improvement, but still raise awkward questions. Paragraph 17 argues that 'Article 1F(c) is only triggered in extreme circumstances by activity which attacks the very basis of the international community's coexistence', a strong assertion of the view that given the lack of clarity attached to the meaning of the 'purposes and principles of the United Nations' in the context of applicants for refugee status, it should be interpreted narrowly. Further, paragraph 24 proposes a proportionality test.

> 24. The incorporation of a proportionality test when considering exclusion and its consequences provides a useful analytical tool to ensure that the exclusion clauses are applied in a manner consistent with the overriding humanitarian object and purpose of the 1951 Convention … As with any exception to a human rights guarantee, the exclusion clauses must therefore be applied in a manner proportionate to their objective, so that the

Offences: the Seriousness Threshold of Article 1F(b) of the 1951 Convention Relating to the Status of Refugees and the UN Drug Conventions', *IJRL* 18 (2006), 81–117 at 110–12.

[35] See *Negusie* v. *Holder, Attorney General* 555 US (2009), Slip Opinion decided 3 March 2009. See also, *R* v. *Ruzic* [2001] SCC 24 and *US* v. *Contento-Pachon* 723 F.2d 691 (9th, 1984), both cited by Gottwald, Asylum Claims, fn. 118.

[36] UNHCR, 'Addressing Security Concerns'.

[37] UNHCR, Background Note to the 2003 Guidelines. NB. The Guidelines only apply to Article 1F, not Article 33.2, which could cause problems for states that have fused the two provisions in their domestic legislation implementing the 1951 Convention.

gravity of the offence in question is weighed against the consequences of exclusion.[38]

On the basis of the very restrictive interpretation of Article 1F(c) in paragraph 17, UNHCR was prepared to accept that the proportionality test ought only to apply to Article 1F(b) crimes and lesser Article 1F(a) crimes, although given the potential consequences for the person seeking refugee status, proportionality should not be completely ruled out for any Article 1F(a) or (c) crimes in appropriate circumstances. On the other hand, the Guidelines also hold that only Article 1F(b) is limited to dealing with pre-entry crimes – Article 1F(a) and (c) can be used to remove refugee status for crimes committed after the person has been granted refugee status.

5. Articles 1F(a) and 1F(c) are concerned with crimes whenever and wherever they are committed. By contrast, the scope of Article 1F(b) is explicitly limited to crimes committed outside the country of refuge prior to admission to that country as a refugee.

The argument is that a refugee committing a crime falling within Article 1F(a) or who is guilty of acts within Article 1F(c) should not continue to enjoy refugee status because they are not deserving. Thus, refugee status can be revoked. There are a number of levels on which this can be challenged, not least that cessation of status is dealt with in Article 1C which makes no provision for taking into account the refugee's post-entry criminal activity[39] and that Article 33.2 is rendered partially redundant. While UNHCR's 2003 interpretation of the temporal scope of Article 1F(a) and (c) cannot be said to be wrong in law and is perfectly justifiable on the basis of the language of the Convention, was it for UNHCR to propose that those two sub-clauses could be used to revoke refugee status as a consequence of post-status activity? UNHCR's

[38] See Article 31 VCLT 1969. The object of the 1951 Convention is to provide international protection to refugees, so clauses excluding applicants from refugee status should be considered restrictively. See also, *Gurung* v. *Secretary of State for the Home Department*, at paragraph 36.

[39] Cf. OAU Convention Governing the Specific Aspects of Refugee Problems in Africa 1969, 1001 UNTS 45, is worded differently and the argument that the exclusion clauses can be used for post-entry crimes carries more weight.

Article 1.4. This Convention shall cease to apply to any refugee if: … (f) he has committed a serious non-political crime outside his country of refuge after his admission to that country as a refugee, or, (g) he has seriously infringed the purposes and objectives of this Convention.

mandate, as set out in paragraph 1 of the 1950 Statute,[40] is to provide international protection to refugees. Such proposals should be left to states that have never been slow to devise ways to restrict refugee status. There was no need to make the argument in the Guidelines.

CASE LAW SINCE 2001

Exclusion from refugee status has been the subject of several cases in domestic courts, while human rights treaty monitoring bodies have also dealt with the potential removal of those who have applied for refugee status and been excluded under the 1951 Convention. Some of the first cases decided after 11 September 2001 suggested that the courts might prove a bulwark of protection against legislatures tightening up procedures relating to refugees so as to be seen to be doing something in the fight against terrorism.[41] However, several subsequent judgments suggest that the courts have rejected a purposive approach to interpreting the ordinary meaning of the terms 1951 Convention in their context and have restricted the protection that ought to be available to those with a well-founded fear of persecution. Much of the subsequent case law has seen judges adopt a more far-reaching application of Articles 1F and 33.2.

The purposive approach

The purposive approach is no more than an acknowledgement of the obligation in Article 31 of the VCLT to give the terms of a treaty their ordinary meaning in context in the light of its object and purpose.[42] The 1951 Convention was established to provide international protection for those unable or unwilling to avail themselves of the protection of their country of nationality for the stated reasons. As such, any limitation on such humanitarian provisions should be interpreted restrictively. Furthermore, another part of the context of

[40] 189 UNTS 150, as amended by the 1967 Protocol, 606 UNTS 267.
[41] See Gilbert, 'The "Law" and "Transnational Terrorism,"' *Netherlands Yearbook of International Law* 26 (1995), 3–32.
[42] See *IH (section 72; 'Particularly Serious Crime') Eritrea.*

the 1951 Convention is to be found in the opening paragraph of its preamble:

Considering that the Charter of the United Nations and the Universal Declaration of Human Rights approved on 10 December 1948 by the General Assembly have affirmed the principle that human beings shall enjoy fundamental rights and freedoms without discrimination.

Human rights are fundamental to refugee protection and the developments in international human rights law since 1951 require courts dealing with refugee status determination to understand Article 1F in the light of those changes. If international human rights law would not allow the *refoulement* of a person, no matter what their previous conduct, international refugee law that is the root of *non-refoulement* needs be interpreted in a consistent fashion.

Double balancing

Double balancing is the process whereby the courts take into account the consequences of returning the refugee or applicant for refugee status to the country of nationality.[43] In *Zaoui*,[44] though, the New Zealand Supreme Court concluded:

that the judgment or assessment to be made under article 33.2 is to be made on its own terms, by reference to danger to the security, in this case, of New Zealand, and without any balancing or weighing or proportional reference to the matter dealt with in article 33.1, the threat, were Mr Zaoui to be expelled or returned, to his life or freedom on the proscribed grounds ...

Given that Article 33.2 expressly revokes the guarantee of *non-refoulement*, an accepted rule of customary international law if not a peremptory norm,[45] it is even more regrettable that the Supreme Court took a narrow view of the role of decision makers, to apply Article 33.2 'on its own terms'.

[43] See Gilbert, 'Current Issues', 450–455.

[44] *Attorney-General* v. *Zaoui and Others* [2005] NZSC 38 at para. 42. See also, Haines, 'National Security and *Non-Refoulement* in New Zealand: Commentary on *Zaoui* v. *Attorney-General (No.2)*' in McAdam (ed.), *Forced Migration*, pp. 63–91.

[45] See Lauterpacht and Bethlehem, '*Non-Refoulement*'.

Membership of a terrorist organization or 'exclusion by association'

The Canadian Supreme Court in *Suresh*[46] was dealing with the Convention Against Torture, not the 1951 Convention, but it accepted that membership alone would not necessarily suffice:

110. We believe that it was not the intention of Parliament to include in the s.19 class of suspect persons those who innocently contribute to or become members of terrorist organizations. This is supported by the provision found at the end of s. 19, which exempts from the s. 19 classes 'persons who have satisfied the Minister that their admission would not be detrimental to the national interest'. Section 19 must therefore be read as permitting a refugee to establish that his or her continued residence in Canada will not be detrimental to Canada, notwithstanding proof that the person is associated with or is a member of a terrorist organization. This permits a refugee to establish that the alleged association with the terrorist group was innocent. In such case, the Minister, exercising her discretion constitutionally, would find that the refugee does not fall within the targeted s. 19 class of persons eligible for deportation on national security grounds.

Comparison should be drawn, however, with the decision of the New Zealand Refugee Status Appeals Authority (RSAA) in Refugee Appeal No.70405/97:[47]

Because the appellant has freely admitted to active involvement in the *Sendero Luminoso* from May 1992 to February 1995 and to having taken part in armed attacks against innocent civilians, the Authority is duty-bound to consider whether Article 1F(a) operates to exclude the appellant from the Refugee Convention. A brief description of the *Sendero Luminoso* is required …

The significance of this information is that when the appellant joined the *Sendero Luminoso* in May 1992 he could have been in no doubt whatsoever of its then 12-year history of violence, terror, human rights abuses and glorification of violence. Thereafter, the appellant's willing, active and armed involvement in the intimidation of civilians and theft of property is the clearest evidence of his knowledge of and deep complicity in the activities of the *Sendero Luminoso*. *In short, there was personal and knowing participation in an organization principally directed to a limited, brutal*

[46] *Suresh* v. *Canada (Minister of Citizenship and Immigration)*, at paras. 75 and 110. Some parts of the following text are taken from the author's chapter, 'Exclusion and Evidentiary Assessment', Noll, *Proof, Evidentiary Assessment and Credibility in Asylum Procedures* (2005), pp.161–177.

[47] 29 May 1997. Cf. *MH (Syria) and DS (Afghanistan)* v. *Secretary of State for the Home Department)*, where membership of the PKK alone was not sufficient.

purpose and the wholesale breach of Common Article 3 of the four Geneva Conventions of 1949. We are satisfied on the facts therefore that there are serious reasons for considering that the appellant has committed crimes against humanity, as defined in the International Instruments drawn up to make provision in respect of such crimes and as interpreted and applied by the principal decisions of the Canadian Federal Court of Appeal, namely *Ramirez* v. *Canada (Minister of Employment and Immigration)* [1992] 2 FC 306 (FC:CA); *Moreno* v. *Canada (Minister of Employment and Immigration)* [1994] 1 FC 298 (FC:CA) and *Sivakumar* v. *Canada (Minister of Employment and Immigration*) [1994] 1 FC 433 (FC:CA) (emphasis added).

The Swedish authorities have equally held that membership of *Sendero Luminoso* was enough to exclude.[48] In *Zrig*,[49] the Canadian Federal Court of Appeal allowed exclusion through association with the terrorist group carrying out the Article 1F(b) crimes. According to the Court:

[94] In order to exclude persons covered by Article 1F(a) and (b), it will be necessary to show that there are 'serious reasons for considering' that the serious crimes identified were committed, but it will not be necessary to attribute any one specifically to the claimant. This test applies to both Article 1F(a) and Article 1F(b)...

[96] In my view, the interpretation of Article 1F(b) which the [applicant] is asking the Court to adopt *conflicts with the very wording of the Article* (emphasis added).

The appellant had argued that only crimes for which extradition might be sought fell within Article 1F(b). While that proposition cannot be sustained, the court's view is equally questionable – Article 1F(b) speaks of there being serious reasons for considering that the applicant for refugee status 'has committed a serious non-political crime', not just that one can be 'ascribed to him as an accomplice by association'.[50] It should be noted that while Decary JA concurred in the result, he did so by reference to Article 1F(c) and rejected

48 *See Paez* v. *Sweden*, App. No. 29482/95, European Commission of Human Rights 18 April 1996.

49 *Zrig* v. *Canada (Minister of Citizenship and Immigration)* (CA) [2003] FCA 178. See the pre-2001 case cited in *Zrig* (para. 56), *Bazargan* v. *Canada (Minister of Citizenship and Immigration)* (1996), 205 NR 282 at paras. 11–12 (FCA).

50 *Zrig* v. *Canada (Minister of Citizenship and Immigration)* (CA), para. 102. See also, *El Hayek* v. *Canada (Minister of Citizenship and Immigration)* 2005 FC 835, at paras. 17 and 18, 17 June

complicity by association. 'In short, complicity by association is a method of perpetrating a crime which is recognized in respect of certain international crimes and applied in the case of international crimes covered by Article 1F(a), and by analogy in the case of acts contrary to the international purposes and principles sought by Article 1F(c). This method of perpetration is not recognized as such in traditional criminal law.'[51]

The Court of Appeal for England and Wales dealt with this issue in some depth in 2009, expanding on the IAT decision in *Gurung*.[52] In *The Queen on the Application of JS (Sri Lanka)* v. *Secretary of State for the Home Department*,[53] the Court of Appeal had to deal with the exclusion of a trusted member of the intelligence unit in the Liberation Tigers of the Tamil Eelam (LTTE). The approach in *Gurung* (paras. 112–14) had been to focus on the organization to which the applicant for refugee status belonged and see whether it had an ultimate political agenda in line with liberal democracy or no political agenda and a focus on terrorism. *JS* rejected this approach of placing the organization on some sort of continuum and opted to look at whether there would be serious reasons for thinking the applicant would be guilty within the terms of the Rome Statute.

> 115. The starting point for a decision maker addressing the question whether there are serious reasons for considering that an asylum seeker has committed an international crime, so as to fall within article 1F(a), should now be the ICC Statute. The decision maker will need to identify the relevant type or types of crime, as defined in articles 7 and 8; and then to address the question whether there are serious reasons for considering that the applicant

2005, and *Jaouadi* v. *Canada (Minister of Citizenship and Immigration)* 2005 FC 1256 at para. 4, 16 September 2005:

> 4. The general principle in matters of exclusion is that mere membership in an organization implicated in the commission of international crimes is not sufficient to establish a basis for exclusion. There is however an exception to the general rule when the very existence of the organization in question is principally directed to a limited, brutal purpose. There is then an irrebuttable presumption of complicity.

Cf. *MH (Syria) and DS (Afghanistan)* v. *Secretary of State for the Home Department*, where membership of the PKK alone was not sufficient.

[51] *Zrig* v. *Canada (Minister of Citizenship and Immigration)* (CA), para. 137. See also, *Tantoush* v. *Refugee Appeal Board*, High Court of South Africa (Transvaal Provincial Division) Case No: 13182/06, 14 August 2007.

[52] *Gurung* v. *Secretary of State for the Home Department*.

[53] [2009] EWCA Civ 364. *JS* (CA).

has committed such a crime, *applying the principles of criminal liability set out in articles 25, 28 and 30 and any other articles relevant in the particular case* (emphasis added).

The Court of Appeal went on to look at Article 25(d) of the Rome Statute and the concept of joint criminal enterprise as expounded by the ICTY to determine the scope of guilt by association, 'that is, where a crime was committed as a foreseeable way of effecting a shared criminal intent and the defendant knowingly took the risk of this happening'.[54] This understanding of exclusion by association only expressly applied to Article 1F(a), but it marked a more individualistic approach more in keeping with the language of the 1951 Convention and international criminal law. When the case went to the Supreme Court, they accepted the basic argument of the Court of Appeal.[55]

30. Rather, however, than be deflected into first attempting some such sub-categorisation of the organisation, it is surely preferable to focus from the outset on what ultimately must prove to be the determining factors in any case, principally (in no particular order) (i) the nature and (potentially of some importance) the size of the organisation and particularly that part of it with which the asylum-seeker was himself most directly concerned, (ii) whether and, if so, by whom the organisation was proscribed, (iii) how the asylum-seeker came to be recruited, (iv) the length of time he remained in the organisation and what, if any, opportunities he had to leave it, (v) his position, rank, standing and influence in the organisation, (vi) his knowledge of the organisation's war crimes activities, and (vii) his own personal involvement and role in the organisation including particularly whatever contribution he made towards the commission of war crimes.

With respect to involvement through joint criminal enterprise, however, the Supreme Court adopted a broader understanding than the Court of Appeal.

38. … Put simply, I would hold an accused disqualified under article 1F if there are serious reasons for considering him voluntarily to have contributed

[54] *JS* (CA), para. 118. See also paras. 119–22. The concept of joint criminal enterprises was nowhere near as developed at the time of *Gurung*, so it is unsurprising that the earlier case did not rely on it with respect to exclusion.

[55] *JS* (SC), *per* Lord Brown with whom the Court concurred. Looking at the nature of the organization to which the applicant belonged may have more relevance to exclusion under Article 1F(b) where there are serious reasons for considering that s/he committed a 'serious non-political crime', but the Court of Appeal and Supreme Court are right to reject it in relation to 1F(a) and, in all likelihood, 1F(c).

in a significant way to the organisation's ability to pursue its purpose of committing war crimes, aware that his assistance will in fact further that purpose.[56]

The nature of the organization is not determinative. Rather, what matters is the part played in the organization by the person seeking refugee status and whether that facilitated the commission of crimes or acts that fell within Article 1F.

The United States case of *In re S-K-*[57] dealt with a statutorily extended understanding of exclusion through association. The Board of Immigration Appeals held that the applicant for refugee status was barred from receiving protection because she had provided material support to a terrorist organization, despite the fact that the organization in question, the Chin National Front(CNF), was seeking the overthrow of the Burmese military junta, a government that the United States government does not recognize as legitimate. As Vice-Chairman Osuna's concurring opinion put it:

In sum, what we have in this case is an individual who provided a relatively small amount of support to an organization that opposes one of the most repressive governments in the world, a government that is not recognized by the United States as legitimate and that has engaged in a brutal campaign against ethnic minorities. It is clear that the respondent poses no danger whatsoever to the national security of the United States. Indeed, by supporting the CNF in its resistance to the Burmese junta, it is arguable that the respondent actually acted in a manner consistent with United States foreign policy. And yet we cannot ignore the clear language that Congress chose in the material support provisions; the statute that we are required to apply mandates that we find the respondent ineligible for asylum for having provided material support to a terrorist organization.[58]

At Osuna V-C's suggestion, the Department for Homeland Security filed a statement acknowledging that applicant was not ineligible for

[56] Cf. *Oberlander*, FCA, at paragraph 18. For a detailed comparison of the approach of the United Kingdom Supreme Court *vis á vis* other appellate courts in the Anglo-American system of law, see Rikhof, Complicity gets complicated: the impact of the *JS* case of the Supreme Court of the United Kingdom, conference paper delivered at York University, Toronto, 2010 (in the possession of the author).

[57] 23 I&N Dec.936 (BIA 2006).

[58] *In re S-K* at p. 950. On a related note, in January 2007 Kenya deported to Somalia not only a 'key international terror suspect', but also wives and children – BBC News website 6309299.stm, 2007/01/29 10:56:39.

asylum, Congress having expressly determined that the CNF was not a terrorist organization. Nevertheless, the broad language of the material support bar remains – 'the statutory language is breathtaking in its scope.[59]

Finally in this section, mere presence at the scene of a crime should not be sufficient to invoke the exclusion clauses. According to cases at the end of World War II, presence was not enough on its own to justify a finding of guilt.[60] In *Prosecutor* v. *Brdjanin*,[61] the Appeals Chamber of the ICTY held that to be guilty through presence, the accused would have to hold a position of authority and be found to be giving tacit approval and encouragement.

Expiation:

The United Kingdom cases of *KK*[62] and *Secretary of State Home for the Department, re AA (Palestine)*[63] dealt in part with expiation. *AA* citing *KK* rejected expiation as a defence to exclusion under Article 1F:[64]

59. *KK* also rejected the notion that expiation, i.e. punishment, pardon or amnesty, and we add remorse or change of heart, is a basis, as a matter of

[59] *In re S-K* at p. 948.

[60] *L and Others*, Supreme Court in the British Occupied Zone, 14 December 1948, cited in Cassese *International Criminal Law*, 2nd edn, (2008), p. 215.

[61] Case No. IT-99–36-A, 3 April 2007.

273. The Trial Chamber might have intended to apply in this case the theory of aiding and abetting by tacit approval and encouragement. An accused can be convicted for aiding and abetting a crime when it is established that his conduct amounted to tacit approval and encouragement of the crime and that such conduct substantially contributed to the crime. This form of aiding and abetting is not, strictly speaking, criminal responsibility for omission. In the cases where this category was applied, the accused held a position of authority, he was physically present on the scene of the crime, and his non-intervention was seen as tacit approval and encouragement (footnotes omitted).

[62] [2004] UKIAT 00101.

[63] [2005] UKIAT 00104.

[64] Of course, if there are doubts as to the legitimacy of the previous conviction, it should not be used as the basis on which to exclude the applicant: see *Al-Sirri* v. *Secretary of State for the Home Department and Another* [2009] EWCA Civ 222 (18 March 2009). Cf. The Canadian position as set out in *Chan* v. *Canada (Minister of Citizenship and Immigration)* [2000] 4 FC 390, upheld in *Santiago Rafael Garcia Rodriguez* v. *Canada (Minister of Citizenship and Immigration)* [2007] FC 462 at para. 18, where completion of a sentence for the serious non-political crime renders it ineffective with respect to Article 1F(b). However, it should be noted that because Garcia Rodriguez had not served his full sentence in the United States but had accepted deportation to the Dominican Republic where he had not completed the sentence, he was still excluded.

Convention interpretation, for not applying the exclusion clause; see paragraphs 91 to 92. It said:

'92. Our conclusion is that we should reject all the arguments put before us for applying glosses to Article 1F, and should instead apply its words exactly as they are written. We appreciate that in so doing we are adopting an approach to the Refugee Convention which is somewhat similar to that which we have criticised when the UNHCR adopts it in relation to the Charter of the United Nations. But the difference is that, in relation to the Refugee Convention, we have been shown no material properly leading to the invocation of Article 31(3)(b) or (c) of the Vienna Convention. So far from being supported by international agreement as to the application of the Refugee Convention, the arguments made on behalf of the Appellant, although to an extent endorsed by the UNHCR,[65] lack authority, sometimes lack coherence and occasionally lack consistency.'

60. The same reasoning applies to remorse or change of heart as expiation.

In this context, where it is contrary to the applicant's interests, the Tribunals both adopted a literalist approach to interpreting Article 1F. Of course, conviction and punishment for a serious non-political crime provide a serious reason for considering that the applicant falls within Article 1F(b). Furthermore, exclusion from refugee status is not a double punishment for the crime – the status determination hearing is not a criminal trial. Nevertheless, the approach adopted in *KK* and *AA* renders any conviction for a serious non-political crime at any time in a person's life a permanent exclusion from refugee status. Expiation by the applicant, not just serving a sentence, but rejection of the previous criminal activity also, should vitiate exclusion under Article 1F.

[65] Cf. Paragraph 23 of the 2003 Guidelines.

23. Where expiation of the crime is considered to have taken place, application of the exclusion clauses may no longer be justified. This may be the case where the individual has served a penal sentence for the crime in question, or perhaps where a significant period of time has elapsed since commission of the offence. Relevant factors would include the seriousness of the offence, the passage of time, and any expression of regret shown by the individual concerned. In considering the effect of any pardon or amnesty, consideration should be given to whether it reflects the democratic will of the relevant country and whether the individual has been held accountable in any other way. Some crimes are, however, so grave and heinous that the application of Article 1F is still considered justified despite the existence of a pardon or amnesty.

See also, Gottwald, 'Asylum claims', pp. 105 et seq.

Rejecting a culture of exclusion

The United Kingdom's then Immigration Appeal Tribunal dealt with Article 1F in *Gurung* v. *Secretary of State for the Home Department*.[66] The case concerned a Nepalese Maoist. The Tribunal held at paragraph 151 as follows:

1. Bearing in mind the need to adopt a purposive approach to the interpretation of the Exclusion Clauses, they are to be applied restrictively. In contrast to the focus under Art 1A(2) on current risk, the focus under Art 1F is on past crimes or acts.
2. In any case in which an adjudicator intends to apply the Exclusion Clauses, he should avoid equating Art 1F with a simple anti-terrorism provision.
3. It would be wrong for adjudicators to adopt an 'exclusion culture' and go searching in every case for exclusion issues under Art 1F. Pragmatism is called for.

According to the Supreme Court of Canada in *Suresh*,[67] it is international law, not just the Convention Against Torture, that rejects *refoulement* to torture. As such, even where the refugee has committed a particularly serious crime and is a danger to the community or if he is a threat to the security of that country, he still should not be sent back to the frontiers of a territory where he would face torture. Therefore, in early 2002 there had been reason to believe that while politicians might not have realized that the 1951 Convention provided all necessary measures to address the situation where an applicant for refugee status might have been involved in terrorism, the judges would apply the exclusion clauses restrictively, as befits a limitation on a fundamental right.[68]

However, while the Tribunal in *AA* expressly referred to the 1951 Convention as a living document that could adapt to the needs of the times whether in terms of the exclusion clauses or protection needs, in that case by reference to terrorism as contrary to the UN's principles, the judges have tended only to use a generous interpretation

[66] *Gurung* v. *Secretary of State for the Home Department*.

[67] *Suresh* v. *Canada (Minister of Citizenship and Immigration)*, see para. 75: 'We conclude that the better view is that international law rejects deportation to torture, even where national security interests are at stake'. Cf. The New Zealand Supreme Court adopting a literalist approach in *Attorney-General* v. *Zaoui and Others*.

[68] See also, *Tantoush* v. *Refugee Appeal Board*.

where it broadens the exclusion clauses, not the scope for protecting the individual through a purposive approach.[69]

The decisions of domestic courts and tribunals since 11 September 2001 have placed great emphasis on the literal language of the 1951 Convention, as if the judges and adjudicators were simply applying an automatic rule with no room for discretion. There is no assumption here that judges should be neutral. One would hope that they were always impartial, but judges are part of the state structure and will defend that against threats to its existence.[70] However, the criticism is that a literalist stance is just as much a form of judicial interpretation. The judge or adjudicator has decided to apply the exclusion clause strictly and hides behind the self-proclaimed 'original meaning' of the text.[71] Such an approach contrasts sharply with the more purposive approach taken towards Article 1A.2 when

[69] The Tribunals in *KK* and *AA* adopted a broad approach to Article 1F(c), not limiting it, as one might have hoped, to acts by senior figures in a state given that the applicant for refugee status has to be 'guilty of acts contrary to the purposes and principles of the United Nations' and those are set out in the Charter that is binding on states' parties. Further, the Tribunals held that the purposes and principles of the UN were not limited to Articles 1 and 2 of the Charter, but could be extended through Resolutions.

[70] Griffith, *The Politics of the Judiciary*, (1997) at pp. 292 and 343.
Neither impartiality nor independence necessarily involves neutrality. Judges are part of the machinery of authority within the State and as such cannot avoid the making of political decisions … [The judges'] principal function is to support the institutions of government as established by law … The confusion arises when it is pretended that judges are somehow neutral between those who challenge existing institutions and those who control those institutions.

[71] For a fuller discussion of judicial interpretation and judicial legislation, see Kennedy, *A Critique of Adjudication {fin de siècle}*, 1997, especially Chapters 5–8.
Denial: not just a river in Egypt

> What does it mean to refer to a judge as 'denying'? … We use the word 'denial' as an interpretation of a piece of behaviour in cases where we agree about what was said or thought and want to figure out what was 'behind' it. We feel the need to go 'behind' because we (the interpreter and the audience for the interpretation) agree on two things:
>
> 1 We agree that what the actor has said is a misrepresentation of his or her own desire, emotion, opinion, or intention, or of important external facts about his or her situation, but in the special sense of a 'refusal to acknowledge', 'refusal to recognize', 'refusal to admit'. The denial requires something like 'refusal', because it presupposes that there is evidence for the thing denied, or an assertion of it by someone in argument. When I say that judges 'deny' the role of ideology in their decisions, it is implicit that in my view it does play a role in fact – the denier is always wrong.
> 2 We agree about the misrepresentation that:
> (a) It is not merely conventional … When judges write their opinions in the language of legal necessity, this is just a convention; when we say that they are engaged in denial, we mean that they at least partly believe the convention. (pp.192–193)

interpreting inclusion – for instance, why should generalized conditions in a state not amount to persecution given that the five grounds for persecution are a separate element in the test? It would seem that the judicial adoption of the purposive approach to treaty interpretation with respect to Article 1F has also run scared since 2001.

Human Rights Treaty monitoring bodies

It is in the light of such an analysis that the lack of an International Refugee Court to oversee the domestic implementation of the Convention Relating to the Status of Refugees 1951 becomes even more apparent. Fortunately, human rights treaty monitoring bodies have supplied a degree of protection where they have jurisdiction to those excluded from refugee status. It should be noted, though, that where it has been considered, the human rights treaty monitoring bodies have held they have no remit to review the fairness of the refugee status determination hearing. Protection, as will be seen, comes, where applicable, through the substantive human rights treaty obligations.

The right to a fair trial under the European Convention for the Protection of Human Rights and Fundamental Freedoms is found in Article 6.

> Article 6 – Right to a fair trial
> 1 In the determination of his civil rights and obligations or of any criminal charge against him, everyone is entitled to a fair and public hearing within a reasonable time by an independent and impartial tribunal established by law.

The European Court of Human Rights has consistently held that a status determination hearing is not the determination of a civil right or obligation or of a criminal charge.[72]

In General Comment 32,[73] the Human Rights Committee reviewed Article 14 of the International Covenant on Civil and Political Rights. The language of Article 14 is broader, referring to 'his rights and obligations in a suit at law' and might have afforded review of fair trial

Nor should judges be allowed to justify their restrictive approach by referring to the general mood at the time. Judges do not make snap decisions, they have time to reflect and their obligation is to the rule of law, not the populace as it is for politicians.

[72] *Maaouia* v. *France* 39652/98, 5 October 2000, at para. 40.

[73] CCPR/C/GC/32, 23 August 2007.

guarantees in cases dealing with refugee status.[74] Indeed, General Comment 32 asserts in paragraph 3 that '[the] first sentence of paragraph 1 [of Article 14] sets out a general guarantee of equality before courts and tribunals that applies regardless of the nature of proceedings before such bodies'. However, General Comment 32 goes on to provide at paragraph 17 as follows:

> 17. On the other hand, the right to access a court or tribunal as provided for by article 14, paragraph 1, second sentence, does not apply where domestic law does not grant any entitlement to the person concerned … This guarantee furthermore does not apply to extradition, expulsion and deportation procedures. Although there is no right of access to a court or tribunal as provided for by article 14, paragraph 1, second sentence, in these and similar cases, other procedural guarantees may still apply.[75]

Nevertheless, a further argument can be made specific to Articles 1F and 33.2 of the 1951 Convention and Article 6 of the ECHR. The European Court of Human Rights has repeatedly held that the way a hearing is designated under domestic law is not conclusive for Strasbourg.[76] The Court will decide whether the proceedings in

[74] International Covenant on Civil and Political Rights, UNGA Res.2200A(XXI), UNGAOR, 21st Sess., Supp.No.16, 52 (1966); 999 UNTS 171; 6 ILM 368 (1967); 61 AJIL 870 (1967): hereinafter, ICCPR.

Article 14

1. All persons shall be equal before the courts and tribunals. In the determination of any criminal charge against him, or of his rights and obligations in a suit at law, everyone shall be entitled to a fair and public hearing by a competent, independent and impartial tribunal established by law.

In *Kwame Williams Adu* v. *Canada*, CCPR/C/60/D/654/1995, 18 July 1997, at paragraph 6.3 the Human Rights Committee found the communication inadmissible for non-exhaustion of domestic remedies and that it therefore did not have to decide if Article 14 applied.

[75] Paragrah 62 of General Comment 32 provides that: 'Insofar as domestic law entrusts a judicial body with the task of deciding about expulsions or deportations, the guarantee of equality of all persons before the courts and tribunals as enshrined in article 14, paragraph 1, and the principles of impartiality, fairness and equality of arms implicit in this guarantee are applicable': see Comm. No. 961/2000, *Everett* v. *Spain*, para. 6.4.

The HRC concluded in its observations on Georgia as follows:

> '[That states] adopt effective legislative and *procedural* safeguards to ensure that nobody is returned to a country where there are substantial grounds to believe that they are at risk of being arbitrarily deprived of their life or being tortured or subjected to other cruel, inhuman or degrading treatment or punishment' (emphasis added): Concluding Observations on: Georgia, CCPR/C/GEO/CO/3, 15 November 2007, paragraph 7(a).

[76] See *Engel* v. *The Netherlands*, Series A, vol. 22, at para. 81, European Court of Human Rights, 18 June 1976.

question, although not designated criminal, could be seen to have the characteristics of a criminal hearing, having particular regard to penalties. As was stated in *Engel* at paragraph 82, the Court's

> supervision would generally prove to be illusory if it did not also take into consideration the degree of severity of the penalty that the person concerned risks incurring.

Where an applicant for refugee status can be excluded and potentially returned to a state where her/his life or freedom would be threatened because there are serious reasons for considering that s/he has committed a war crime, a crime against peace, a crime against humanity, a serious non-political crime or is guilty of acts contrary to the purposes and principles of the United Nations, then there is a strong argument that the refugee status determination proceeding should be treated as a 'criminal charge against him' – unlike extradition law, *refoulement* would not necessarily result in a trial to determine whether s/he has committed a crime under Article 1F(a) or (b) or is guilty of 1F(c) acts, so status determination is much closer to a criminal trial with the possibility of the most serious of consequences.[77] On that basis, it is suggested that Article 6 of the ECHR and Article 14 even more so should properly be engaged in cases where someone is excluded from refugee status.

Where applicable, international human rights law treaties guarantee rights to everyone within the jurisdiction of a state party, including applicants for refugee status and even excluded applicants for refugee status. On 28 February 2008, the European Court of Human Rights held in *Saadi* v. *Italy*[78] no one could be deported to where there was a serious risk that their right to be free from torture, inhuman or degrading treatment or punishment would be violated contrary to Article

[77] On the relationship between Article 1F and extradition law, see Gilbert, 'Current issues', 446–49. Cf. The concurring opinion of Bratza J in *Maaouia* v. *France*.

[78] *Saadi* v. *Italy*, paras. 146–148.

146. In these circumstances, the Court considers that in the present case substantial grounds have been shown for believing that there is a real risk that the applicant would be subjected to treatment contrary to Article 3 of the Convention if he were to be deported to Tunisia. That risk cannot be excluded on the basis of other material available to the Court. In particular, although it is true that the International Committee of the Red Cross has been able to visit Tunisian prisons, that humanitarian organisation is required to maintain confidentiality about its fieldwork … and, in spite of an undertaking given in April 2005, similar visiting rights have been refused to the independent human-rights-protection organisation Human Rights Watch … Moreover, some of the acts of torture reported allegedly took place while the victims were in police custody or pre-trial detention on the premises of the Ministry of the Interior … Consequently, the visits by the International

3 ECHR. Article 3 of the Convention Against Torture establishes an absolute prohibition on return to Article 1 Torture. In *Agiza* v. *Sweden*,[79] the Committee Against Torture went so far as to hold that:

> 13.4 … The procurement of diplomatic assurances, which, moreover, provided no mechanism for their enforcement, did not suffice to protect against this manifest risk.

Committee of the Red Cross cannot exclude the risk of subjection to treatment contrary to Article 3 in the present case.

147. The Court further notes that on 29 May 2007, while the present application was pending before it, the Italian Government asked the Tunisian Government, through the Italian embassy in Tunis, for diplomatic assurances that the applicant would not be subjected to treatment contrary to Article 3 of the Convention … However, the Tunisian authorities did not provide such assurances … It was only in a second note verbale, dated 10 July 2007 (that is, the day before the Grand Chamber hearing), that the Tunisian Ministry of Foreign Affairs observed that Tunisian laws guaranteed prisoners' rights and that Tunisia had acceded to 'the relevant international treaties and conventions' … In that connection, the Court observes that the existence of domestic laws and accession to international treaties guaranteeing respect for fundamental rights in principle are not in themselves sufficient to ensure adequate protection against the risk of ill-treatment where, as in the present case, reliable sources have reported practices resorted to or tolerated by the authorities which are manifestly contrary to the principles of the Convention.

148. Furthermore, it should be pointed out that even if, as they did not do in the present case, the Tunisian authorities had given the diplomatic assurances requested by Italy, that would not have absolved the Court from the obligation to examine whether such assurances provided, in their practical application, a sufficient guarantee that the applicant would be protected against the risk of treatment prohibited by the Convention … The weight to be given to assurances from the receiving State depends, in each case, on the circumstances prevailing at the material time.

See also, *DD and AS* v. *Secretary of State for the Home Department* SIAC SC/42 and 50/215, 27 April 2007.

[79] *Agiza* v. *Sweden*, Comm. No. 233/2003, UN Doc. CAT/C/34/D/233/2003 (2005). This decision marked a change of approach from its earlier decision in *Hanan Ahmed Fouad Abd El Khalek Attia* v. *Sweden*, Comm. No. 199/2002, UN Doc. CAT/C/31/D/199/2002 (2003).

13.5 In light of this assessment, the Committee considers it appropriate to observe that its decision in the current case reflects a number of facts which were not available to it when it considered the largely analogous complaint of Hanan Attia, where, in particular, it expressed itself satisfied with the assurances provided. The Committee's decision in that case, given that the complainant had not been expelled, took into account the evidence made available to it up to the time the decision in that case was adopted. The Committee observes that it did not have before it the actual report of mistreatment provided by the current complainant to the Ambassador at his first visit and not provided to the Committee by the State party (see paragraph 14.10 below); the mistreatment of the complainant by foreign intelligence agents on the territory of the State party and acquiesced in by the State party's police; the involvement of a foreign intelligence service in offering and procuring the means of expulsion; the progressively wider discovery of information as to the scope of measures undertaken by numerous States to expose individuals suspected of involvement in terrorism to risks of torture abroad; the breach by Egypt of the element of the assurances relating to guarantee of a fair trial, which goes to the weight that can be attached to the assurances as a whole; and the unwillingness of the Egyptian authorities to conduct an independent investigation despite appeals from

The Human Rights Committee in *Alzery* v. *Sweden*[80] dealt with the potential breach of Article 7 ICCPR as a consequence of expulsion:

11.4 The Committee notes that, in the present case, the State party itself has conceded that there was a risk of ill-treatment that – without more – would have prevented the expulsion of the author consistent with its international human rights obligations (see … para. 3.6). The State party in fact relied on the diplomatic assurances alone for its belief that the risk of proscribed ill-treatment was sufficiently reduced to avoid breaching the prohibition on *refoulement*.

11.5 The Committee notes that the assurances procured contained no mechanism for monitoring of their enforcement. Nor were any arrangements made outside the text of the assurances themselves which would have provided for effective implementation. The visits by the State party's ambassador and staff commenced five weeks after the return, neglecting altogether a period of maximum exposure to risk of harm. The mechanics of the visits that did take place, moreover, failed to conform to key aspects of international good practice by not insisting on private access to the detainee and inclusion of appropriate medical and forensic expertise, even after substantial allegations of ill-treatment emerged. In light of these factors, the State party has not shown that the diplomatic assurances procured were in fact sufficient in the present case to eliminate the risk of ill-treatment to a level consistent with the requirements of article 7 of the Covenant. The author's expulsion thus amounted to a violation of article 7 of the Covenant.

This active involvement post-surrender has been reflected in a Resolution on the Transfer of Persons of the former Sub-Commission for the Protection and Promotion of Human Rights.[81]

4. Confirms that where torture or cruel, inhuman or degrading treatment is widespread or systematic in a particular State, especially where such practice has been determined to exist by a human rights treaty body or a special procedure of the Commission on Human Rights, there is presumption that any person subject to transfer would face a real risk of being subjected to

the State party's authorities at the highest levels. The Committee observes, in addition, that the calculus of risk in the case of the wife of the complainant, whose expulsion would have been some years after the complainants, raised issues differing from to the present case.

More effective again would be for the State seeking assurances to persuade the other State to ratify the draft Optional Protocol to the Convention Against Torture permitting regular visits to all places of detention by the Subcommittee on Prevention of Torture, and Other Cruel, Inhuman or Degrading Treatment or Punishment of the Committee against Torture – adopted on 18 December 2002 at the fifty-seventh session of the General Assembly of the United Nations by resolution A/RES/57/199.

[80] CCPR/C/88/D/1416/2005, 10 November 2006.

[81] E/CN.4/Sub.2/2005/L.12, 4 August 2005. See also, Human Rights Watch's report, Still at Risk, referred to in *Guardian*, 15 April 2005, p. 19.

such treatment and recommends that, in such circumstances, the presumption shall not be displaced by any assurance, undertaking or other commitment made by the authorities of the State to which the individual is to be transferred;[82]

6. Strongly recommends that, in other cases, where the question of a real risk of torture arises in a particular case, no transfer shall be carried out unless:

(a) The State authorities effecting the transfer seek and receive credible and effective assurances, undertakings or other binding commitments from the State to which the person is to be transferred that he or she will not be subjected to torture or cruel, inhuman or degrading treatment;[83]

(b) Provision is made, in writing, for the authorities of the transferring State to be able to make regular visits to the person transferred in his/her normal place of detention, with the possibility of medical examination, and for the visits to include interviews in private during which the transferring authorities shall ascertain how the person who has been transferred is being treated;

(c) The authorities of the transferring State undertake, in writing, to make the regular visits referred to.

Thus, it can be seen that mere paper assurances should not prove sufficient. Indeed, it is arguable that where the person would be surrendered to a State with a persistent record of torture or inhuman and degrading treatment, it is hard to believe that there could ever be a system that could provide effective, verifiable monitoring. Furthermore, obtaining diplomatic assurances for the individual to be surrendered implicitly condones the torture or inhuman and degrading treatment that is endemic in that society.

CONCLUSION

Human rights have been curtailed generally in the fight against terrorism as anyone travelling by air since 2001 can testify. Thus, it would have been harder for persons seeking refugee status to obtain

[82] NB. Transfer of certain persons to the United States from where they might be subject to extraordinary rendition to a state where they face torture or other inhuman or degrading treatment or punishment should also be outlawed by this requirement. See *Guardian*, 12 March 2002, p. 4; 4 October 2003, p. 14.

[83] The adequacy of such assurances must be subject to review by a court according to *Turkish National Extradition Case (Case No. 4)* 106 *International Law Reports* 298 at 301. Cf. The United States handed a Guantanamo detainee back to Egypt without contacting his lawyer and he cannot now be traced, although the Pentagon did claim that appropriate assurances had been received that Sami al-Laithi would continue to be treated humanely – BBC News website 4307310.stm, 2005/10/04 09:05:20.

international protection regardless of any special measures taken by states. The fact that the United Nations emphasized unspecified but potential dangers from granting asylum in the Security Council Resolutions passed as a consequence of the attacks of 11 September 2001 certainly gave states a green light to revisit the law and procedure relating to exclusion. It is less than fortunate that the 2003 UNHCR Guidelines gave states even more leeway in interpreting Article 1F. Moreover, domestic judges dealing with applicants for refugee status have been prepared to hide behind an 'ordinary meaning' smokescreen to limit refugee rights even further. The only bright light shining through this gloom has been the decisions of the human rights treaty bodies asked to adjudicate on the issue. The only problem is that not all states' parties to the 1951 Convention are parties to an international or regional human rights treaty where individuals can bring complaints to the relevant treaty body.

It might be considered strange that the 1951 Convention is being restricted while human rights treaties are interpreted as dynamic, living instruments of protection. Where is the progressive development of the 1951 Convention? On the other hand, it should be noted that refugee status determination is carried out at the domestic level. As indicated previously, judges should be impartial, but they are not neutral.[84] Domestic judges have a role in protecting the state from threats to its security, something that the 1951 Convention provides for through the exclusion clauses. Those sitting on supranational human rights treaty monitoring bodies have a different role. To be sure, human rights conventions give scope for states to interpret rights in a way that allows them to protect their national interests, but the focus of the monitoring body is on balancing the interests of the two parties, the individual and the state. Whether that indicates the need for an international refugee court in order to achieve progressive development of the 1951 Convention is an interesting but, ultimately, purely academic question as things stand. As such, the responsibility lies with academics, advocates and practitioners to ensure that those devising and implementing national laws on refugee status are reminded that Articles 1F and 33.2 are limitations on internationally recognised humanitarian provisions and that they should therefore be interpreted restrictively.

[84] See Griffith, *The Politics of the Judiciary*.

CHAPTER 4

Asymmetrical sovereignty and the refugee: diplomatic assurances and the failure of due process, Agiza *v.* Sweden *and* Alzery *v.* Sweden

Elspeth Guild

THE VISIBLE STATE

Refugee protection forms a small but troublesome part of a wider picture within which the international community deals with the consequences of conflict.[1] Refugees trigger states' duty to provide international protection for those whose states of nationality are unable or unwilling to protect them. The duty comes into existence when there is a serious risk of persecution or torture which are often a by-product of conflict within states and/or among them. The sovereign interstate system, represented by the United Nations, is based on the visibility of the state alone as the actor on that stage. The recognition of Kosovo as a state in March 2008 by a number of European states to the chagrin of Serbia and the Russian Federation's decision in August 2008 to recognise South Ossetia in spite of Georgian resistance are only some examples of the political contestation which surrounds efforts to acquire that visibility and in so doing, sovereignty.[2] They also exemplify the conflict which may surround visibility struggles as the fact of recognition by some states does not necessarily result in sovereignty. If most of the world refuses to recognise a territory as a state, such as has happened in respect of Northern Cyprus, then the territory does not

[1] In this chapter, I have built on research contained in chapter 5 of my book *Security and Migration in the 21st Century* (London: Polity, 2009). The focus and development of the research is, however, fundamentally different here.

[2] J. Caporaso, 'Changes in the Westphalian Order: Territory, Public Authority and Sovereignty' *International Studies Review* 2 (2) (2000), 1–28. Caporaso posits the idea of more or less sovereign, building on the four properties associated with sovereignty – territory, recognition, autonomy and control.

acquire sovereignty within the state system.[3] However, once accepted into the interstate system, the state is entitled to enjoy equality with other states within the international community.

The starting place is the principle that all states are equally sovereign. Article 2(1) of the UN Charter states that '[t]he Organization is based on the principle of the sovereign equality of all its Members'. However, following the declaration of a 'war on terror' by the US President in September 2001, sovereignty has become increasingly asymmetrical. The claims to sovereignty of one state impinge on the sovereignty of other states in particular as regards non-citizens. The political and human rights debacle of the USA's extraordinary rendition programme according to which US agents kidnap individuals from the state where they are present and take them to other states where the individuals are subjected to torture (or to the US military base in Guantanamo Bay), is only the most obvious of the problems which are resulting from asymmetry in sovereignty.[4]

THE INVISIBLE INDIVIDUAL

Refugees, by their existence, constitute an irritant to the sovereign interstate system. This system is intended to be based exclusively on states which are responsible for the human rights of their citizens and the foreigners on their territory. The state has a sovereign right to choose its citizens and does so through the adoption of rules on acquisition of nationality. The state also has the right to choose its foreigners; a right it exercises according to its national rules. The protection of the human rights of foreigners only rarely has consequences for the power of the state to expel foreigners it does not want to their state of nationality.[5] The scope of state obligations to ensure respect for human rights is ring-fenced by its borders (the borders of jurisdiction – though an increasing number of exceptions are being

[3] R. J. B. Walker, *Inside/Outside: International Relations as Political Theory* (Cambridge University Press, 1993).

[4] A. Worthington, *The Guantanamo Files, The Stories of the 774 Detainees in Americas Illegal Prison* (London, Pluto Press, 2007); C. Stafford Smith, *Bad Men: Guantanamo Bay and the Secret Prisons* (London, Phoenix Press, 2007); P. Sands, *Torture Team: Deception, Cruelty and the Compromise of Law* (London, Allen Lane, 2008).

[5] R. Hussain and N. Blake QC, *Immigration, Asylum and Human Rights* (Oxford University Press, 2003).

recognised in international law, for instance as regards the actions of state agents outside the state).[6] Thus the individual remains invisible in the interstate system – though if he or she is on the wrong side of a state border, the manifestation of sovereignty inherent in the state's right of choice permits the state to expel the individual to his or her country of citizenship or country of former habitual residence for those who are stateless.

The refugee, however, cannot be placed back into his or her state of nationality so easily. The UN Convention relating to the Status of Refugees 1951 and the Protocol 1967 (the Geneva Convention) requires states to examine whether the person who claims to be a refugee is indeed one before it can refuse to allow the individual onto the territory.[7] Only once the state has determined whether the individual fulfils the criteria of a well-founded fear of persecution on the basis of race, religion, nationality, membership of a social group or political opinion (article 1A) or that the individual can be excluded either on grounds of international security (article 1F) or on the basis of a national security or public order claim (article 33(1)) can he or she be expelled to the state of origin. Thus persons who claim to need international protection have an oblique right to remain on the territory of a state irrespective of the wishes of the state until the claim has been determined.

The state retains sovereign control over the determination procedure – the meaning of the Geneva Convention depends on the administrations and the courts of each of the signatory states. The result is substantial differences in recognition rates of refugees with the same nationality and circumstances in different host states.[8] The speed with which applications are dealt with is also a matter

[6] E. Guild, *Security and European Human Rights: Protecting Individual Rights in Times of Exception and Military Action* (Nijmegen, Wolf Press, 2007).

[7] G. Goodwin-Gill, and J. McAdam, *The Refugee in International Law*, 3rd edn, (Oxford University Press, 2007). Some states claim a right to send persons claiming to be refugees to countries other than the one from which they fear persecution, usually on the basis that the individuals have already been there and have a right to return there.

[8] The case of recognition rates of Iraqis in European states in 2007 has been particularly problematic: see UNHCR Research Paper No 144 Sperl M, *Fortress Europe and the Iraqi 'intruders': Iraqi asylum seekers and the EU 2003–2007*, October 2007; in 2006 no Iraqis were recognised as refugees in Greece while 90 per cent of Iraqi asylum seekers were recognised as refugees in Sweden.

of national sovereignty. Whether a state takes years to determine a claim or a few hours is a matter for their authorities. However, the state remains constrained in the period between the arrival of the refugee and his or her acceptance or departure by the Geneva Convention.

State obligations to protect individuals do not end with the Geneva Convention. Article 7 of the UN International Covenant on Civil and Political Rights 1966 (ICCPR) prohibits torture, inhuman or degrading treatment (including return to it). Article 3 UN Convention against Torture Inhuman and Degrading Treatment or Punishment 1984 (UN Convention against Torture) prohibits return of a person to a country where he or she is likely to be subjected to torture. Torture, according to article 1 of the UN Convention involves actions causing pain carried out at the instigation of or with the consent or acquiescence of a public official, or other person acting in an official capacity, intentionally for a purpose, for instance, to make the person confess to an offence or provide information. It must be inflicted intentionally 'for such purposes as obtaining from him or a third person information or a confession, punishing him for an act he or a third person has committed or is suspected of having committed or intimidating or coercing him or a third person, or for any reason based on discrimination of any kind …'.

Both the ICCPR and UN Convention against Torture include human rights monitoring bodies capable of considering complaints by individuals, so long as the state party has accepted the bodies' jurisdiction. So, while national procedures still apply to the determination of refugee claims, there is the possibility for the individual to escape state sovereignty as regards the determination of his or her claim to protection and complain to an international human rights monitoring body against a prospective (or actual, as we will see in the cases I examine below) expulsion back to a country where the individual fears torture. While states retain the sovereign right whether to sign up to the jurisdiction of the monitoring bodies as regards the Conventions, once they have done so, they cannot pick and choose which cases they will permit to be adjudicated by the monitoring bodies. The asymmetry in the adjudication of protection claims where states have the last word as regards the interpretation of the Geneva Convention but not (or not necessarily) in respect of the ICCPR or the UN Convention against Torture means that where a conflict between an individual and a state regarding the validity of a protection claim becomes particularly acute, the resolution of the matter may change from one relating to refugee status under the Geneva Convention to one engaging state obligations under the ICCPR or UN Convention against Torture and thereby find a venue of expression beyond the state institutions themselves.

THE INVISIBLE INDIVIDUAL IN THE VISIBLE STATE

The refugee, by the nature of his or her claim to protection, challenges the authorities of his or her state of origin. In the most benign form, the claim to protection is on the basis that the state authorities are no longer able to provide protection although they would like to (this appears to have been the case in Iraq in 2006). In its more confrontational form, the claim of the refugee is that the state is actively persecuting him or her in defiance of international human rights obligations. The host state must determine the validity of the claim unless it uses the security or public order card to refuse responsibility. This card only works as regards the obligations of the Geneva Convention, it does not provide a mechanism to avoid determination of a protection claim which is based on a fear of torture (article 3, UN Convention against Torture). The individual, by arriving at the border of a state and making a protection claim, first, disrupts the sovereign power of the state to refuse entry on to the territory and secondly, requires the state to make a decision regarding the future treatment which he or she might receive at the hands of another state.

At the best of times this can be problematic for states – at the very least they must accept that their sovereignty is modified by the inclusion of the refugee into the territory at least for the period of determination of the claim to protection. In times of asymmetrical sovereignty this causes substantially more problems for states whose claims to sovereignty are put under pressure by an ally.

ASYMMETRICAL SOVEREIGNTY AND THE REFUGEE

The relationship of the state to the refugee is often one of conflict and suspicion.[9] Many western states dispute the identity of those claiming international protection, doubt the validity of their claims and fear that they are security risks.[10] However, in the intersection of refugee claims and sovereignty, the right of the state to treat the protection seeker according to its own rules up until and including expulsion from the state has been fiercely defended. The development of asymmetrical sovereignty has resulted in a weakening of the position of the refugee as states bow to the superior sovereignty claims of a stronger state power, which are expressed in security terms.

To examine this issue, I will take the cases of Mr Agiza and Mr Alzery, two Egyptians who sought international protection in Sweden. Their treatment by the Swedish authorities became a focus for profound questions about the nature of security and sovereignty both by institutions within Sweden, here I will examine the report of the Swedish Parliamentary Ombudsman, and beyond Sweden, here I will look at the determinations of the UN Committee against Torture in May 2005 in respect of the complaint of Mr Agiza and that of the UN Human Rights Committee in November 2006 regarding Mr Alzery. These men are two of the many unexpected victims of 11 September 2001 on a number of grounds: (a) they failed to receive procedural safeguards in respect of their asylum claims in Sweden; (b) the Swedish authorities permitted state agents from their country of origin, accompanied and aided by US state agents, to subject them to inhuman and degrading treatment if not torture on Swedish soil; and, (c) the Swedish authorities permitted agents of the men's country of origin accompanied by US agents to refoule them to Egypt, the country where they feared torture.[11] The ground for the men's treatment by the Swedish authorities remains murky. While the refusal of the men's asylum claims were

[9] D. Joly, *Global Changes in Asylum Regimes: Closing Doors*. (Houndmills, Palgrave, 2002).

[10] S. Kneebone and F. Rawelings-Sanaei, *New Regionalism and Asylum Seekers* (New York, Bergham Books, 2007).

[11] E. Guild, 'International Terrorism and EU Immigration, Asylum and Borders Policy: The Unexpected Victims of 11 September 2001', *European Foreign Affairs Review* 8 (2003), 331–346.

based on information provided to the Swedish Migration Board by the Swedish Security Police, the involvement of US state agents throughout the events which led to the men's expulsion was intense as the Swedish Ombudsman's report indicates. What state security claims led to the men's summary refoulement has not been revealed as the men never received a sufficiently reasoned determination of their asylum claims to clarify this nor was the rejection of their asylum claims accompanied by the procedural safeguards which would have revealed information about the state security grounds for their rejection.

The unwillingness of parts of the Swedish state to resist the security claims which appear to have been promoted by the US but which resulted in a breach of Swedish sovereignty had the unexpected consequence of making these two men visible in the international system. Their claims for protection escaped the framework of national sovereignty and were determined, in the end, beyond the state by the UN bodies. The failure to provide protection and the necessary procedural safeguards to ensure the adequacy of the way in which protection claims are determined led to the condemnation by two international human rights monitoring bodies of a state with an honourable human rights record. At the heart of the case is a fundamental breach of the principle of the rule of law which is linked with the failure of the Swedish authorities to exercise their sovereignty on their own territory. I will examine the events that gave rise to the two cases before the UN bodies step-by-step examining them in relation to the jurisprudence of international human rights monitoring bodies. The most extensive jurisprudence comes from the European Court of Human Rights (ECtHR), the supranational judicial instance charged with the final determination of whether a state has breached its obligations contained in the European Convention on Human Rights 1950. All countries which are members of the Council of Europe, such as Sweden, are obliged to accept the jurisdiction of the ECtHR. The key provisions of the European Convention on Human Rights of relevance to this discussion are article 1 – the jurisdictional scope of the Convention; article 3 – the prohibition on torture, inhuman or degrading treatment and article 13 – the right to an effective remedy.

THE INVISIBLE MEN WHO BECAME VISIBLE

Mr Agiza, an Egyptian national born in 1962 alleged that he was subject to persecution and torture in Egypt on account of his activities at university in the Islamic movement throughout the 1980s. Accordingly, he fled Egypt in early 1991 first to Saudi Arabia, then Pakistan and finally after a failed attempt to get to Europe, Iran. In 1998, he was convicted in absentia in Egypt of terrorist activity against the state in a collective trial before the Superior Court Martial along with over one hundred other accused. At this time Agiza was in Iran but, as relations between Iran and Egypt improved, two years later he began to fear possible return to Egypt so together with his family, he went to Sweden where they applied for asylum.[12]

Mr Alzery, another Egyptian national, was a chemistry and physics teacher who was active in an organisation involved in Islamic opposition to the Egyptian government. According to the description contained in the UN Human Rights Committee decision, his activities were limited to distributing flyers and participating in meetings and lectures and reading the Koran to children in his village.[13] After harassment then arrest by the Egyptian authorities, he fled to Saudi Arabia in 1991 and from there to Syria in 1994. However, in 1999 after a number of Egyptians were extradited from Syria to Egypt he fled again this time to Sweden where in August 1999 he applied for asylum. His claim was based on the substantial risk that he would suffer torture if returned to Egypt (the only country where he has a right of entry). At this point the cases of the two men converge.

The Swedish Migration Board, which was responsible for considering the men's applications, took over a year to deliberate. The Board was advised by Swedish Security Police that Agiza held a leading position in a terrorist organisation and had responsibility for actions of the organisation and that his application should be rejected. According to the UN Human Rights Committee, the Swedish Security Police also submitted a report to the Board on Mr Alzery recommending that his application be rejected on security grounds. The rejection of the claims to protection of both men took place with

[12] *Agiza* v. *Sweden* Comm. No. 233/2003, 24 May 2005 (UNCAT).

[13] *Alzery* v. *Sweden* Comm. No. 1416/2005, 10 November 2006 (UNHRC).

such rapidity and with the means for the refoulement immediately available so as to make any legal challenge to their expulsion effectively impossible.

The ECtHR was faced with a not dissimilar situation which it determined on 5 February 2002, after the events in Sweden. A family of Romanian Roma who had been expelled from Belgium in what the ECtHR found to have been an illegal collective expulsion had been unable to access an effective remedy which in theory existed under Belgian law and could theoretically have been used to permit a court to consider whether the expulsion would be lawful or not before it was carried out.[14] The ECtHR considered the potential right of appeal to the Belgian Conseil d'Etat was too uncertain to fulfil the requirements of an effective remedy under article 13 ECHR (in conjunction with the prohibition on collective expulsion contained in article 4 Protocol 4). The speed with which the expulsions took place after the decision (and detention of the family) together with the lack of access to the means to exercise the appeal right were important factors in the ECtHR's decision.

Although the decisions of the Swedish Migration Board to refuse the protection claims took place on 18 December 2001, the Swedish government had entered into discussions with their Egyptian counterparts in early December 2001 to explore whether the men could be returned to Egypt without violating Sweden's international obligations (including, that not to return a person to a country where there is a substantial risk that he will suffer torture, inhuman or degrading treatment or punishment and that he and his family would not suffer persecution by the Egyptian authorities). The Egyptian authorities responded: 'We herewith assert our full understanding to all items of this memoire, concerning the way of treatment upon repatriate (sic) from your government, with full respect to their personal and human rights. This will be done according to what the Egyptian constitution and law stipulates.'[15] By contacting the Egyptian authorities seeking assurances about the possible treatment of the men if returned there, the Swedish authorities appear to have violated the essential requirement of confidentiality of the refugee proceedings. As a decision had

[14] *Conka* v. *Belgium* App. No. 51564/99, 5 February 2002.

[15] *Alzery* v. *Sweden*, (UNHRC), para. 3.7.

not yet been taken on their refugee claims, an essential requirement of refugee determination proceedings was not respected.[16]

The two men's asylum applications were rejected on 18 December 2001. According to the Human Rights Committee's review of the facts, the Swedish authorities assessed the risk of persecution, sentence of death, torture or severe ill treatment if they were returned to Egypt (all of which would constitute an absolute bar on Sweden's expulsion of the men). The authorities decided, however, that the assurances provided by the Egyptian authorities were sufficient to comply with Sweden's non-refoulement obligation.

The ECtHR had been faced with the problem of diplomatic assurances by a country of origin in respect of the expulsion of a foreigner who was considered to be a national security risk in the host state in a case from the UK decided in 1996.[17] In that case the ECtHR had considered that the diplomatic assurances provided by India, the state of origin of Mr Chahal, were not effective to provide protection. 'Although the Court does not doubt the good faith of the Indian Government in providing the assurances mentioned above (paragraph 92) it would appear that, despite the efforts of that Government, the NHRC and the Indian courts to bring about reform, the violation of human rights by certain members of the security forces in Punjab and elsewhere in India is a recalcitrant and enduring problem … Against this background the Court is not persuaded that the above assurances would provide Mr Chahal with an adequate guarantee of safety' (paras 105 and 106).

The information, which non-governmental organisations and the lawyers of the two men had put to the Swedish government about the endemic nature of human rights abuses in Egypt carried out by the security forces, was not dissimilar to that considered by the ECtHR in the *Chahal* decision. A more careful consideration of

[16] UNHCR examined, in detail, the international duty of confidentiality in asylum proceedings in its submission, 2005, to the Australian Senate Foreign Affairs, Defence and Trade References Committee Inquiry into asylum for consular officials and the deportation, search and discovery of Vivian Solon. The basis of the right, in international human rights law is the right to privacy in article 12, Universal Declaration of Human Rights and article 17, ICCPR coupled with the right to protection from torture and the protection of refugees: www.unhcr.org.au/pdfs/SubmissionVivianSolon.pdf.

[17] *Chahal* v. *United Kingdom* [1996] ECHR 54; App. No. 70/1995/576/662, 15 November 1996.

the implications of the judgment for Sweden might have assisted the Swedish authorities to avoid committing violations of the UN Convention against Torture and the International Covenant on Civil and Political Rights (see below).

The ECtHR decision in *Chahal* regarding need to take great care in respect of diplomatic assurances where an individual claims that he or she will suffer torture, inhuman or degrading treatment on return to a country was confirmed by the ECtHR in a 2008 judgment in respect of Italy.[18] The Italian authorities sought diplomatic assurances from the Tunisian authorities regarding the treatment of Mr Saadi, a Tunisian national, should he be returned there (which efforts were not successful). The ECtHR stated 'even if, as they did not do in the present case, the Tunisian authorities had given the diplomatic assurances requested by Italy, that would not have absolved the Court from the obligation to examine whether such assurances provided, in their practical application, a sufficient guarantee that the applicant would be protected against the rights of treatment prohibited by the Convention'. (para. 148). Because of the way in which the Swedish authorities permitted the expulsion of the two Egyptians, there was no opportunity for a court to consider the sufficiency of the diplomatic assurances which the Swedish authorities had obtained from their Egyptian counterparts.

On the same day as the refusal of the asylum applications of Agiza and Alzery, they were arrested by Swedish Security Police and escorted to the Bromma airport. I have already dealt with above the issue of access to a judicial remedy. Clearly the alacrity with which the Swedish authorities acted effectively prevented the exercise of judicial remedies which might have halted the events which led to Sweden committing serious breaches of its international human rights obligations. At the airport the men were handed over to ten foreign agents in civilian clothes and hoods. The Swedish Ombudsman's investigation subsequently disclosed that the ten men were US and Egyptian security agents.[19] Later that day they were expelled to Egypt on the plane which had brought the foreign agents to Sweden.

[18] *Saadi* v. *Italy* App. No. 37201/06, 28 February 2008.
[19] *Alzery* v. *Sweden* (UNHRC), paras. 3.8 – 3.10.

There is no question that in international human rights law, the Swedish authorities retained responsibility for the men's treatment as long as they were on Swedish territory. The fact that they were handed over to foreign agents did not have the effect of relieving the Swedish authorities of their duty under article 1 ECHR to ensure the protection of the human rights of all persons within their jurisdiction. Elsewhere I have examined the jurisprudence of the ECtHR on sovereign responsibility, in particular where states take action outside their own territory.[20] Suffice it here to reiterate that there was no ground in international human rights law to consider that the treatment of the men at a Swedish airport by agents of other countries would not engage Swedish human rights obligations.

The treatment of the two men recorded in the review of the complaint by the Human Rights Committee (and repeated in the record of the UN Committee against Torture)[21], while they were still at the airport in Sweden is remarkable. 'The author states that the hooded agents forced him into a small locker room where they exposed him to what was termed 'security search', although Swedish police had already carried out a less intrusive search. The hooded agents slit the author's clothes with a pair of scissors and examined each piece of cloth before placing it in a plastic bag. Another agent checked his hair, mouth[s] and lips, while a third agent took photographs, according to Swedish officers who witnessed the searches. When his clothes were cut off his body, he was handcuffed and chained to his feet. He was then drugged per rectum with some form of tranquilliser and placed in diapers. He was then dressed in overalls and escorted to the plane, blindfolded, hooded and barefoot. Two representatives from the Embassy of the United States of America were also present during the apprehension and treatment of the applicant.'[22] It is worth remembering that in December it is very cold in Sweden.

I have already given the definition of torture in article 1 UNCAT above. The question of the treatment of the men at the Swedish airport would exercise both the UNCAT and the UNHRC when they heard the cases. There was unanimity that the treatment constituted

[20] E Guild, *Security and European Human Rights*.
[21] *Agiza* v. *Sweden* (UNCAT), paras. 12.28 – 12.29.
[22] *Alzery* v. *Sweden* (UNHRC), para. 3.11.

inhuman and degrading treatment, there was less clarity on whether it constituted torture outright. Already in 1999 the ECtHR had considered what inhuman and degrading treatment was. It stated:

In order to determine whether a particular form of ill-treatment should be qualified as torture, the Court must have regard to the distinction, embodied in article 3, between this notion and that of inhuman or degrading treatment. As the European Court has previously found, it appears that it was the intention that the Convention should, by means of this distinction, attach a special stigma to deliberate inhuman treatment causing very serious and cruel suffering.

The acts complained of were such as to arouse in the applicant feelings of fear, anguish and inferiority capable of humiliating and debasing him and possibly breaking his physical and moral resistance. The Court therefore finds elements which are sufficiently serious to render such treatment inhuman and degrading (see the *Ireland* v. *The United Kingdom* judgment cited above, pp. 66–67, § 167, and the *Tomasi* judgment cited above, p. 42, § 115). In any event, the Court reiterates that, in respect of a person deprived of his liberty, recourse to physical force which has not been made strictly necessary by his own conduct diminishes human dignity and is in principle an infringement of the right set forth in Article 3 (see the *Ribitsch* judgment cited above, p. 26, § 38, and the *Tekin v. Turkey* judgment of 9 June 1998, *Reports* 1998-IV, pp. 1517–18, § 53).[23]

By allowing the two Egyptians to be treated in the way they were at Bromma Airport, the Swedish authorities should have known that a breach of article 3 ECHR was taking place.

Mr Agiza's wife went into hiding in Sweden. In January 2002 the Swedish ambassador to Egypt met with Mr Agiza who was in prison but noted nothing untoward about his appearance. On the same day Mr Agiza's parents were allowed to see him for the first time. They alleged that he was in a shocking state, clearly having been the object of torture which he confirmed to them.[24] Various other people visited Mr Agiza in prison over the next twelve months, including a journalist. His parents were able to visit regularly and once the Swedish Ambassador visited him. The Swedish Ambassador similarly met with Mr Alzery though not in private and when Mr Alzery complained of ill treatment in front of both the Ambassador and

[23] *Selmouni* v. *France* App. No. 25803/94, 28 July 1999.

[24] *Agiza* v. *Sweden* (UNCAT), para.2.6.

the Egyptian warden, the latter took notes. When the Ambassador asked for further information about the treatment of Mr Alzery, the Egyptian authorities rejected the claims saying this was what could be expected of 'terrorists'. Mr Alzery was transferred subsequently to another prison where he was subject to very serious torture.[25]

The facts regarding the torture of the two men on their return to Egypt are disputed. While there is evidence that they were subjected to torture, the Swedish Ambassador, who saw both men, did not find any evidence of it. From the perspective of international human rights law, the key issue is whether the Swedish authorities should have been aware of the risk of torture in the event of the men being returned to Egypt. The ECtHR spelled this out in 1989.[26] The test for a breach of the duty to protect an individual from torture or inhuman and degrading treatment on expulsion to a third country is whether there were distinguishing features of the case, which ought to have enabled the state to foresee the substantial risk of the prohibited treatment.

HOW THE MEN BECAME VISIBLE IN THE INTERNATIONAL COMMUNITY

The allegations against Sweden arising from these cases were expressed before two human rights monitoring bodies: the UN Committee against Torture and the UN Human Rights Committee. Mr Agiza complained to the UN Committee against Torture that Sweden had failed to comply with its duty to protect him from torture; including return to a country where there is a substantial risk he would be tortured as required by article 3 UNCAT. In light of the information, which the Swedish authorities had at the time they expelled him to Egypt, Mr Agiza claimed that they should have known that there was an unacceptably high risk that he would be tortured. His complaint was supported by international reports on the use of torture in Egypt and the high risk of torture for persons suspected of being Islamic fundamentalists. In their defence, the Swedish authorities relied

[25] *Alzery* v. *Sweden* (UNHRC).

[26] *Vivlarajah and Others* v. *United Kingdom* App. Nos. 13163/87; 13164/87; 13165/87; 13447/87; 13448/87 para.112, 10 October 1989.

substantially on the diplomatic assurances which they had received from the Egyptian authorities before expelling him.

The UN Committee against Torture in its decision on 24 May 2005 found Sweden had breached its duty to protect Mr Agiza from torture by sending him back to Egypt. It stated:

> The State party was also aware of the interest in the complainant [Mr Agiza] by the intelligence services of two other States: according to the facts submitted by the State party to the Committee, the first foreign State offered through its intelligence service an aircraft to transport the complainant to the second State, Egypt, where to the State party's knowledge, he had been sentenced in absentia and was wanted for alleged involvement in terrorist activities. In the Committee's view, the natural conclusion from these combined elements, that is, that the complainant was at a real risk of torture in Egypt in the event of expulsion, was confirmed when immediately preceding expulsion, the complainant was subject on the State party's territory to treatment in breach of, at least article 16 of the Convention[27] by foreign agents but with the acquiescence of the State party's police. It follows that the State party's expulsion of the complainant was in breach of article 3 of the Convention. The procurement of diplomatic assurances, which, moreover, provided no mechanism for their enforcement, did not suffice to protect against this manifest risk.[28]

There were three key findings from UN Committee against Torture:

- The evident interest in Mr Agiza (and possible collusion) of two foreign states' security services, one of which having a record of consistent and widespread use of torture against detainees, should have put the Swedish authorities on notice that sending Mr Agiza to one of them, Egypt, would place him at unacceptable risk of torture;

[27] 1. Each State Party shall undertake to prevent in any territory under its jurisdiction other acts of cruel, inhuman or degrading treatment or punishment which do not amount to torture as defined in article 1, when such acts are committed by or at the instigation of or with the consent or acquiescence of a public official or other person acting in an official capacity. In particular, the obligations contained in articles 10, 11, 12 and 13 shall apply with the substitution for references to torture or references to other forms of cruel, inhuman or degrading treatment or punishment.

2. The provisions of this Convention are without prejudice to the provisions of any other international instrument or national law which prohibit cruel, inhuman or degrading treatment or punishment or which relate to extradition or expulsion.

[28] *Agiza* v. *Sweden* (UNCAT), para. 13.4.

- The treatment of Mr Agiza in Sweden by the US and Egyptian agents constituted at least inhuman and degrading treatment if not torture and thus showed the Swedish authorities that he was at risk of further torture if removed to Egypt;
- The Egyptian diplomatic assurances where valueless not least because there was no mechanism to protect Mr Agiza from their breach.

In this finding, the UN Committee against Torture developed its own jurisprudence on the conditions under which a risk of torture is evidenced. Very sensibly, the UNCAT did not make a finding on the treatment of Mr Agiza in Egypt, rather it extrapolated from his treatment in Sweden what a reasonable state authority should conclude regarding the risk of torture in the country of origin. The Swedish Chancellor of Justice Goran Lambertz announced that the authorities would pay Agiza SEK 3 million[29] in compensation for his expulsion and related human rights abuses. The announcement is dated 6 October 2008 and followed a tort action against the Swedish authorities.[30] There are echoes here of the case of the dual Canadian/ Syrian national, Maher Arar, who was captured by US authorities when transiting the USA in September 2002 and sent to Syria (where he explicitly did not want to go as he feared torture) and where he was tortured. Following a Royal Commission inquiry into the participation of Canadian authorities in the treatment of Mr Arar, the Canadian Government offered him an apology and CAN$10.5 million in compensation.[31]

The second decision of an international complaint body was by the UN Human Rights Committee (HRC), which determined Mr Alzery's complaint on 10 November 2006. The Committee considered

[29] Approximately €291,405.

[30] Swedish Helsinki Committee 6 October 2008 www.shc.se/en/4/110/1324/.

[31] The full history of the case and the official documents can be found at www.maherarar.ca/; see also Thomas Poole, 'Recent Developments on the "War on Terrorism" in Canada', *Human Rights Law Review*, 7: (3) (2007), 633–642 and A Macklin, 'From Cooperation to Complicity to Compensation: The War on Terror, Extraordinary Rendition and the Cost of Torture', *European Journal of Migration and Law* 10 (1) (2008), 11–30(20). The Euro equivalent is €6.77 million – very substantially more than for the Egyptian. One wonders about the differential in terms of the treatment of a citizen (Mr Arar) versus the treatment of a foreigner (Mr Agiza).

the same facts as the Committee against Torture and came to very similar conclusions. Its key findings were:

- Sweden accepted, by its efforts to obtain diplomatic assurances from the Egyptian authorities the fact that there was a real risk that Mr Alzery would be subject to torture, inhuman or degrading treatment if returned there;
- The diplomatic assurances given were inadequate not least as there was no mechanism for monitoring or enforcement and thus the expulsion was contrary to article 7 ICCPR;
- The acts of the US agents at the Swedish airport took place with the acquiescence of the Swedish authorities and therefore must be imputed to the Swedish authorities. The treatment which Mr Alzery suffered at the airport in Sweden (cutting off of his clothes, intimate body search, handcuffing, shackling, etc.) violated article 7 International Covenant Civil and Political Rights 1966 (ICCPR)[32] not least as it was disproportionate to any law enforcement purpose.

The HRC also found that the Swedish authorities had attempted to frustrate judicial supervision of their expulsion of Mr Alzery by providing inaccurate information to his advisers regarding whether his asylum application had been rejected. The advisers were told that no decision had been taken when the decision had, in fact, already been taken. As can been seen from the report of the Swedish Ombudsman, one of the reasons for this subterfuge was to make it impossible for the advisers to seek an injunction from one of the international courts to prevent Mr Alzery's expulsion from Sweden.[33] The use of subterfuge by state authorities to effect the expulsion of foreigners was condemned by the ECtHR in the *Conka* decision (see footnote 15). In that case the Belgian authorities had sent letters to

[32] 'No one shall be subjected to torture or to cruel, inhuman or degrading treatment or punishment. In particular, no one shall be subjected without his free consent to medical or scientific experimentation.'

[33] The Parliamentary Ombudsman, *A review of the enforcement by Security Police of a Government decision to expel two Egyptian citizens* Adjudication Number 2169–2004; 22 March 2005, section 2.4.2: 'K.J. has stated that the officials at the Ministry of Foreign Affairs told him that during the presentation there was some concern that either the UN Committee against Torture or the European Court of Human Rights would have time to issue a staying order before enforcement could take place.'

the foreigners asking them to attend at the police office to resolve their files. When the individuals attended they were detained and expelled. The ECtHR held that: 'Although the Court by no means excludes its being legitimate for police to use stratagems in order, for instance, to counter criminal activities more effectively, acts whereby the authorities seek to gain the trust of asylum seekers with a view to arresting and subsequently deporting them may be found to contravene the general principles stated or implicit in the Convention.' (para. 41).

The HRC required two measures in respect of the breach: an effective remedy, which included compensation for Mr Alzery (in an amount unspecified); and that Sweden take steps to ensure that there is no re-occurrence of such a breach. It welcomed the establishment of an independent immigration court with power to review expulsion decisions, including where a security aspect is present. On 3 July 2008 the Swedish Chancellor of Justice announced that compensation of SEK 3 million[34] would be paid to Mr Alzery.[35]

The case has thrown a long shadow over the international reputation of Sweden. For example, when Sweden was under examination as regards its compliance with the UN Convention against Torture in June 2008 under the general reporting requirements, the matter of Mr Agiza and Mr Alzery came back to haunt the Swedish authorities. The UNCAT Consideration of Reports: Sweden[36] regretted the lack of full implementation of the key elements of the two decisions and in particular, the lack of an in-depth investigation and prosecution of those responsible. Following this exchange, the Swedish authorities compensated the two men for the harm they had suffered.

WHOSE CLAIM? WHOSE RESPONSIBILITY?

The events surrounding the departure of Mr Agiza and Mr Alzery from Sweden for Egypt presented their own particular problems around the question of sovereignty and refugee protection. Not only

[34] Approximately €291,405.

[35] Swedish Helsinki Committee 3 July 2008 www.shc.se/en/4/110/1324/?tpid=81&tpl=214.

[36] Committee against Torture; 40th Session, 28 April – 16 May 2008; CAT/C/SWE/CO/5; 4 June 2008.

did they cause consternation in international venues but they also perturbed national settlements about the nature of Swedish sovereignty. These concerns found their clearest voice in the report of the Swedish Parliament Ombudsman on the matter.[37]

The facts regarding the case of the two men as revealed in the Ombudsman's report coincide with those found by the two UN bodies. However, as the remit of the Ombudsman's inquiry was different further facts were revealed which I will set out here before looking at the findings of the Report. First, the Swedish Security Police had been investigating the two men since the Spring of 2001, at the same time that the Swedish Migration Board was investigating their claims to asylum. In October 2001 the Swedish Security Police lodged objections to the two men's asylum applications. The Migration Board duly referred the applications to the Swedish Government for a decision in November 2001. It appears that the Ministry of Foreign Affairs had the lead in this matter while the Ministry of Justice appeared to be more and more marginalised as the events unfolded.

In the same month, the Security Police decided that expulsion could be required and began planning. Although the advisers were told that a decision on the asylum claims would be made in January 2002, the Security Police file revealed that the Swedish Government planned to take the decision on 13 December 2001 with expulsion following on 15 December. However, at a time unspecified but well before any decision was taken, the Swedish Security Police received an offer from the American Central Intelligence Agency (CIA) of the use of a plane for the expulsion with a guarantee that the plane could fly over Europe without having to touch down thus avoiding the need to negotiate with any other state (though according to the report, one official at least recalled some discussion that the problem of airspace would be resolved with US help or help from 'colleagues in the West').

The timing changed again, this time with the Ministry of Foreign Affairs advising, on 5 December 2001, that a decision on the asylum applications would not be made until 20 December. However, there is a journal entry in the Security Police file of 14

[37] The Parliamentary Ombudsman, *A review of the enforcement by Security Police*5.

December that the decision on the applications would be taken on 18 December and that a plane for their expulsion had been booked for 19 December. It is clear from the report that the decision, in the end, to use the CIA plane and to expel the men on 18 December was made at the highest levels in the Foreign Affairs Ministry and after substantial discussion and consultation with the Security Police and Migration Board.

WHO CONTROLS WHAT HAPPENS ON THE TERRITORY?

The events of 18 December 2001 in Stockholm relating to Mr Agiza and Mr Alzery fall into two very distinct periods. First, the two men are arrested quietly and without any use of force or resistance by Swedish police. They were notified that their asylum applications had been rejected, that they were about to be expelled to Egypt and they were subject to a body search. They were then taken to the airport. At this point the second stage begins when the two men were handed over to the US and Egyptian agents. The CIA plane landed just before 9 pm and contained, in addition to its crew, a security team of seven or eight persons including two Egyptian officials and a doctor. All were wearing hoods. Curiously by this time there were no longer any senior Swedish Security Police officers present and of those junior officers who were present no one had been assigned operational command at the airport. None considered that they were ultimately responsible for the expulsion. Instead it was the US and Egyptian agents who carried out the cutting off of clothing, intimate body searches, handcuffing and shackling, hooding and administration of sedatives anally (an act which none of the Swedish officers present accepted that they saw, each with a separate excuse for the lapse of attention or presence at that critical moment).

An individual reported the events of 18 December 2001 to the Swedish Public Prosecutor for consideration of whether any crime had been committed in connection with the enforcement of the expulsion order. The then Acting Director of Public Prosecution decided there were no grounds for assuming that any offence subject to public prosecution had been committed.

Following a television documentary on the events of 18 December, which was broadcast on 25 May 2004, the Swedish Ombudsman opened an inquiry on his own initiative. The central issue was twofold: the actions of the Swedish Security Police and the use of public authority by foreign officials on Swedish territory. Sovereignty and its exercise is the stake in the competing claims of security which revolve around the expulsion of the Egyptians. The UN Human Rights Committee, as noted above, found that Sweden is responsible in international human rights law for the acts which take place on its territory and with which it has acquiesced. The Ombudsman examined the nature of Swedish sovereignty and to what extent the events of 18 December 2001 are compatible with it.

The Swedish constitution is set out in the Instrument of Government. It is the expression of Swedish sovereignty and sets out in the form of law what that sovereignty means and how it must be exercised. The Swedish constitution, like those of other liberal democracies, is founded on the assumption that judicial and administrative measures which take place on the territory are the concern of the Swedish authorities. According to the Ombudsman, only Swedish police officers are empowered to use force or coercive measures including against individuals or to exercise their authority in any other form on Swedish territory. There is no exception in respect of expulsion. The Ombudsman examined Swedish criminal law to determine the legality of the events of 18 December and their consistency with the Swedish constitution. National criminal law controls on the use of body searches is the first target: as one of the most coercive measures permitted to the state they can only be carried out by state actors – in this case the police. While the Ombudsman recognised the importance of contact between Swedish and foreign security agencies, where this cooperation moved beyond the exchange of information to permitting foreign police officers or security agents to take an active part in police operations and to exercise public authority in Sweden a completely different, and unacceptable, state of affairs had been reached.

Among the key reasons why the action of foreign security agents in Sweden was contrary to Swedish sovereignty, according to the Ombudsman, is because the national rules on the conduct of the police and on liability for misuse of office in the event of transgression by the police only apply to national police. Thus the individual who is the object of these protections is no longer able to access them if the principle of sovereignty is not respected. He stated: 'In my opinion, it would be unacceptable to have a system which enabled foreigner officials to exercise public authority in Sweden without being subject to the liability laid down in the Criminal Code for misuse of office.'[38]

The Swedish constitution, in common with those of other liberal democracies, does not limit protection against unlawful police action to citizens. It applies to all persons who encounter unlawful action. As the Ombudsman states 'it is self-evident that in a democratic state, subject to the rule of law, police officers must treat all those who become the object of police actions in a humane and dignified manner. This means that nobody may be subject to degrading or humiliating treatment in the course of a police operation'.[39] He found that the body searches and hooding constituted such treatment. Further (and perhaps in explanation of the failure of any of the Swedish officers to observe the administration of tranquillizers to the two men) he noted that coercive medication is one of the kinds of coercive physical measures specifically prohibited in the constitution and thus requires the support of law to be permitted.

ASYMMETRIC SOVEREIGNTY AND THE SOVEREIGN STATE

The Ombudsman examined Swedish sovereignty as expressed in its constitution against the actions taken by the Swedish authorities to permit their allies to carry out their security objectives in Sweden and found that the principle of sovereignty itself had been compromised. The interests of Swedish sovereign security were offended by acts carried out in the name of collective security including Sweden, the USA and Egypt and allowed to take place on Swedish territory. As a result of concern regarding the events of 18 December 2001,

[38] The Parliamentary Ombudsman, *A review of the enforcement by Security Police.*
[39] *Ibid.*

the Swedish Security Police have been re-organised to enable better strategic planning and to enhance, substantially, direction and monitoring of its operations. Thus one of the costs of the subordination of Swedish security to that of its allies has been the reining in of the Swedish agency held most responsible for the event and it is subjected now to greater democratic scrutiny. Another cost relates to the safeguarding of rule of law and the treatment of the Swedish Migration Board. Its independence was completely undermined in both cases as all the key decisions about the fate of the two men were made exclusively at the political level. The failure to provide effective procedural guarantees (an issue which was heavily criticised by the UN Human Rights Committee) was critical to the breakdown of the exercise of Swedish sovereignty in accordance with the constitution in Sweden. Had the Board been empowered to provide an effective remedy as required by the ECHR and the ICCPR to the aggrieved men it is much less obvious that the miscarriage of justice would have occurred. The centrality of all state institutions in ensuring full respect for constitutional sovereignty even in the face of external pressure is one of the main lessons of the matter.

The example I have used to examine asymmetrical sovereignty is intentionally one where all the countries involved: Egypt, Sweden and the USA have undisputed claims to being functioning states. Two of the three also enjoy unchallenged claims to be liberal democracies. Yet, the treatment of two men claiming a need for international protection revealed a very unsettling relationship of power among the states. The asymmetry of the relationships among the countries is startling. From the reports of the UN treaty monitoring bodies and the Ombudsman, it appears that Sweden accepted the US claims to exercise sovereign power on its territory notwithstanding the fact that this was in contravention of its constitution. The Egyptian authorities, on the other hand, refused to relinquish any sovereignty to Sweden – providing only the most cursory of assurances that they would not torture the men if they were sent back to Egypt and refusing any form of monitoring of the assurances other than accompanied visits from time to time by the Swedish Ambassador to the men in prison after their return to Egypt.

The treatment of the men in both Sweden and following their return to Egypt indicates that they were indeed at risk of torture. As the UN Human Rights Committee noted, the interest of the Egyptian authorities in the two men was sufficient to put Sweden on notice that there was a real risk that returning the men there would result in a breach of the state's international human rights commitments. It is through the treatment of these refugees that the changing nature of sovereignty is revealed.

CHAPTER 5

Economic harm as a basis for refugee status and the application of human rights law to the interpretation of economic persecution

Kate Jastram

I INTRODUCTION

The 1951 Refugee Convention is so strongly linked in people's minds to the protection of civil and political rights that refugee status is often referred to as "political asylum." Yet claims to refugee status based on economic forms of persecution[1] and on persecution for reasons of economic status[2] have long been recognized as falling within the Convention definition.[3] Although refugee judges routinely assess such claims,[4] consensus remains elusive on the extent to which the Convention properly encompasses violations of economic, social or cultural rights. Commentators note troubling inconsistencies in approach to economic claims within and between jurisdictions, as well as the de jure or de facto imposition of more restrictive standards for harm, risk, ground and/or nexus than are employed for claims based on violations of civil and political rights.[5]

[1] See Part 1. See also G. Goodwin-Gill and J. McAdam, *The Refugee in International Law*, 3rd edn. (Oxford University Press, 2007), p. 92: "[L]ess overt measures may suffice [for persecution], such as the imposition of serious economic disadvantage, denial of access to employment, to the professions, or to education."

[2] See Goodwin-Gill and McAdam, *The Refugee in International Law*, pp. 74–9, noting that former capitalists were apparently the intended beneficiaries of the social group ground, and discussing various other economic class-related social groups.

[3] "[W]hilst there will always be heavy factual obstacles in the way of a finding that socio-economic circumstances can constitute persecution, there is no reason of principle why a claim of this kind cannot succeed." *AM & AM (armed conflict: risk categories) Somalia CG* v. *Secretary of State for the Home Department* [2008] UKAIT 00091, paras. 78–79.

[4] "[C]laims of economic persecution are common in this Circuit," *Mirzoyan* v. *Gonzales*, 457 F.3d 217 at 224 (2nd Cir. 2006).

[5] For a comprehensive survey, see M. Foster, *International Refugee Law and Socio-Economic Rights* (Cambridge University Press, 2007); for US approaches to economic persecution, see

Some argue that there is further capacity for recognition of economic claims to refugee status. This case has been put most comprehensively by Michelle Foster, who contends that refugee law has so far largely failed to reflect the growth of a more sophisticated and complex understanding within the human rights realm of the content of economic, social and cultural rights. She argues that the growing maturity of this aspect of human rights law provides a principled basis for refugee judges to re-assess the Convention's scope.[6]

However, there are diverging views as to whether the Convention can and should include a wider range of economic claims. Some refugee receiving countries with important asylum jurisprudence, notably Australia and the United States, do not explicitly employ a human rights framework in analyzing claims, so that it is not clear that arguing for greater acceptance of economic forms of persecution on the basis of developments in human rights law is necessarily persuasive. Countries of asylum with their own resource constraints are apt to look askance at the notion of enlarging protection to encompass claims based on denials of economic rights. Nor are wealthy countries necessarily more welcoming. David Martin urges caution on the basis that refugee protection is a scarce resource to be preserved for only a limited category of harms,[7] and has welcomed the US Board of Immigration Appeals' recent endorsement of a higher standard for economic persecution.[8] Even in the context of complementary protection regimes, states are evidently wary of such claims. Jane McAdam concludes that at present, there is scant support for a right to remain for socio-economic reasons or due to a severe paucity of resources in the country of origin.[9] One notable instance of this

J. Falkler, "Comment: Economic mistreatment as persecution in asylum claims: towards a consistent standard," *U. Chi. Legal F.* (2007), 471–501.

6 See Part 3.2, below, and Foster, *International Refugee Law*, generally. See also F. Gabor and J. Rosenquest IV, "The Unsettled Status of Economic Refugees from the American and International Legal Perspectives – A Proposal for Recognition under Existing International Law," *Tex. Int'l L. J.* 41 (Spring 2006) 275.

7 D. Martin, "The Refugee Concept: On Definitions, Politics, and the Careful Use of Scarce Resources" in H. Adelman (ed.), *Refugee Policy: Canada and the United States* (1991) 30, reprinted in D. Martin et al., *Forced Migration Law and Policy* (Thomson/West 2007), pp. 59–65.

8 D. Martin, "Major Developments in Asylum Law Over the Past Year: A Year of Dialogue Between Courts and Agencies," *Interpreter Releases* 84 (35) (Sept. 10, 2007), 2069–77 at 2072. The case is *In re T-Z-*, 24 I&N Dec. 163 (BIA 2007), discussed in Part 2.1.

9 J. McAdam, *Complementary Protection in International Refugee Law* (Oxford University Press, 2007), pp. 163–4.

reluctance is the near complete exclusion of claims based on lack of access to adequate health care from the Convention as well as from complementary protection provisions.[10]

UNHCR has not addressed economic claims to refugee status as such but should consider doing so for at least two reasons. First, it is critical to UNHCR's protection mandate to assist states in maintaining the distinction between refugees and migrants.[11] Second, UNHCR itself carries out refugee status determination in over seventy-five countries.[12] Certainly, greater attention to the issue is warranted.[13] While it is difficult to quantify the number of economic claims or their trends, it is safe to say that in light of the growing disjunction between global economic pressures that fuel migration and restrictive immigration policies of many states,[14] refugee judges are called upon to make increasingly fine distinctions between "genuine" refugees and "economic migrants." Furthermore, the exploration of appropriate responses to displacement related to famine[15] and other threats,[16] including climate change,[17] requires an

[10] For example, Canada's Immigration and Refugee Protection Act, sec. 97(1)(b)(iv) excludes situations of risk to life or risk of cruel and unusual treatment or punishment caused by the inability of the country of origin to provide adequate health or medical care.

[11] A recent UNHCR discussion paper on migration issues notes that asylum seekers leave countries simultaneously affected by "human rights violations, armed conflict, ethnic discrimination, unemployment and deteriorating public services," yet observes merely that "high quality refugee status determination procedures, supported by accurate and timely country of origin information, make it possible to differentiate between those people who are in need of international protection and those who are not." UNHCR *Discussion Paper: Refugee protection and durable solutions in the context of international migration*, UNHCR/DPC/2007/Doc. 2 (19 Nov. 2007), paras. 33–4. Available at www.unhcr.org/protect/PROTECTION/4742a6b72.pdf (last visited Feb. 4, 2009).

[12] UNHCR Refugee Status Determination Unit Background, updated July 2008. www.unhcr.org/pages/4a16b1d06.html. (last visited April 5, 2009.)

[13] Foster, *International Refugee Law*, notes the paucity of judicial or scholarly attention, pp. 88, 151–4.

[14] For UNHCR's recent initiatives to address this challenge, see UNHCR's *Dialogue on Protection Challenges* (Dec. 2007), and *Refugee Protection and Mixed Migration: A 10-Point Plan of Action* (Rev. 1, Jan. 2007), both available at www.unhcr.org/protect/473db6522.html (last visited Feb. 4, 2009).

[15] E. Chan and A. Schloenhardt, "North Korean Refugees and International Refugee Law," *International Journal of Refugee Law*, 19 (2) (2007), 215–245.

[16] M. Afzal, *"A violation of his or her human security" – New grounds for the recognition of refugee status: A proposal for reform*, UNHCR New Issues in Refugee Research Paper No. 140 (Dec. 2006).

[17] E. Piguet, *Climate change and forced migration*, UNHCR New Issues in Refugee Research Paper No. 153 (Jan. 2008).

agreed understanding of the scope of the tools presently available to the international community.

The aim of this chapter is to provide an overview of the standards governing economic persecution claims and their current application in order to assess arguments both for a more restrictive approach based on the limitations of the Refugee Convention and for a more expansive approach based on developments in human rights law. A number of issues are identified as worthy of further judicial and scholarly exploration, as well as the considered attention of UNHCR. These include the legal justification for the use of a higher standard to assess persecution when it takes the form of economic harm as well as the proper scope of policy concerns in interpreting the refugee definition. The chapter concludes that considerable work remains to be done before socio-economic rights jurisprudence can provide a useful basis for refugee law judges confronted with claims of economic persecution.

Part Two outlines the two tests used to assess economic forms of persecution and surveys their application in recent cases decided in Australia, Canada, New Zealand, the United Kingdom, and the United States. It concludes that notwithstanding the formal difference in standards, in practice most cases are decided by reference to the more stringent of the two tests and queries whether this is an appropriate reading of the Convention. Part Three critiques two contrasting perspectives on the place of economic claims under the Convention. It questions the wisdom of importing restrictive policy considerations so blatantly into definitional issues, while also suggesting a number of reasons that an economic rights framework may prove particularly challenging for refugee judges. Part Four concludes that the jurisprudential value of a human rights framework for economic persecution claims has yet to be demonstrated, and urges judges, scholars, and UNHCR toward a more critical engagement with both the legal and policy issues raised by such claims.

Two preliminary comments on the scope of the chapter are in order. First, the focus is on persecution. Considerations of space preclude discussion of other elements of the definition where economic factors may be relevant to the analysis, particularly interpretation of membership of a particular social group. Review of the recent cases confirms that socio-economic characteristics such as poverty, medical condition, occupation, and wealth are accepted in combination with others as establishing a particular social group, but that greater attention should be given to the proper analysis of poverty or wealth alone in defining a social group.[18] Second, within the chapter's focus on economic forms of persecution, space constraints preclude consideration of a common category of such claims, those based on denials of access to adequate healthcare. Recent cases raise a number of interesting issues that merit a fuller discussion than is possible here, including the difficulties judges face in examining policy decisions regarding resource allocation in the country of origin,[19] and the relationship of Convention protection to complementary protection in jurisdictions where the latter is available.[20]

Finally, two notes on terminology may be helpful. First, for simplicity's sake, the term economic claim is used as a general reference for claims involving persecution in the form of socio-economic harm or socio-economic factors as a ground for persecution. The term economic persecution refers to various types of socio-economic harms.[21] Finally, for the sake of brevity, this paper uses the term judge to refer generally to all executive, administrative, and judicial officials who make or review determinations of refugee status.

2 ECONOMIC FORMS OF PERSECUTION

Part Two examines how judges decide whether economic harms such as interference with education or employment, and the imposition

[18] See, e.g., the ongoing dialogue between the US Board of Immigration Appeals and the Second Circuit Court of Appeals concerning social group claims based on wealth, in *Matter of A-M-E- & J-G-U-*, 24 I&N Dec. 69 (BIA 2007), *aff'd by Ucelo-Gomez* v. *Mukasey*, 509 F.3d 70 (2nd Cir. 2007) and in *Romero* v. *Mukasey* 2008 WL 268682 (2nd Cir. 2008 unpublished). See also "Second Circuit Upholds BIA Decision that 'Affluent Guatemalans'" Do Not Constitute a Particular Social Group," 84 *Int. Rel.* 2874 (Dec. 10, 2007).

[19] See, e.g., *Reference 071295385* [2007] RRTA 109, (20 June 2007), analyzing the sufficiency of Sri Lanka's attempts in light of available resources to provide adequate pensions and health care to the elderly.

[20] See, e.g., *RPD TA5–11242*, Savage (9 Mar. 2007), finding that an Ethiopian woman with bipolar disorder met the Convention definition, but not that of complementary protection due to the medical exemption provision.

[21] The International Covenant on Economic, Social and Cultural Rights (ICESCR) does not categorize rights as specifically economic, social, or cultural. No diminution of the importance of social rights, or the social aspect of economic rights, is implied by the terminology used in this chapter.

of punitive fines, rise to the level of persecution. In formal terms, some jurisdictions prescribe a more rigorous test for economic forms of persecution (in essence, that it be life-threatening) while other jurisdictions describe only one standard to assess all forms of persecution. Despite this apparent divergence in approach, a review of recently decided claims reveals in nearly all cases results consistent with the more exacting test. This part concludes that imposition of such a demanding standard is not justified under the Convention.

2.1 The analytical framework: two approaches

Economic forms of persecution are recognized by statute in Australia and by case law in Canada, New Zealand, the United Kingdom and the United States. As compared to other forms of persecution, economic harm must meet a higher test in Australia, and in some US federal courts of appeal and the US Board of Immigration Appeals. In Canada, New Zealand, the UK and other US federal courts of appeal, economic harm is assessed against a standard the same as or similar to the general test for persecution. As a partial explanation for the lack of consistency in the US on this question, it should be noted that in comparison to the other countries under discussion, US asylum adjudication is highly decentralized.[22]

[22] Two structural features of the US asylum adjudication system tend to discourage consistency. First, in addition to decisions taken by the Department of Homeland Security's Asylum Offices, which are not published, there are thirteen authoritative sources of precedent. Asylum decisions may be published by the Board of Immigration Appeals (BIA), an administrative appellate body within the Department of Justice having nationwide jurisdiction, and also by each of the twelve geographically based federal courts of appeal. Although the federal courts of appeal are superior to the BIA and can overrule its decisions, many BIA decisions are not appealed and so stand on their own. The federal courts themselves are co-equal and are not bound by each other's precedent. Circuits can and do adopt different analytical approaches as they see fit; J. Ramji-Nogales et al., "Refugee Roulette: Disparities in Asylum Adjudication," 60 *Stanford L. Rev.* 2 (Nov. 2007), 295–412 at 361–71 documents varying outcomes in similar asylum cases in different federal courts of appeal. Second, when a federal court of appeal adopts a legal interpretation contrary to the BIA's, the BIA is obliged to follow the federal court's reasoning only in cases arising under that court's jurisdiction. Differences of approach among the circuits and between one or more circuits and the BIA can be resolved only by the Supreme Court, which rarely hears cases involving interpretation of the refugee definition.

2.1.1 A higher standard for economic persecution: Australia and the US (some courts)

Australia's Migration Act 1958 provides a non-exhaustive list of six examples of serious harm, one of the elements required to establish persecution.[23] The examples are:

(a) a threat to the person's life or liberty;
(b) significant physical harassment of the person;
(c) significant physical ill-treatment of the person;
(d) significant economic hardship *that threatens the person's capacity to subsist;*
(e) denial of access to basic services, *where the denial threatens the person's capacity to subsist;*
(f) denial of capacity to earn a livelihood of any kind, *where the denial threatens the person's capacity to subsist* (emphasis added).[24]

Three of the examples of serious harm are economic in nature, and each one requires that the economic harm threaten the person's capacity to subsist. This requirement is comparable to the first example of serious harm listed, which is "a threat to the person's life or liberty."[25] In contrast, the other two serious harms listed, physical harassment or ill-treatment, need only be "significant."[26]

Although the additional requirement places a "significant constraint" on finding that economic harm constitutes persecution,[27] recent Australian cases have emphasized that it does not require a showing of complete inability to subsist;[28] and that it may be met by cumulative economic harms such as discrimination in education and employment.[29]

In the US, the federal courts are fairly evenly divided between a more restrictive standard and a standard more consistent with other

[23] Section 91R(1) of the Migration Act 1958 provides that persecution involves (a) serious harm and (b) systematic and discriminatory conduct.

[24] Migration Act 1958, sec. 91R(2).

[25] Migration Act 1958, sec. 91R(2)(a).

[26] Migration Act 1958, sec. 91R(2)(b) and (c).

[27] *MZWPD* v. *Minister for Immigration and Multicultural and Indigenous Affairs* [2006] FCA 1095 (18 Aug. 2006), para. 82.

[28] *M93 of 2004* v. *Minister for Immigration & Another* [2007] FMCA 252 (Feb. 24, 2006), para. 42.

[29] *MZWPD* v. *Minister for Immigration and Multicultural and Indigenous Affairs*, para. 84; *See also Reference 0802865* [2008] RRTA 307 (Aug. 20, 2008) (finding severe restrictions on Palestinian applicant's movements to cause significant economic hardship that threatens his capacity to subsist).

tests for persecution. The more restrictive test, used by a minority of courts, is usually phrased as "economic deprivations or restrictions so severe that they constitute a threat to an individual's life or freedom."[30] In contrast, the majority of courts use the "substantial economic disadvantage" test,[31] seen as more in keeping with the general test for persecution.[32]

Until very recently, the Board of Immigration Appeals' (BIA) approach to economic persecution was unclear as a result of its use over time, with little explanation, of at least four different standards.[33] In response to a remand from the Court of Appeals for the Second Circuit seeking clarification of its standard,[34] the BIA in 2007 adopted a new two-prong test of "severe economic disadvantage or deprivation of liberty, food, housing, employment or other essentials of life."[35] The BIA's new test is intended to raise the bar for economic persecution claims. The first prong of the test rejects the "substantial" economic disadvantage standard in favor of one requiring "severe" economic disadvantage.[36] Although the test itself does not explicitly

[30] *Matter of Acosta*, 19 I&N Dec. 211 (BIA 1985). This or a very similar test has been adopted in at least four circuits and has been followed as recently as 2007. See *Hen* v. *Attorney General*, 230 Fed.Appx. 131 (3rd Cir. 2007 unpublished); *Li* v. *Gonzales*, 405 F.3d 171 (4th Cir. 2005); *Ahmed* v. *Ashcroft*, 396 F.3d 1011 (8th Cir. 2005); *Zehatye* v. *Gonzales*, 453 F.3d 1182 (9th Cir. 2006). The BIA itself did not cite *Matter of Acosta* in an economic persecution case again until 2007.

[31] *Kovac* v. *INS*, 407 F.2d 102 (9th Cir. 1969). This or a very similar test has been adopted in at least six circuits and has been followed as recently as 2007. See *Guan Shan Liao* v. *USDOJ*, 293 F.3d 61 (2nd Cir. 2002); *Yong Hao Chen* v. *USINS*, 195 F.3d 198 (4th Cir. 1999); *Jaars* v. *Gonzales*, 148 Fed.Appx. 310 (6th Cir. 2005 unpublished); *Koval* v. *Gonzales*, 418 F. 3d 798 (7th Cir. 2005); *Gormley* v. *Ashcroft*, 364 F.3d 1141 (9th Cir. 2004); *Satriawan* v. *Gonzales*, 227 Fed.Appx. 757 (10th Cir. 2007 unpublished). The BIA used this standard as recently as *Matter of H-M-*, 20 I&N Dec. 683 (BIA 1993).

[32] The Convention definition appears in sec. 101(a)(42) of the 1952 Immigration and Nationality Act. Persecution has been defined in various terms in the case law, including as "the infliction of suffering or harm upon those who differ (in race, religion or political opinion) in a way regarded as offensive," see *Ghaly* v. *INS*, 58 F.3d 1425, 1431 (9th Cir. 1995); and as "punishment for political, religious, or other reasons that our country does not recognize as legitimate," see *Osaghae* v. *INS*, 942 F.2d 1160, 1163 (7th Cir. 1991), both quoted in D. Martin et al., *Forced Migration Law*, p. 97.

[33] *Mirzoyan* v. *Gonzales*, pp. 221–2. See also Falkler, "Comment."

[34] *Ibid.*

[35] *In re T-Z.* The decision was written by Board Member Filppu, with Board Member Cole dissenting. The test is not actually new, but until now was rarely cited by the BIA since its first appearance in *Matter of Laipenieks*, 18 I&N Dec. 433 (BIA 1983), *rev'd on other grounds*, 750 F.2d 1427 (9th Cir. 1985), which in turn adopted it from a 1978 Report to the US House of Representatives.

[36] *In re T-Z-*, p. 173.

refer to life-threatening harm, the previously accepted language of the restrictive approach, the BIA stated that the second prong of the test regarding deprivation of basic necessities should be equated with the threat to life standard.[37]

Whether the BIA's reasoning in tightening the persecution standard will be sufficiently clear and persuasive to guide the appellate courts and command their deference is yet to be determined.[38] At least one court is on record specifically rejecting the life-threatening standard as imposing an impermissibly high test for economic persecution,[39] and several of the judicial decisions that have cited the BIA's new standard reveal some confusion in applying the test,[40] or disagreement as to whether it is even a new standard at all.[41] Nevertheless, it is notable that not one of the eight recent employment–related claims reviewed under the new *T-Z*-standard was found to rise to the level of persecution. The availability of other means of earning a livelihood precluded a finding of persecution in all but two of the cases, which were denied on the basis of credibility and/or lack of evidence.

[37] *In re T-Z-*, p. 171.

[38] Falkler, "Comment," argues that the BIA's interpretation should not be given the deference normally due an agency's construction of a statute precisely because of its former inconsistency. There is also a larger debate regarding judicial deference to agency decisions, *See National Cable & Telecommunications Assn* v. *Brand X Internet Services*, 547 U.S. 967 (2005).

[39] *Koval* v. *Gonzales* 805.

[40] In *Makatengkeng* v. *Gonzales*, 495 F.3d 876, 887 (8th Cir. 2007), the concurring opinion seems to treat the *T-Z-* standard as a unitary test and states that it appears to be less harsh than the threat to life or freedom standard. In contrast, the court in *Ji* v. *Mukasey*, 2008 WL 344778 (2nd Cir. 2008) (unpublished) also appears to collapse the two prongs of the *T-Z-* standard into one but equates it with the threat to life or freedom standard. In *Vicente-Elias* v. *Mukasey*, 532 F.3d 1086, 1090 (10th Cir. 2008), the court rejected the applicant's argument that the standard used by the immigration judge (loss of all means of earning a living) was unduly strict, saying that it supplemented rather than superseded the threat to life or freedom standard. In *Vafaev* v. *Mukasey*, 2008 U.S. App LEXIS 23358, 3–4 (2nd Cir. Oct 28, 2008) the court cites an old BIA case (*Matter of Salama* 11 I&N Dec. 536 (BIA 1996) to say that "discrimination can, in extraordinary cases, be so severe and pervasive as to constitute persecution," but then later cites the *T-Z-* standard requiring a showing of "deliberate imposition of substantial economic disadvantage."

[41] *Yuan Qing Wang* v. *Mukasey*, 2008 WL 217844 (2nd Cir. 2008) (unpublished) stated that *T-Z-* did not change the Board's policy, but merely clarified the standard. *Accord*, *Beck* v. *Mukasey*, 527 F.3d 737, 740 (8th Cir. 2008). But see *Jiang* v. *Mukasey*, 2008 U.S. App. LEXIS 9857 (2nd Cir. May 6, 2008) (unpublished) ("We do not reach the question here of whether the BIA used a standard comparable or fundamentally identical to the one it later articulated in *In re T-Z-* for evaluating economic persecution, or otherwise comment on the BIA's interpretation of economic persecution under applicable statutes").

2.1.2 A consistent standard for all forms of persecution: Canada, New Zealand, the UK, and the US (some courts)

At least formally, all types of persecution are assessed against the same standard in Canada, New Zealand, the UK, and some US courts. In Canada, the Immigration and Refugee Board (IRB) has summarized the case law on persecution[42] as requiring serious harm, to be determined by examining what interest might be harmed, and to what extent the subsistence, enjoyment, expression or exercise of that interest might be compromised; it quotes with approval James Hathaway's formulation of persecution as the sustained or systemic violation of basic human rights demonstrative of a failure of state protection.[43] The IRB's summary of Canadian cases does not identify a specific test for economic forms of persecution, but simply includes a number of economic claims in its compilation of judicial observations on forms of persecution.[44]

[42] The Convention definition is found in sec. 96 of the Immigration and Refugee Protection Act (IRPA) of 2002.

[43] Legal Services, Immigration and Refugee Board of Canada, *Interpretation of the Convention Refugee Definition in the Case Law*, 3–1 to 3–5 (31 Dec. 2005). Available at www.irb-cisr.gc.ca/en/references/legal/rpd/crdef/crdef03_e.pdf (last visited Feb. 4, 2009).

[44] The IRB compilation includes (internal footnotes omitted; subheadings added for ease of reference):

Employment

Where the state interferes substantially with the claimant's ability to find work, the possibility of the claimant's finding illegal employment is not an acceptable remedy.

Permanently depriving an educated professional of his or her accustomed occupation and limiting the person to farm and factory work constituted persecution.

Education

Education is a basic human right, and a nine-year-old claimant who could have avoided persecution only by refusing to go to school was deemed a Convention refugee.

It is not an act of persecution to ban certain groups of children from attending public schools, if they are permitted to have their own schools.

Punitive fines

Economic penalties may be an acceptable means of enforcing a state policy, where the claimant is not deprived of his or her right to earn a livelihood.

Extortion may be one of the indicia of persecution, depending on the reason for the extortion and the motivation of the claimant in paying.

By itself, confiscation of property is not sufficiently grave to constitute persecution.

General / cumulative

Serious economic deprivations may be components of persecution.

A child who would experience hardships including deprivation of medical care, education opportunities, employment opportunities and food would suffer concerted and severe discrimination, amounting to persecution.

Ibid., 3–10 to 3–15.

In New Zealand, the Refugee Status Appeals Authority (RSAA) has similarly adopted Hathaway's definition of persecution.[45] It is "well-established" that a refugee claim may be founded on a violation of a right contained in the International Covenant on Economic, Social and Cultural Rights, and that like other rights violations, the breach must go to the core of the right and must occasion serious harm. In contrast, a breach at the margins of a right or one that does not bring about serious harm, will not reach the threshold of persecution.[46]

In the United Kingdom, persecution is defined by reference to the European Union Qualification Directive,[47] which provides that acts of persecution must:

(a) be sufficiently serious by their nature or repetition as to constitute a severe violation of basic human rights, in particular the rights from which derogation cannot be made under Article 15(2) of the European Convention for the Protection of Human Rights and Fundamental Freedoms; or
(b) be an accumulation of various measures, including violations of human rights which is sufficiently severe as to affect an individual in a similar manner as mentioned in (a).[48]

No specific test for economic forms of persecution is provided; the non-exhaustive list of examples in the Qualification Directive does not include economic forms of persecution.

In the US, as noted above, the most widely accepted test for economic harm is substantial economic disadvantage.

[45] The Convention definition is referenced in sec. 129D of the Immigration Act of 1987.

[46] *Refugee Appeal No. 76015*, RSAA (14 Nov. 2007), para. 37; *Refugee Appeal No. 76112* RSAA (28 Feb. 2008), para. 91–92.

[47] Council Directive 2004/83/EC of 29 April 2004 on Minimum Standards for the Qualification and Status of Third Country Nationals or Stateless Persons as Refugees or as Persons who Otherwise Need International Protection and the Content of the Protection Granted. OJ L. 304, 30/09/2004, P. 0012 – 0023. Available at http://eur-lex.europa.eu/LexUriServ/LexUriServ.do?uri=CELEX:32004L0083:EN:HTML (last visited 4 Feb. 2009). The Qualification Directive has been implemented in the UK by the Refugee or Person in Need of International Protection (Qualification) Regulations 2006, SI 2006/2525 and the Statement of Changes in Immigration Rules, Cm 6918. See *GG (political oppositionists) Ivory Coast CG* v. *SSHD* [2007], UKAIT 00086 (14 June 2007), paras. 73–9.

[48] EU Qualification Directive, Art. 9(1).

2.2 The standard(s) as applied: recent case law on economic persecution

This section surveys the latest (January 2006–January 2009) case law on economic persecution in the five countries in order to have a common, current appreciation of some of the claims presented to judges and how they are resolved.[49] Recent claims based on economic forms of persecution included interference with employment and/or education, and the imposition of punitive fines.

It can be difficult to formulate a precise statement of the law on economic persecution.[50] Such claims are often cumulative in nature, and frequently are combined with additional non-economic harms such as detention, physical violence, or harassment; judges do not always disaggregate their analysis of the various elements. Nevertheless, it appears that in practice, most of these recent cases were tested against a more rigorous standard.

2.2.1 Employment

Recent claims based on denial of employment/right to work across the five jurisdictions appear to require the complete unavailability of other means of support in order to find persecution, suggesting that the de facto standard for economic persecution may still be the total economic proscription test described by Atle Grahl-Madsen in 1966.[51] All of the following claims were based at least in part on denial of or interference with employment for Convention reasons. All were rejected, at least in part because other means of support were available:

A Colombian who had to abandon his business due to threats from FARC, but who had an alternative occupation or business reasonably open to him that would eliminate the risk of harm (case decided in Canada);[52]

[49] In light of Foster's comprehensive survey of economic claims which covered developments as of the end of 2005 in the same five countries, *International Refugee Law*, p. xi, this chapter focuses on cases decided in Jan. 2006 and thereafter. The law under review in this chapter is current as of January 2009.

[50] Foster, *International Refugee Law*, p. 105.

[51] Economic proscription so severe as to deprive a person of all means of earning a livelihood constitutes persecution, cited in Foster, *International Refugee Law*, pp. 90–1.

[52] *Sanchez* v. *Canada (Minister of Citizenship and Immigration)*, 2007 FCA 99 (8 Mar. 2007) affirmed the IRB's denial on both Convention and complementary protection grounds. The question certified was whether a person is obliged to make lifestyle or other employment changes which would offer protection from persecution, and if so, what the test

An Indonesian man who was unable to find employment but who was able to start his own business and support his family (US case under threat to life standard);[53]

An Indonesian man who lost his business due to extortion but who was able to find work elsewhere (US case under substantial economic disadvantage standard);[54]

A single Iranian woman who had the possibility of support from her family (UK case); [55]

A Chinese man who was demoted, then fired, and was unable to find new employment but who received severance pay and a pension, and whose wife was able to support the family (US case under threat to life standard);[56]

An Iranian Baha'i couple who faced difficulties in practicing their profession, but were able to do so, with an additional finding that "substantial discrimination" against Baha'is in Iran extending to education, work and ownership of property did not amount to persecution (UK case);[57]

A Czech Roma who had little prospect of obtaining permanent employment but who could likely maintain his livelihood by casual work (New Zealand case);[58]

A Chinese Uighur whose employment opportunities would be limited, but not foreclosed (Australian case);[59]

An Uzbekistani man who suffered discrimination at work and lost his job did not suffer persecution where he was unemployed for eleven months, but able to live off his savings (US case under substantial economic disadvantage standard);[60]

An ethnic Hungarian woman who was denied a promotion in favor of a co-worker who was male and ethnically Romanian (US case under threat to life standard);[61]

should be for making such a determination? Analogizing to internal flight alternative analysis which requires a claimant to avail himself of a safe haven in his own country, the Court of Appeal found that the claimant had a reasonable alternative that would eliminate the risk of future harm, namely, complying with FARC's demands to cease his secondary employment. The Court of Appeal found that denial of the side-business interest would not affect a fundamental principle of human rights. In answering the certified question, the court held that persons claiming to be in need of protection solely because of the nature of their occupation or business generally will not be found to be in need of protection unless there is no alternative occupation or business reasonably open to them that would eliminate the risk of harm. See also *Liberato Gonzalez* v. *Canada (Minister of Citizenship and Immigration), 2008 FC 983*. A similar result is found in *Refugee Appeal No. 76230*, RSAA (6 Aug. 2008).

53 *Makatengkeng* v. *Gonzales.* 54 *Satriawan* v. *Gonzales.*

55 *SR (Iran)* v. *SSHD* [2007] EWCA Civ 460 (17 May 2007).

56 *Ji* v. *Mukasey.*

57 *SH (Baha'is) Iran CG* v. *SSHD* [2006] UKAIT 00041 (27 April 2006).

58 *Refugee Appeal No. 76043*, RSAA (7 Dec. 2007).

59 *Reference V05/18276* [2006], RRTA (12 May 2006).

60 *Vafaev* v. *Mukasey.*

61 *Ghilduta* v. *Mukasey*, 263 Fed. Appx. 111, 112 (2nd Cir. 2008) (unpublished).

A Nigerian health care professional unable to obtain work in a government hospital because he lacked powerful tribal and political connections but was nevertheless able to secure a good education and steady work (Australian case);[62] and

A Pakistani Ahmadi financial professional who experienced unfavorable treatment and was passed over for promotion in his government post (Australian case).[63]

Three other recent employment-related claims were rejected without discussion of possible alternative means of support. A single Nigerian woman without family support who feared, among other harms, being forced to provide sexual favors in order to obtain employment was found to be at risk only of discrimination, not persecution.[64] An Eritrean woman whose father's business was confiscated and trade license revoked was not able to show that these harms constituted persecution under the strict US life-threatening standard.[65]

In only one recent US claim did a court find there "might be" persecution under the more generous US substantial economic disadvantage test, in the case of an Indonesian man whose shop was burned in ethnic rioting.[66] In an Australian claim, a Federal Magistrate required the Refugee Review Tribunal (RRT) to reconsider the denial of protection to an Indo-Fijian couple who had been forced off their leased land in Fiji. The Federal Magistrate found that even though the couple had relocated and changed employment, the permanent deprivation of land as a means of earning a livelihood might be considered persecution.[67]

The consistency of approach (are other means of support available?) and outcome (no persecution) in these recent employment cases suggests that surface differences in the persecution standard may be eclipsed by de facto acceptance of the higher

[62] *Reference N0801104* [2008] RRTA 200 (16 April 2008).

[63] *Reference N0800834* [2008] RRTA 165 (12 May 2008). The case was remitted, on other grounds, for reconsideration with the direction that the applicant was a person to whom Australia had protection obligations.

[64] *AI (Nigeria)* v. *SSHD* [2007] EWCA Civ 707 (21 June 2007).

[65] *Zehatye* v. *Gonzales*; *See also Weijun Kong* v. *Mukasey*, 273 Fed. Appx. 46 (2nd Cir. 2008) (unpublished).

[66] *Satriawan* v. *Gonzales*. The claim was rejected, however, because he was not able to show that the government was unable or unwilling to control the rioters, thus failing to establish a nexus to a Convention ground.

[67] *S2012/2003* v. *Minister for Immigration and Another* [2008] FMCA 954 (July 31, 2008), para. 23.

standard.[68] Perhaps as a result of the high standard applied, recent employment claims were recognized or remitted only where there was cumulative economic persecution.[69]

2.2.2 Education

Three claims recently decided in Australia gave favorable treatment to education-related persecution. Two cases concerned denial of primary education to a minor child, while the third case involved interference with, not denial of, education at the tertiary level. In the first case, which involved a young girl from Thailand, a Federal Magistrate made a specific finding that denial of education to a minor child is serious harm that threatens the child's capacity to subsist.[70] Interestingly, the Federal Magistrate found that denial of education also falls under the (non-economic) serious harm example of significant physical ill-treatment, in that it constitutes a deprivation of the child's physical and mental development, although the reasoning for this finding was not explained.[71]

The other two Australian cases were based on cumulative economic harm, but nevertheless provide additional support for education claims. In one case, the RRT found serious harm resulting from cumulative economic harms to a Russian single mother and her child, including denial of access to employment, denial of education to the minor child, and denial of health care and other social services.[72] The Federal Court remitted a claim from a Latvian man that included interference with tertiary education, emphasizing that determinations of serious harm must take into account the cumulative nature of discrimination in education and employment, as well as the ongoing impact of prior interference with education on current and future employment possibilities.[73]

68 Foster also documents the imposition of a standard for economic persecution significantly higher than that generally required in refugee adjudication, see n. 5 above, 123–32.

69 *Refugee Appeal Nos. 75829, 75830, 75831, 75832 & 75833*, RSAA (7 Mar. 2007); *Refugee Appeal Nos. 75948, 75949, 75950 & 75951*, RSAA (12 March 2007); *Reference N0653159* [2006], RRTA (19 May 2006); *MZWPD* v. *Minister for Immigration and Multicultural and Indigenous Affairs* (remitted). See also Foster, *International Refugee Law*, pp. 132–6 on the "automatic requirement" of accumulation.

70 *M93 of 2004*, paras.41–5. 71 Ibid., para. 42.

72 *Reference N0653159* [2006], RRTA (19 May 2006).

73 *MZWPD* v. *Minister for Immigration and Multicultural and Indigenous Affairs*, para. 62.

2.2.3 Punitive fines

Several recent cases have considered economic persecution in the form of punitive fines, reaching contrary results. In the US, imposition of a financial penalty equivalent to ten years' income for violation of China's family planning policies was found to be "severe" and therefore persecutory, even under the BIA's new heightened standard.[74] A recent Australian decision found economic hardship where the Chinese applicant had a child out of wedlock and faced exorbitant fines and a low prospect of gainful employment.[75] In contrast, in New Zealand, imposition of substantial fines beyond the appellant's ability to pay, along with a prison sentence, for violation of China's Marriage Act was not so "draconian" as to amount to persecution.[76] Ability to pay the fines appears to undermine a finding of economic persecution.[77]

Recent case law indicates that the standard for economic persecution commonly employed is a rigorous one, requiring severity rising to the level of a threat to life or the capacity to subsist. Such an approach is contrary to the well-established proposition that persecution is a more expansive concept than threats to life or freedom.[78] Even where a higher standard is sanctioned in domestic law, the Convention does not provide a legal basis for differentiating among various forms of harm. The choice of a more demanding standard for economic harm may reflect policy considerations or an outdated

[74] *Zhen Yu Chen* v. *Mukasey*, 269 Fed. Appx. 17 (2d Cir. 2008) (remanded for additional fact-finding to determine if the fine was actually imposed). Although this case was remanded, there are many other cases involving punitive fines and the Chinese one-child policy that have been denied following *In re T-Z-*, often for lack of evidence attesting to the hardship caused by the fine or information on the applicant's ability to pay. See generally *Zhu* v. *Bd. of Immigration Appeals*, 2008 U.S. App. LEXIS 23149 (2d Cir. Nov. 5, 2008); *Bin Wu* v. *Mukasey*, 2008 U.S. App. LEXIS 22552 (2d Cir. Oct. 21, 2008); *Xiao Fei Dong* v. *Mukasey*, 2009 U.S. App. LEXIS 1118, 3–4 (2d Cir. Jan. 22, 2009); *Jian Hui Shao* v. *Mukasey*, 546 F.3d 138, 161 (2d Cir. 2008).

[75] *Reference 071945034* [2008] RRTA (28 March 2008).

[76] *Refugee Appeal No. 75973* [2007] RSAA (9 Mar. 2007); the claim was recognized on cumulative grounds, however.

[77] *Hanquan Liang An Li Ou* v. *Minister of Citizenship and Immigration*, 2008 FCA 450 (8 April 2008) (holding the IRB's conclusion that there was no economic deprivation reasonable given that the applicants were able to pay the fine and to travel to Canada).

[78] UNHCR, *Handbook on Procedures and Criteria for Determining Refugee Status Under the 1951 Convention and the 1967 Protocol Relating to the Status of Refugees*, UN Doc. HCR/IP/4/Eng/REV.1, (1979, re-edited Jan. 1992), para. 51. See also Foster, *International Refugee Law*, pp. 92–3 and cases cited therein; and Falkler, "Comment."

understanding of human rights law. Both subjects are taken up in Part Three, which surveys the larger debate over the place of economic claims in refugee law.

3 COMPETING PERSPECTIVES ON ECONOMIC CLAIMS

Perspectives on economic claims under the Convention vary, depending on whether interpretation of the definition is thought to be best framed by the overall goal of ensuring support for international protection, or of maintaining consistency with international human rights law.

3.1 The importance of caution

Arguments in favor of a cautious approach to economic claims stress the Convention's limited purpose, the instrumental relationship of refugee law to human rights law, and the political constraints on international protection. These arguments have been advanced most consistently and cogently by David Martin.[79]

3.1.1 The limited purpose of the Refugee Convention

With respect to the purpose of the Refugee Convention, Martin has criticized the dominant US test for assessing economic forms of persecution (the "substantial economic disadvantage" test) as overly lenient, arguing that it is "not really consistent with the underlying purposes of the refugee treaties."[80] Martin hailed the BIA's recent decision to raise the bar for economic persecution claims, discussed above, as a "welcome tightening of the ['substantial economic disadvantage'] standard" and expressed concern that the new test might still go "a bit too far" in the direction of including less than severe cases.[81]

In Martin's view, the purpose of the Refugee Convention is essentially to assign a scarce resource, namely, asylum. He contends that

[79] Martin, "The Refugee Concept," 59–65; and Martin, "Major Developments," 2069. See also: D. Martin and D. Vagts, "Review of *The Law of Refugee Status*," *Am. J. Int'l. L.* 87 (April 1993). 348

[80] Martin, "Major Developments," 2072. [81] *Ibid.*

asylum is not indispensable in responding to need in the realm of economic and social rights because governments in countries of origin usually welcome relief and/or development aid. The refugee definition is engaged only when governments are not receptive to such aid, a resistance which would suggest a political element to the deprivation.[82]

In contrast to Martin's view, most commentators locate the purpose of the Refugee Convention in the Preamble's reference to the Universal Declaration of Human Rights and its concern for the widest possible exercise of fundamental rights and freedoms.[83] In accordance with the generally accepted view, the open-ended notion of persecution is understood as providing for the progressive development of the sorts of harm encompassed by the Convention. Martin's argument that the failure of state protection is a relevant consideration in fact reflects the mainstream of refugee jurisprudence and is taken into account when assessing economic claims.

3.1.2 The instrumental relationship of refugee law to human rights law

Contending that "the institution of asylum is not coterminous with human rights policy," Martin argues that the purpose of the Refugee Convention is not "to express sympathy, to note human rights abuses whenever they appear, or to register disapproval of a practice."[84] In his view, asylum can best serve human rights by being relatively inaccessible. He suggests that asylum states should not be encouraging individuals (via low threshold requirements for refugee status) to escape from societies beset by human rights problems, since such individual solutions undermine communal struggles in the home country.[85]

Martin's arguments regarding asylum and human rights law are not apt. No serious commentator contends that the Convention is intended to cover all human rights violations; it is well established that not all violations of civil and political rights, much less of economic, social and cultural rights, will merit recognition as a refugee.

[82] Martin, "The Refugee Concept," 62.
[83] See, e.g., Goodwin-Gill and McAdam, *The Refugee*, pp. 7–8.
[84] Martin, "Major Developments," 2072.
[85] Martin, "The Refugee Concept," 64.

His suggestion that people suffering from human rights abuses be encouraged by a narrow reading of the refugee definition to stay home and fight for better conditions in their country is unrealistic at best. The widespread tendency to suspect asylum seekers of being economic migrants already distorts consideration of economic claims.[86] Adoption of Martin's mode of thinking would tend to introduce an additional irrelevant factor: the asylum seeker would need to establish not only that he is not opportunistically abusing the asylum system for reasons of personal convenience, but also that he is not selfishly putting his own interests above his country's. Although Martin is careful to say that he is not proposing "heroism" as the standard for recognition as a refugee, surely his logic could equally be extended to even the most high-profile, at-risk opposition leaders. Why grant asylum at all, when we could improve human rights simply by requiring victims to return home and resume their struggle? Nor is Martin's instrumental argument persuasive. Human rights in countries of origin are probably better served by allowing exiles, who have more political freedom and usually greater economic resources in their countries of asylum, to work for change from a safe distance.[87]

3.1.3 Political constraints on protection

Martin's concern regarding any expansion of economic claims is grounded in his conviction that international protection in the form of asylum is a scarce political resource that must be limited to a "relatively modest" number of people.[88] Pointing to the negative public reaction in Western countries when the number of refugee claimants becomes uncomfortably high, he maintains that asylum must be restricted in order to maintain political support. Efforts to expand the scope of protection run the risk of endangering the fragile consensus in favor of those currently protected. He insists on the importance of recognizing that "restrictive pressures seek an outlet" and considers

[86] Foster (*International Refugee Law*, pp. 2–21, 238–47) skillfully deconstructs the impact of this dichotomy.

[87] UNHCR has noted the positive role of refugees vis-à-vis their countries of asylum, not only in sending remittances home, but also in reducing competition for jobs and other scarce resources (by living in the country of asylum) and thereby contributing to the peacebuilding process. *UNHCR Discussion Paper on International Migration*, para. 51.

[88] Martin, "The Refugee Concept," 62.

denial of access to territory much more disturbing than tightening the substantive requirements of the definition.[89] He warns that we must learn how to "shape our legal doctrine to sustain the political conditions" needed to keep asylum vital.[90]

Martin's point regarding the political constraints on protection is well taken, particularly in cases where the country of asylum faces socio-economic rights challenges of its own. His concern to preserve asylum is shared widely, not least by UNHCR, which nevertheless does not advocate restricting the reach of the refugee definition but rather focuses on promoting the development of other tools to advance human rights, help states host refugees, manage migration, and address negative perceptions of asylum seekers. Although anxiety over opening the floodgates is often an implicit and sometimes an explicit concern in status determination, it is not a legal argument and should not influence interpretation of the definition.

Interpreting the Convention in light of desired policy outcomes could politicize and discredit the refugee regime, which carries its own risk of loss of public support. In addition, a deliberate practice of restricting the development of refugee law for strategic reasons poses the danger of making refugee status such a scarce resource that it becomes irrelevant both to states and to persons in need of protection. The growth of complementary protection regimes is, in part, a response to such restrictive interpretations.[91]

Martin is the first to admit that his is a minority viewpoint on economic claims, at least among scholars.[92] Nevertheless, he articulates the concerns animating many states and his objections deserve further consideration. A different perspective on economic claims takes human rights law as a point of departure.

3.2 The importance of coherence

The importance of coherence between refugee law and human rights law has been recognized by the International Association of

89 *Ibid.* at 60. 90 *Ibid.*

91 McAdam (*Complementary Protection*, p. 15) notes that excluding known groups from protection does not eliminate them, it simply creates new categories of unprotected persons.

92 "I intend, perhaps inadvisedly, to swim against [the tide]." Martin, "The Refugee Concept," 59.

Refugee Law Judges, which recommends that the term persecution be interpreted by reference to accepted international human rights instruments.[93] The case in favor of expanded recognition of economic rights-based claims to refugee status has been developed most fully by Michelle Foster, who similarly locates the principled basis for such an interpretation in international human rights law.[94] Her argument rests on two basic premises: that human rights law is integrally related to refugee law and provides the appropriate frame of reference for determining refugee claims; and that refugee judges must ensure their analysis of human rights standards is consistent with the increasingly sophisticated understanding of those standards elaborated by the relevant authoritative treaty bodies in recent years.

3.2.1 Refugee law in a human rights framework

In many jurisdictions, human rights law provides the framework for moving beyond the agreed understanding that persecution comprehends more than threats to life or freedom. Hathaway's formulation of persecution as the sustained or systemic denial of core or basic human rights demonstrative of a failure of state protection has been accepted in Canada, New Zealand, and in a more restrictive variation, in the EU Qualification Directive.[95] In contrast, Australia and the US define, and often analyze, persecution without specific reference to human rights.[96]

The practical impact of this analytical divide is not clear. Foster cites a study which concluded that the "violation of basic human rights" is the only essential criterion applied in status determination, either expressly or implicitly, in fifteen countries including the US.[97] Certainly, in at least some types of cases, outcomes seem broadly similar across jurisdictional lines. For example, Foster argues that the expanded recognition of gender-related claims is a key example of the importance of using human rights norms to analyze persecution,[98] yet US judges contributed to this development without the benefit of a

[93] J.C.Simeon, "Human Rights Nexus Working Party Rapporteur's Report," in *The Changing Nature of Persecution*, International Association of Refugee Law Judges, 4th Conference, Oct. 2000, Berne, Switzerland, (Institute of Public Law, University of Bern, Switzerland, 2001), 305.

[94] Foster, *International Refugee Law*.

[95] See Part 2.1.2, above.

[96] See Part 2.1.1, above.

[97] Foster, *International Refugee Law*, p. 31, fn.14.

[98] Foster, *International Refugee Law*, p. 16.

strong basis in human rights law.[99] Similarly, sexual orientation claims have been recognized in all five countries discussed in this paper.[100]

Foster argues that using human rights law as an external and "objective" source for interpreting the refugee definition promotes the goal of consistency in decision-making.[101] She criticizes the "subjective" formulations of persecution in the US as leading to inconsistency in US case law.[102] However, as noted above, the decentralized US asylum adjudication system places significant structural obstacles in the way of achieving consistent outcomes.[103] The problem of US inconsistency has at least as much to do with the lack of a single authoritative arbiter as it does with an overly subjective analytical framework.[104] The emergence of similar concerns with respect to varying interpretations of the EU Qualification Directive appears to bear out this analysis.[105]

3.2.2 The limits of human rights law in status determination

It is difficult to dispute that refugee law and human rights law are integrally connected. As a matter of political commitment as well

99 For example, in *Matter of Kasinga*, 21 I&N Dec. 357, 365 (BIA *en banc* 1996), the BIA found that FGM is persecution on the basis of their past definitions of the term. The INS *Considerations for Asylum Officers Adjudicating Asylum Claims from Women* (1995) employs a human rights framework, but is not binding on immigration judges or the BIA. For a review of these guidelines, see L. Scialabba, "The Immigration and Naturalization Service Considerations for Asylum Officers Adjudicating Asylum Claims for Women," *International Journal of Refugee Law*, Special Issue, Autumn 1997, UNHCR Symposium on Gender-Based Persecution, Geneva, 22–23 February 1996, 174–181.

100 See R. Haines, *The Domestic Application of International Human Rights Standards in New Zealand: The Refugee Convention* (Sept. 2004), paras. 43–45, for a comparison of the Australian and New Zealand approaches to this question. Available at www.refugee.org.nz/Reference/spring.html#Identifying_Core_Human_Rights (last visited 4 Feb. 2009).

101 Foster, *International Refugee Law*, p. 38.

102 Foster, *International Refugee Law*, pp. 37–9.

103 See Part 2.1, above. Another critical factor is the insufficiency of resources, which limits possibilities for training and professional development, and imposes unrealistically high case completion requirements.

104 For a proposal to centralize asylum review in order to promote a more uniform national jurisprudence, see *Address by the Honorable Carlos T. Bea, Judge, US Court of Appeals for the Ninth Circuit, to the Board of Immigration Appeals and Immigration Judges* (10 Aug. 2007), available at http://lawprofessors.typepad.com/immigration/files/bea_address_to_bia_and_ij_2007_annual_convention.pdf (last visited 4 Feb. 2009).

105 UNHCR, *Asylum in the European Union: A Study of the Implementation of the Qualification Directive* (Nov. 2007). Available at www.unhcr.org/protect/Protection/47302b6c2.pdf (last visited 4 Feb. 2009).

as legal understanding, it is important that states approach refugee protection in the broadest sense as a human rights issue.[106] However, there are significant limits to the role human rights law can play in status determination, some arising from the imperfect fit between the two bodies of law, which can result in over-inclusiveness or under-inclusiveness, and some inherent in human rights law, whose indeterminate norms and diverse authorities can be difficult to translate into the exacting requirements of interpreting the refugee definition. These limits are particularly problematic for economic claims.

Human rights law is often over-inclusive for refugee purposes, for the obvious reason that not all violations of all human rights rise to the level of persecution. This understanding is reflected in the language of "seriousness" or "severity" used to narrow the persecution inquiry. Refugee judges must delve more deeply than most human rights experts into an understanding of the nature and limits of the right under consideration.[107] Hathaway's hierarchical approach provides a simple matrix to determine when a core human right has been violated,[108] but Foster argues persuasively that his system of categorization no longer reflects the state of human rights law and has impeded proper consideration of economic claims.[109]

Human rights law can also be under-inclusive. If a judge cannot locate specific textual support in human rights law relevant to his or her understanding of the harm at issue, the persecution analysis may be cut short or miss its mark. In this regard, Goodwin-Gill and McAdams note the deleterious impact of the House of Lords' unsuccessful search for a human right of conscientious objection to

[106] Hence the value of Executive Committee Conclusions affirming the link, e.g. *Conclusion on the Provision on International Protection Including Through Complementary Forms of Protection*, No. 103 (2005).

[107] Goodwin-Gill and McAdam, *The Refugee in International Law*, p. 92 describe persecution analysis as "turn[ing] on an assessment of a complex of factors, including (1) the nature of the freedom threatened, (2) the nature and severity of the restriction, and (3) the likelihood of the restriction eventuating in the individual case."

[108] The hierarchy consists of four levels: (1) non-derogable rights found in the ICCPR, violation of which is always persecution; (2) derogable rights in the ICCPR, violation of which is usually persecution unless requirements for derogation were met; (3) rights in the ICESCR, violation of which is not usually persecution unless based on discrimination or failure to take steps toward progressive realization despite adequate resources; and (4) rights in the Universal Declaration but not in either Covenant, violation of which is not persecution. J. Hathaway, *The Law of Refugee Status* (Butterworths, 1991), 108–12.

[109] Foster, *International Refugee Law*, pp. 113–52, 168–81, 190–2.

military service in *Sepet and Bulbul*, when the right actually at risk was the right to freedom of conscience.[110]

Human rights law is often not sufficiently detailed to help judges engaged in refugee status determination. Pirjola observes that:

> [l]inking persecution with rights guaranteed in human rights conventions does not, as such, clarify the concept, however. The articles of human rights conventions to which Hathaway turns to define persecution have been written in abstract language and, in practice, their content often remains vague or undefined.[111]

This has posed a particular challenge for judges analyzing economic claims, since the International Covenant on Economic, Social and Cultural Rights (ICESCR) has a higher quotient of abstract and undefined terms than the International Covenant on Civil and Political Rights, most notably the notion of progressive realization. Proper consideration of economic claims can require assessment of concepts such as taking steps, maximum available resources, and minimum core obligations. Refugee judges may feel they lack the political authority or institutional expertise to inquire into policies governing resource allocation in a country of origin.

A final limitation, related to indeterminacy of norms, is the diversification and fragmentation of human rights law. Human rights law is an expansive and evolving field, based on a large and growing number of international and regional treaties, as well as customary international law.[112] Beyond these binding obligations are a multitude of norms of varying weight and legitimacy, and a variety of interpretive authorities and actors. The content of a norm may

110 Goodwin-Gill and McAdams, *The Refugee in International Law*, p. 114.

111 J. Pirjola, "Shadows in Paradise – Exploring Non-refoulement as an Open Concept," *International Journal of Refugee Law* 19(4) (2007), 639–600. McAdam (*Complementary Protection*, pp. 179–80) makes a related point regarding the indeterminacy of the best interests of the child principle in the Convention on the Rights of the Child.

112 There are seven human rights treaties with reporting requirements and expert committees currently in force at the international level. Two new treaties, one with a non-refoulement provision, are not yet in force but will have reporting requirements supervised by expert committees: the Convention on the Rights of Persons with Disabilities (adopted 13 Dec. 2006) and the International Convention for the Protection of All Persons from Enforced Disappearance (adopted 20 Dec. 2006), art. 16 of which provides that: "No State Party shall expel, return ('refouler'), surrender or extradite a person to another State where there are substantial grounds for believing that he or she would be in danger of being subjected to enforced disappearance."

not be fully defined, the relationship of one norm or authority to another is not always readily apparent, and human rights law as a whole lacks a coherent structure. Regional treaties can contribute to different understandings of the same right in different systems, with the European Court of Human Rights, in particular, developing jurisprudence far beyond that at the international level.

With the emergence of economic, social and cultural rights from a position of relative marginalization and neglect, the Committee on Economic, Social and Cultural Rights (ESC Committee), related United Nations mandates,[113] national courts,[114] scholars,[115] and advocates[116] are elaborating a rich, complex and diverse set of interpretations and opinions on the content and meaning of the rights involved. Foster rightly stresses the importance of judges ensuring that any use of human rights law to analyze economic claims reflects these developments. For that reason, she cautions against further use of Hathaway's hierarchical model and proposes instead that judges adopt the core obligations approach developed by the ESC Committee.[117]

113 The UN Human Rights Council has appointed special rapporteurs or independent experts on adequate housing, the effects of economic reform policies, education, food, health, extreme poverty, and access to safe drinking water.

114 A growing body of literature on justiciability issues focuses, in particular, on the influential South African jurisprudence. See e.g., E. Christiansen, "Adjudicating Non-Justiciable Rights: Socio-Economic Rights and the South African Constitutional Court," *Columbia Human Rights L. Rev.* 38(2) (2007), 321–86; A. Pillay, "Courts, Variable Standards of Review and Resource Allocation: Developing a Model for the Enforcement of Social and Economic Rights," *European Human Rights L.Rev.* 6 (2007), 616–36; B. Ramcharan (ed.), *Judicial Protection of Economic, Social and Ccultural Rights: Cases and Materials* (M. Nijhoff Publishers, 2005); Y. Ghai and J. Cottrell (eds.), *Economic, Social and Cultural Rights in Practice: The Role of Judges in Implementing Economic, Social and Cultural Rights* (Interights, 2004); D. Brand and S. Russell (eds.), *Exploring the Core Content of Socio-economic Rights: South African and International Perspectives* (Protea Book House, 2002).

115 Recently published works include S. Leckie and A. Gallagher (eds.), *Economic, Social, and Cultural Rights: A Legal Resource Guide* (University of Pennsylvania Press, 2006); M. Sepúlveda, *The nature of the obligations under the International Covenant on Economic, Social and Cultural Rights* (Intersentia, 2003); A. Chapman and S. Russell (eds.), *Core Obligations: Building a Framework for Economic, Social and Cultural Rights* (Intersentia, 2002); I. Merali and V. Oosterveld (eds.), *Giving Meaning to Economic, Social and Cultural Rights* (University of Pennsylvania Press, 2001).

116 See, e.g., Amnesty International, *Human Rights for Human Dignity: A Primer on Economic, Social and Cultural Rights* (2005), available at: www.amnesty.org/en/library/info/POL34/009/2005. (last visited 1 March 2009).

117 Foster, *International Refugee Law*, pp. 194–253.

3.2.3 The core obligations approach to analyzing economic claims

In analyzing the nature of state obligations under the Covenant, the ESC Committee has concluded that "a minimum core obligation to ensure the satisfaction of, at the very least, minimum essential levels of each of the rights is incumbent upon every State party."[118] The Committee is in the process of defining more fully the content of the minimum core obligation for each right.[119] The minimum core obligation is an immediate obligation, along with the duty not to discriminate and the duty to take steps toward progressive realization of the Covenant.

The main thrust of Foster's argument is that a violation of the core obligation of a right, in human rights terms, should be understood as persecution in refugee terms.[120] She contends that analyzing persecution in terms of violation of a core obligation would promote consistent decision-making by providing a common framework of understanding. It also has the advantage of bringing this aspect of refugee law into closer alignment with the accepted approach in human rights law, providing judges with a doctrinal basis for expanded recognition of economic claims. The following observations neither do justice to her thorough and thoughtful analysis, nor offer a fully developed critique of it.[121] They are intended rather to highlight areas that merit further consideration and discussion.

First, because refugee judges must assess whether there has been a violation of a core obligation of the right in order to find persecution, there is a risk of circularity. Foster alludes to this when she says that the core/periphery approach "provides a useful tool for conceptualizing what it is that refugee judges are attempting to do when they undertake the persecution assessment. Indeed, analysis of the case law reveals that this is what decision-makers are effectively doing."[122] She cites employment cases as an example, where judges

[118] CESCR, General Comment No. 3: The nature of States parties obligations (1990), para. 10.

[119] The ESC Committee's General Comments on specific rights are: No. 7 on adequate housing (1997); No. 12 on food (1999); No. 13 on education (1999); No. 14 on health (2000); No. 15 on water (2002); No. 16 on equal rights of men and women (2005); No. 18 on work (2005); and No. 19 on social security (2008).

[120] Foster, *International Refugee Law*, pp. 197–8.

[121] Foster (*International Refugee Law*, pp. 75–86) discusses some possible objections to a human rights approach.

[122] Foster, *International Refugee Law*, p.198.

will find persecution if there is complete denial of the right to work, which she characterizes as a violation of the core of the right, but not if there is simply minor discrimination in the workplace, which she characterizes as a peripheral violation.[123]

Second, the extent to which the core obligations approach would actually lead to a wider range of economic harms being recognized as persecution remains to be seen. Either possibility could raise concerns, depending on one's view of the desirability of that goal. If the core obligations approach is largely reflective of current practice, its contribution would go more to framing analysis than expanding it. If, however, greater understanding of the content of core obligations of economic rights provides a strong basis for arguing that refugee law has been too dismissive of economic forms of harm, then there is a risk that the approach may be discarded as out of step with states' policy concerns. It is easy to imagine a restrictive interpretation of the core obligation approach that would require, for example, a "severe" violation of the "nucleus" of the core of a "core right." If that were to occur, the goal of ensuring coherence between refugee law and human rights law would be jeopardized.

As a final observation, it is unlikely, at least in the short run, that adoption of the core obligations approach would in fact promote the goal of greater consistency in determining when economic harm amounts to persecution. Notwithstanding the significant interpretive advances made by the ESC Committee and other human rights scholars and judges, considerable work needs to be done to translate their analysis into terms meaningful to refugee scholars and judges. For example, a central precept of ICESCR analysis, that non-discrimination is a core and immediate obligation of states with respect to economic, social and cultural rights,[124] is an over-inclusive norm for refugee purposes and would need further elaboration to provide a consistent benchmark for status determination.[125]

A more specific example of an issue to be clarified may be of interest: Foster refers to violation of the core of the right to work as

[123] Foster, *International Refugee Law*, p. 198.

[124] CESCR, General Comment No. 3: The nature of States parties obligations (1990), para. 1.

[125] Foster (*International Refugee Law*, pp. 142–7) notes the misunderstanding of discrimination in socio-economic rights on the part of some refugee judges.

including denial of the right to work in relation to a specific occupation.[126] Refugee claims made on this basis, for example, that a person with professional training is able to obtain only menial work, are a source of some controversy. Some claims of this nature have been recognized, while others have been rejected.[127] Martin is adamant that this form of economic hardship should not be considered to fall within even a generous reading of the refugee definition.[128] The interpretation Foster suggests does not appear to find support in the ESC Committee's General Comment on the right to work, which raises again the concern of circularity, reasoning backward from the persecution finding to analyze the core of the right.

Use of the core obligations approach in refugee status determination poses significant interpretive challenges that could benefit from greater engagement by judges, scholars, and UNHCR. UNHCR guidelines and position papers on various topics vary greatly in how extensively, if at all, economic factors are addressed and even in how fully human rights law generally is incorporated into the analysis.[129] Consideration of the potential relevance of economic rights to the interpretive issue at hand should be included in future UNHCR guidelines regardless of topic.

4 CONCLUSION

There is an evident need to consider how best to bridge the interpretive gap between human rights law and refugee law in respect of economic claims. The ongoing expansion of economic, social

[126] Foster, *International Refugee Law*, p. 198.

[127] Foster (*International Refugee Law*, pp. 97, 99–101) discusses this case law; see also *Scavenger* v. *Mukasey*, 2008 U.S. App. LEXIS 24360 (6th Cir. 2008).

[128] See, Martin, "The Refugee Concept," 2072–3.

[129] Positive examples of drawing on human rights law to interpret the definition may be found in UNHCR's *Guidelines on International Protection No. 6: Religion-Based Refugee Claims*, HCR/GIP/04/06 (28 April 2004) and in the *Guidelines on International Protection No. 7: The Application of Article 1A(2) to Victims of Trafficking and Persons At Risk of Being Trafficked*, HCR/GIP/06/07 (7 April 2006). In contrast, UNHCR's *Note on Issues Related to Eligibility for International Protection in the Context of Fumigations* (30 July 2007) is less complete in that regard; it refers to the Convention on the Rights of the Child and other international instruments, but neglects, for example, to discuss the right to health under the ICESCR and the ESC Committee's General Comment No. 14 on the right to health (2000).

and cultural rights law provides an opportunity if not an obligation to reconsider the scope of Convention protection. However, given the highly adverse protection climate, where some government policies scarcely seem to distinguish between refugees, unauthorized migrants, and terrorists, the risks of further confusion and backlash are obvious. While there is an enormous appeal to the notion of bringing refugee law more fully into coherence with human rights law, the significant differences between human rights analysis and refugee status determination suggest a large degree of caution.

Invoking the link between human rights and refugee law does not by itself provide sufficient guidance to refugee judges. It is a truism that not all human rights violations are considered persecution under the 1951 Convention. Hathaway's 1991 human rights framework for analyzing persecution appears to be of only limited assistance, notwithstanding its adoption by some courts. Notably, it is rarely if ever followed in either Australia or the United States, two countries that play a key role in refugee jurisprudence. The existing human rights framework appears to be more an explanatory device rather than a jurisprudential tool, and, as interpreted, has not kept pace with developments in human rights law.

The re-orientation and re-alignment of refugee law toward new thinking in human rights law with an aim of promoting coherence between the two does not yet appear to be either necessary or desirable. First, general appeals to human rights law are not likely to solve the particular problems of restrictive interpretations of the refugee definition. Pledging adherence to human rights norms bears limited "costs" for most states: they are either observing such standards already, or they do not intend to do so.[130] In contrast, recognizing claims to refugee status has a high, and immediate, "cost." If human rights law is used more widely as a point of reference in status determination, it will either be largely rhetorical or it will risk promoting fragmentation, as a result of the pressures on asylum. It would be better not to import refugee policy-driven legal precedents into human rights law.

[130] See, e.g., Oona A. Hathaway, "Do Human Rights Treaties Make a Difference?" *Yale Law Journal* 111(8) (2002), 1935.

Second, the external framework provided by human rights law is not likely to result in more consistent asylum decisions within and between jurisdictions. Inconsistency is a serious problem facing international protection but one that is due in large part to structural issues such as lack of resources, and extra-legal factors such as negative public opinion toward immigrants. After all, the 1951 Convention definition already offers a universal standard, yet asylum outcomes vary widely even for similar cases.

If the goal is interpretive harmony, it would be helpful for jurisdictions that use a human rights framework and those who promote the link to take the lead in developing with greater specificity the content of potential human rights law contributions to refugee status determination. One point of departure, for example, could be an examination of the similarities and differences between human rights law and refugee jurisprudence on a well-established civil or political right such as the right to freedom from torture, and on an evolving socio-economic right such as the right to work. Any such examination should also include refugee jurisprudence from countries that do not use a human rights framework, in order to assess the role human rights law actually does play in status determination and to ensure that any proposed use of human rights law tends toward greater harmony and not greater divergence of result.

Jurisdictions that do not generally use a human rights framework and those who question its utility should similarly clarify and justify their interpretation of socio-economic claims. The US BIA's murky decision in *Matter of T-Z* is not a helpful example of analysis even of its own jurisprudence, much less that of the federal appellate courts.

UNHCR's role, as always, is to engage in a creative and protection-oriented dialogue with states, guided by its experience and expertise. Since many refugee receiving states have not adopted a human rights framework even for adjudication of claims based on violations of civil and political rights, it is not necessarily persuasive to insist that they utilize it now for claims based on violations of economic and social rights. The practical value of resort to human rights law in interpreting persecution evidently needs to be developed more fully in order to be adopted more widely. Given the rapidly evolving expansion of socio-economic rights analysis, it does not yet seem advisable to try to crystallize such insights for immediate application by refugee law judges. Nevertheless, there is ample scope for further inquiry and reflection on economic claims under the 1951 Convention and the 1967 Protocol. The questions raised in this chapter may suggest some useful points of departure.

CHAPTER 6

The fragmented nature of the international refugee regime and its consequences: a comparative analysis of the applications of the 1951 convention

Nergis Canefe

I INTRODUCTION

This chapter critically examines the emergence of a global regime of accountability in international law in the area of refugee protection since the end of the Second World War. The 1951 United Nations Convention Relating to the Status of Refugees [1951 Convention hereafter] puts forward the claim of universal jurisprudence that supposedly overrides private norms and domestic legal practices in the area of refugee protection. However, in their application, the Convention and later developments in the area of domestic renditions of refugee jurisprudence systematically fell short of this intent. The chapter posits that the main reason for this failure is that the current international refugee regime was mainly designed to provide a *back-up source* for the protection of seriously at-risk persons. Its primary function, since its Westphalian origins, has been to support the state-centric status quo in international politics. The chapter regards international refugee law and, in particular, the 1951 Convention as an overly guarded safety net used only in the event that a state entirely fails to meet its most basic protective responsibilities towards its citizens and within constraints protecting the needs of the refugee-receiving states first and foremost.[1] This observation is supported by the fact that the 1951 Convention and subsequent refugee

[1] The United Nations Convention Relating to the Status of Refugees is an international convention that defines who is a refugee, and sets out the rights of individuals who are granted asylum and the responsibilities of nations that grant asylum. The Convention also sets out which people do *not* qualify as refugees, such as war criminals. Finally, it provides for visa-free travel arrangements for holders of travel documents issued under the Convention. The

jurisprudence disperses the duty of protection in a piecemeal fashion towards other states and international institutions. Furthermore, the Convention's applications vary immensely even among the states who are party to it.

It is true that the current international refugee regime, built upon the premise of universal jurisprudence, clearly implies that the "international community" is meant to be a forum of resort for the persecuted. The protection afforded to refugees responds to acute rather than to ongoing crises. The protection provided is on a temporary basis in the expectation that they will, eventually, return to their country of origin. In this sense, refugee jurisprudence is predicated upon legalizing a "surrogate" function regarding countries of asylum and the protection they may offer for persons in dire need for safety. Thus, people who face even egregious risks, but who can presumably secure meaningful protection from their own government through internal displacement or in a regional refugee camp, are increasingly deemed as not eligible for Convention refugee status. As a result, the protective shield that is provided by the international refugee regime and sanctified by the 1951 Convention and its addendum has become increasingly dubious. In this context, the chapter also questions the internal limits of the Convention itself in addition to the pitfalls created by the customary methods of its application in the context of domestic law.

II UNIVERSAL APPLICATION OF REFUGEE JURISPRUDENCE: AN ELUSIVE TASK?

Refugee law is a branch of public international law that specifically deals with the rights and protection of people at grave risk in their country of origin or habitual residence. As a body of jurisprudence and customary practices, it is related to but distinct from both international human rights law and international humanitarian law. Standard sources of refugee law are the 1951 Convention itself, modified by the 1967 *Protocol Relating to the Status of Refugees*, the

Convention was approved at a special United Nations conference on July 28, 1951 and it was initially limited to protecting European refugees after the Second World War. However, the 1967 Protocol removed the geographical and time limits and expanded the Convention's scope to implicate universal jurisdiction in principle.

1966 *Bangkok Principles on Status and Treatment of Refugees* adopted at the Asian-African Legal Consultative Committee, the 1969 *Organization of African Union Convention Governing the Specific Aspects of Refugee Problems in Africa*, the 1984 *Cartagena Declaration on Refugees for Latin America*, the 1976 *Council of Europe's Recommendation 773 (1976) on the Situation of de facto Refugees*, and, the 2004 *European Union's Council Directive on Minimum Standards for the Qualification and Status of Third Country Nationals and Stateless Persons as Refugees or as Persons who Otherwise Need International Protection*. In all these legal documents and consequent jurisprudence, the essence of the definition of a refugee has been protected as it has been set out in Art. 1(A)(2) of the 1951 Convention.[2] The Convention thus clearly circumscribes the identification of persons who are entitled to claim protection in a contracting state against the risk of persecution in their own country. Meanwhile, this legally prescribed duty of state parties to provide surrogate protection arises only in relation to persons who are either unable to benefit from the protection of their own state, or who are unwilling to accept that state's protection because of a well-founded fear of persecution. It therefore follows that to the extent that meaningful protection against the risk of persecution is genuinely available to an asylum-seeker, Convention refugee status need not be recognized. In light of this proposition, the majority of the signatories to the 1951 Convention have long required asylum seekers to exhaust all reasonable domestic protection possibilities before asserting their entitlement to refugee status.

Still, until the mid-1980s, we did not face the routine denial of asylum on the grounds that protection against an acknowledged risk could be secured in another part of the applicant's state of origin. And yet, with the arrival of increasing numbers of refugees from countries that were politically, racially, and culturally

[2] Article 1 of the Convention, as amended by the 1967 Protocol, provides the definition of a refugee in the following terms: A person who "owing to well-founded fear of being persecuted for reasons of race, religion, nationality, membership of a particular social group or political opinion, is outside the country of his nationality and is unable or, owing to such fear, is unwilling to avail himself of the protection of that country; or who, not having a nationality and being outside the country of his former habitual residence as a result of such events, is unable or, owing to such fear, is unwilling to return to it."

"different" from asylum-granting countries, the legal and political interpretation of the 1951 Convention took a turn towards a displaced commitment to avoid, when possible, admission of refugees. The so-called "internal flight" doctrine emerged precisely from this context of heightened sensitivity to refugees arriving from the Global South and, in particular, in response to asylum seekers arriving from ex-European colonies to Western metropoles. This is despite the fact that as formulated by the United Nations High Commissioner for Refugees (UNHCR) in its *Handbook on Procedures and Criteria for Determining Refugee Status*,[3] the fear of being persecuted need not always extend to the *whole* territory of the refugee's country of nationality. For instance, in ethnic clashes or in cases of grave disturbances involving civil war conditions, persecution of a specific ethnic or national group may occur in only one part of the country. In such situations, a person at grave risk or danger should not be excluded from refugee status merely because he or she could have sought safety in another part of the same country. Notwithstanding this signpost in refugee jurisprudence in international law, precisely on the basis of this particular directive of internal flight option, Sikh activists clearly at risk in the Punjab have been repeatedly denied refugee status and returned to other regions of India; Tamils to southern Sri Lanka; and Turkish Kurds to Istanbul. This is only but one example of how the 1951 Convention is at times used as a deterrence tool rather than as a means to extend protection for genuine asylum seekers despite the original intent and the legal content of the Convention itself.

It is true that in some cases, there may indeed be true protection options available inside the asylum seeker's country of origin. Since most refugees in today's political climate flee complex internal and regional conflicts, reaching safety and security is often plotted in ways that were not plausible during the height of the Cold War, the historical reference point for the 1951 Convention. Yet, the often radically disparate ways in which the "duty" to seek internal protection has been conceived and implemented by refugee-accepting states suggest that it often ends up being used as the legal foundation for

[3] *Handbook on Procedures and Criteria for Determining Refugee Status* can be found at www.unhcr.org/publ/PUBL/3d58e13b4.pdf (last accessed on September 6, 2009).

limiting access to refugee status. Indeed, comprehensive reviews of the refugee jurisprudence in leading asylum countries, such as the one compiled for the formulation of the *Michigan Guidelines on the Internal Protection Alternative*,[4] clearly indicate that there is a true need for the refinement of currently available frameworks for adjudicating asylum seeker applications in closer consonance with the 1951 Refugee Convention. Similar findings have been endorsed by authoritative international organizations such as the International Association of Refugee Law Judges, as well.[5] In so many areas of refugee law and policy, the viability of a universal commitment to protection is challenged by divergences in state practices as far as the implementation and application of the 1951 Convention is concerned. Neither is this phenomenon limited by the behavior of states in the Global North. In the Global South, the symptoms of idiosyncratic appropriation of the 1951 Convention in particular, and refugee jurisprudence in general, are somewhat different. Nonetheless, the end result is the same and it reveals the weaknesses of the current refugee regime as a global accountability regime if dictated *only* by existing refugee jurisprudence in international law and its variant domestic applications.

In the remainder of this chapter, the limits of the 1951 Convention are discussed with reference to some of the contemporary practices of asylum states both in the Global North and the Global South. In the light of these findings, limitations of the Convention's predication of universal jurisdiction are examined and an alternative model of understanding the international refugee regime is posed in order to formulate remedies for systemic problems in the interpretation and application of the 1951 Convention. For instance, both the risk of persecution and availability of countervailing protection have traditionally been assessed directly in relation to an asylum seeker's place of origin. Contemporary practice in some states of asylum in the Global North did evolve to take account of regionalized variations of risk within countries of origin. However, a detailed risk

[4] The full document could be accessed at www.refugeelawreader.org/files/pdf/230.pdf (last accessed on September 6, 2009).

[5] See Association of Refugee Law Judges documents on the 1951 Convention at http://iarlj.eear.eu/IARLJ/SearchForms/IARLJ_Database_Start.htm (last accessed on September 6, 2009).

assessment is not simply a matter of examining whether an asylum seeker might have avoided departure from her or his country of origin through internal flight. Nor is it to be reduced to the determination of whether the risk of persecution could be avoided somewhere inside the asylum seeker's country of origin via internal relocation. Embodying an alternative approach developed from within the Global South, state parties to the Organization of African Unity's *Convention Governing the Specific Aspects of Refugee Problems in Africa* have obligated themselves to protect not only Convention refugees, but also persons at risk due to "[e]xternal aggression, occupation, foreign domination or events seriously disturbing public order in either part or the whole of [the] country of origin or nationality."[6] This chapter makes a case that this kind of innovative and region-specific response, combined with a backing from international human rights law, is perhaps where we should turn our attention in order to undo the roadblocks against universal jurisdiction in the area of refugee protection, particularly in the case of the Global South where the majority of the world's refugee population is housed or incarcerated. Only through composite readings of the 1951 Convention that can counter the pressure of regional demands and domestic reservations could we expect to enlarge the circle of influence for its purported claim of universal jurisdiction.

III A CRITICAL LOOK AT THE INTERNATIONAL REFUGEE REGIME: THE 1951 CONVENTION AS THE EDICT OF NANTES FOR THE WESTPHALIAN ORDER

International law scholars whose expertise falls in the area of refugees undeniably claim that refugees and asylum seekers are an integral part of the international legal system. Accordingly, the international refugee regime is assumed to have foundationalised the core legal documents such as the 1951 Convention and the 1967 Protocol, and, it is claimed to be sustained and defended by institutions such as

[6] The full text of the Convention can be found at www.africa-union.org/Official_documents/Treaties_%20Conventions_%20Protocols/Refugee_Convention.pdf (last accessed on September 6, 2009).

the United Nations High Commission for Refugees (UNHCR), International Organization for Migration (IOM), as well as several prominent non-governmental organizations.[7] However, this definition of an international refugee regime sorely lacks the critical component of national or domestic jurisprudence, as well as local and regional realities that determine the outcome of the applications of refugee jurisprudence. It gives hardly any consideration to legal, bureaucratic or political actors who put into effect the core documents of international refugee law and who endorse or reject the mandate of international organizations pertaining to the international refugee regime as defined above.

Since the Treaty of Westphalia in 1648, the international refugee regime has evolved along with the modern state system.[8] However, responding to a history of religious and political persecutions, the first signs of a comprehensive refugee regime could be argued to have emerged only after the First World War and under the League of Nations.[9] This regime then underwent dramatic changes during the Second World War and witnessed the creation of a permanent legal and institutional framework. Added to this equation were the UNHCR and the 1951 Convention to cope with the acute post-war "refugee problem." This is the standard narrative pertaining to the history of the international refugee regime as we know it today. Notwithstanding this somewhat cleansed historical account, suffice it to say that refugees matter not *only* because of the substantive challenge they pose to the relatively calcified state-citizen relationship of the Westphalian international order. The ideal of a mutually constitutive relationship between states and their citizens according

[7] The 1951 Convention relating to the Status of Refugees is the key legal document in defining who is a refugee, their rights and the legal obligations of states. The 1967 Protocol removed geographical and temporal restrictions from the Convention. The full text of the Convention is available at www.unhcr.org/cgi-bin/texis/vtx/protect/opendoc.pdf?tbl=PROTECTION&id=3b66c2aa10 (last accessed on September6, 2009). The 1967 Refugee Protocol is available at www.unhchr.ch/html/menu3/b/o_p_ref.htm (last accessed on September 6, 2009).

[8] See Laura Barnett, "Global Governance and the Evolution of the International Refugee Regime," *International Journal of Refugee Law* 14 (2), (3) (2002), 238–262 and the classic piece by Gil Loescher, "The International Refugee Regime: Stretched to the Limit?" *Journal of International Affairs* 47(2) (1994), 351–377.

[9] Michael Barnett, *Eyewitness to a Genocide: The United Nations and Rwanda*(Ithaca, N.Y., Cornell University Press, 2002).

to which states guarantee a predetermined set of rights in exchange for legitimacy has long proved to be a not entirely reliable bargain. Nonetheless, such a deal looks relatively attractive in the event of prior citizens becoming not only deprived of their rights but also anchorage to a place to claim or contest such rights, a condition otherwise known as statelessness.[10] In this context, the purported refugee regime provides a population relief valve of sorts both regarding those who are displaced within the borders of their home state harbouring an intent of leaving their country of origin if they could, and for people who actually flee or are forced out of their country of origin and are rendered "stateless."

As such, the current refugee regime serves a hidden as well as a blatant, albeit often ignored, function. In the first instance, those dispossessed by their own states or put in danger by their own societies, at least in principle, are to be provided with sanctuary and protection by other states that can accept them as refugees. This is done without violating the "violent" state's sovereignty despite the fact that its behaviour must have caused the displacement of peoples and human catastrophe at hand. In the second instance, the international refugee regime allows states to deal with unwanted populations by "allowing them to leave," perhaps the gruesome alternative being mass murder, ethnic cleansing or genocide. In order to avoid the potentially rogue element of stateless populations circulating along the borderlines of the international system of states, the refugee regime thus provides a built-in escape mechanism allowing the system to sustain itself without undergoing major revisions as far as the legitimacy of states or their borders are concerned.[11]

Both international relations and international law theorists have long posited that a network of formal and informal institutions allow states to achieve a sense of stability in an otherwise anarchic environment. This suggestion of a framework conducive to cooperative interaction between states, hinging on the idea of institutional practices transcending power relations and self-interest, also assumes that the legal field is a handmaiden for such promises of

[10] Hannah Arendt and Jerome Kohn, *Between Past and Future: Eight Exercises in Political Thought* (New York, Penguin Classics, 2006).

[11] Gil Loescher and James Milner, *Protracted Refugee Situations: Domestic and International Security Implications* (Adelphi Papers. Oxford University Press, 2005).

regulated coexistence.[12] In this context, several regime-based practices are named that hold the Westphalian state system together. Among these, national constitutional structures and domestic legal regimes are identified as foundational. This is due to the fact these are generally assumed to comprise the constitutive values that define legitimate statehood and rightful state action from within. Then, there are issue-specific regimes, which exist in order to enact basic institutional practices in inter-state relations.[13] Finally, there are transnational regimes dictating the rules of the overall game. The international refugee regime is an issue-specific regime from the perspectives of both international law and international relations. Meanwhile, it would be apt to argue that there have been at least two distinct embodiments of it in its long history, operating according to different core norms. If we go back as far as the seventeenth century, this is where the origins of the *first* international refugee regime is to be found. Of that era, the formative period (1648–1685) fell in the immediate aftermath of the Westphalia Treaty. The main characteristic of that era is the establishment of a *laissez-faire* framework with no clear cooperation among states, or rules of best practice or conduct for that matter, above and beyond the tacit understanding that states would accept one another's dispossessed at times of crisis. This state of affairs concerning the stateless people or the displaced political subjects in general continued until the end of First World War. At that point, and more precisely between 1918 and 1951, we witness the collapse of the ad hoc and *laissez faire* frameworks of practice that existed before. As already mentioned, the emergence of a new and institutionalized refugee regime, based on the 1951 *Refugee Convention*, signifies the attempt to legally define what a refugee is. The 1967 additional protocol then proceeded to establish clear norms against the forcible removal of refugees based on the claimed right of non-refoulement. They also incorporated the element of protection from prosecution for crossing international boundaries in order to claim asylum.[14]

[12] John Gerard Ruggie, "Reconstituting the Global Public Domain – Issues, Actors, and Practices," *European Journal of International Relations* 10 (4) (2004), 499–531.

[13] Christian Reus-Smit, "Politics and International Legal Obligation," *European Journal of International Relations* 9 (4) (2003), 591–625.

[14] Heather Rae, *State Identities and the Homogenisation of Peoples* (Cambridge University Press, 2002).

Needless to say, this purported regime has been under attack and faced multiple challenges in terms of its perception by domestic legal orders not only due to the ever-increasing number of refugees in the world, but also because of the sometimes forced acceptance of the rules of this regime as part of a bargain in international relations. These two factors led to the emergence of a deficit of required political will to uphold the regime's foundational premises. In this context, a third transition in the international refugee regime, which began in the early 1980s, is becoming increasingly more visible. The forced expansion of an international refugee regime to include states that do not possess sufficient or even minimum internal legitimacy in the eyes of their own citizens is but one aspect of the regime's repeated failure. An equally important dimension, relating to the erosion of legitimacy of the 1951 Convention as the cornerstone of the international refugee regime, has been the increasing per centage of states making use of "safe third country" legislation according to which refugees can be returned to countries that they previously resided in, provided that it is determined by their destination country that they are not at risk of harm if returned.

Meanwhile, critical human rights scholarship has long established that rights are not things that a person can be conceived of as having outside of or prior to social and political institutions, arrangements and practices.[15] This reality proves particularly cumbersome for the drafters and supporters of international norms to be adhered to by states, which are political authorities traditionally acting as the sole arbiters of legitimate controls and regulations in modern societies.[16] Indeed, the Peace of Westphalia played a critical role in the emergence of key normative institutions and

[15] Alison Brysk and Gershon Shafir (eds.), *People out of Place: Globalization, Human Rights, and the Citizenship Gap* (New York: Routledge, 2004).

[16] See Stephen Krasner, *Sovereignty: Organized Hypocrisy* (Princeton University Press, 1999). In this classic volume, Krasner contends that states have never been as sovereign as some have supposed. Throughout history, rulers have been motivated by a desire to stay in power, not by some abstract adherence to international principles. Accordingly, organized hypocrisy – the presence of long-standing norms that are frequently violated – has been an enduring attribute of international relations. Though this is a very pessimistic take on international law in particular. It does balance the overly optimistic belief in first order rules and universal principles.

principles, especially sovereignty. The original refugee regime itself also emerged only after the Peace of Westphalia as a way to deal with religious minorities. However, this agreement is foreshadowed in the Peace of Augsburg, in 1555. The latter treaty concluded a settlement under which the formula *cuius regio, eius religio* ("whose the region, his the religion") allowed rulers in Germany to determine whether their states would be either Lutheran or Catholic.[17] The Peace of Westphalia built upon this foundation by arguing for the right of *jus emigrandi* – the right to emigrate with one's personal property – as a universal right. It is in this very context that the term *refugee* emerged. In its historic form, it denoted a separate class of people from ordinary migrants, and was first used in reference to the Huguenots, French Protestants. Close to 200,000 Huguenots fled France following the Revocation of the Edict of Nantes by Louis XIV. The Revocation not only declared Protestantism illegal in France, but also officially denied exit to the protestant community.[18] It was with reference to this particular event that such a group became differentiated and given a separate title as *refugee* compared to groups who had previously been similarly excluded and had to migrate. The original refugee regime, therefore, emerged during a time of great transition in Europe, in conjunction with the emergence of principles of state sovereignty and of territorial sanctity of borders. It came into being as a way to deal with individuals who otherwise might be stateless, and would thus constitute either a burden, or a threat, or both, to the nascent Westphalian nation-state system.[19] Still, each nation reacted to refugees and refugee crises in its own way and on an entirely ad hoc basis between the sixteenth and twentieth centuries. In addition, a complementary albeit ad hoc refugee regime developed

[17] See Brian Turner, "Religion and State-Formation: a Commentary on Recent Debates," *Journal of Historical Sociology* 1 (3) (1988), 322–333.

[18] See Heather Rae, *States*.

[19] See Andreas Osiander, *The States System of Europe, 1640–1990* (Oxford University Press, 1994). This work provides a canonical analysis of the evolution of the states system of Europe since the mid-seventeenth century. Osiander looks at the four major European congresses: Munster and Osnabruck, Utrecht, Vienna, and Paris, and shows how a prevailing consensus on certain structural concepts has influenced the evolution of the system and determined its stability. This work is generally cited by regime theorists in international relations as a foundational text.

thanks to the existence of "open territories" in the new world that allowed settlement by the dispossessed via colonisation.

In hindsight, it is therefore possible to argue that the Westphalian state system may not have held up had colonies not existed, or wars not led to massive displacement of people who were then absorbed by the newly created political units in the domain of Old World Empires such as the Ottomans, Russians or the Habsburgs. Furthermore, well before the twentieth century, states were already engaged in intensive regulation of population flows. For instance, during the demographic undoing and redoing of the Balkans at the end of the Ottoman Empire and the breakup of the Austro-Hungarian Empire, border changes, undertaken at the Peace of Paris, resulted in the creation of large minority groups in a number of new states in Eastern Europe. In order to protect these groups, monitoring and guaranteeing of minority rights' provisions were entrusted to the League of Nations.[20] This is despite the fact that the High Commissioner created "Nansen Passports" – legal documents that gave refugees a recognizable status and allowed them to travel freely and created the category of refugees as possessors of a legal and juridical status.[21]

Given this background, the criticisms raised against the current international framework for protecting refugees as being fragmentary could perhaps be put into a better perspective. Still, the truth remains that there is a disconcerting multiplicity of categories of persons deemed as in need of protection, and, a cacophony of organizations for addressing their problems in addition to problems related to the wide-ranging interpretation and varying applications of international refugee law at the domestic level. Though these symptoms, which indicate the limits of the international refugee law as the foundational pillar of an accountability regime, exhibit themselves differently in the Global North and the Global South, they do have common characteristics. These include the prioritization of protection of state borders from unwanted influxes of peoples regardless of their need or the rightfulness of

[20] See Mark Mazower, "The Strange Triumph of Human Rights, 1933–1950," *The Historical Journal* 47 (2004), 379–398.

[21] Louise Holborn, *Refugees, a Problem of Our Time: The work of the United Nations High Commissioner for Refugees, 1951–1972* (Metuchen, N.J. Scarecrow Press, 1975).

their demand for access or asylum; securitization and bureaucratization of the refugee selection and admittance procedures to the degree that sometimes it takes years for an asylum seeker to be recognized as a refugee, conditional and stifled application of the 1951 Convention and the 1967 Protocol in a wide range of cases whereby either acute crises or political conflicts are concerned, and, regionalization of the problem and dispersal of state responsibilities in the name of burden sharing – often leading to the warehousing of refugees in camps for years. The conclusion to be derived from these observations is that despite the front of unity at the level of refugee jurisprudence, the international refugee regime, as we know it today and in its third phase, is still highly fragmented and preserves many of the key features it inherited from the early Westphalian era at a time widely deemed as post-Westphalian or even post-national.

IV BEWARE THE GIFT OF THE WHITE ELEPHANT: VARIANT APPLICATIONS OF THE 1951 CONVENTION

For over half a century the 1951 Convention has served as the cornerstone of international refugee law. Recognized as the primary legal document – along with the 1967 Protocol – governing refugee matters, the Convention is lauded for elaborating a series of principles that have been used to provide protection to millions of refugees since the Second World War. Meanwhile, these very principles have also been subject to a great deal of debate and interpretation over the years. Key provisions set forth in the Convention include the definition of the term refugee with five stated grounds. These are grouped under three sets of clauses: the "cessation clauses," which enumerate circumstances when an individual should cease being a refugee; the "exclusion clauses," which spell out who should be excluded from refugee status; and the rights and obligations of refugees in a host country, particularly the right not to be refouled or returned to a country where an individual fears persecution. States that sign onto the Convention and Protocol are obligated to implement these provisions in their national legislation. Meanwhile, the precise method and manner of this implementation are to be determined by national decision-making bodies.[22] During these processes of implementation, adaptation and putting the Convention into actual practice, even the key principles of the 1951 Convention and the 1967 Protocol receive markedly different readings, as a result of which the treatment of refugees worldwide takes the form of a highly fragmented as opposed to a unified regime.

In this section, I briefly examine interpretations of the 1951 Convention and the 1967 Protocol in select areas of the world where there are ongoing, large-scale and protracted refugee problems. The three examples chosen from the Global South for this purpose are Guinea in Africa, Turkey in the Middle East, and China in Asia. Of these three, needless to say, China does not count as a developing country. However, in terms of its history and its distinct identity as a political regime, it is customarily included within the Global South rather than in the West. In contrast to these examples, I then analyze some of the current practices crowned by the European Union (EU) immigration legislation and refugee policies to underline the fact that what was outlined in the previous section as the characteristics of the current international refugee regime as a fragmented accountability regime holds true in both the Global South and Western countries.

Issues from the Global South: Select profiles

To start with, the plight of eight million African refugees, the majority of whom subsist under very poor conditions in some of the most dangerous parts of the world, is an issue that scholarship on refugees simply cannot ignore.[23] Since the 1990s, refugees in Africa make up

[22] See UNHCR, "States Parties to the 1951 Convention relating to the Status of Refugees and the 1967 Protocol," 15 February 2005 (last accessed on September 6, 2009).

[23] Meanwhile, it is important to note that according to the statistics provided by the World Refugee Survey, the ten worst refugee situations in the world today are in Bangladesh where there are 177,600 refugees and asylum seekers, China (323,600 refugees and asylum seekers), European Union (252,000 refugees and asylum seekers), India (420,400 refugees and asylum seekers), followed by Iraq, Kenya, Malaysia, Russia, Sudan and Thailand. These are destinations where refugees and asylum seekers are deemed most vulnerable to abuse, violence, and unstable conditions. For details, see www.refugees.org/article.aspx?id=2324&subm=179&area=About%20 Refugees& (last accessed on September 6, 2009).

more than one-third of all refugees worldwide. Of the many African countries, Guinea hosts about half a million refugees who ran away from conflicts in neighbouring Sierra Leone and Liberia. In effect, the refugee population in Guinea is the largest such grouping on the continent. Meanwhile, conditions under which refugees survive in Guinea are markedly worrisome.

The problem of refugee reception and protection is a manifold one in many of the countries in the Global South and African societies constitute no exception in this sense. Specifically in Guinea, there are continued tensions between refugees and the host community as refugees have been receiving more services than nationals. Under pressure, in January 2008, the Office of the UN High Commissioner for Refugees (UNHCR) had to turn two refugee camps, housing around 8,000 Liberian refugees, over to the Government. Similarly, the Jesuit Refugee Service handed its projects in Kouankan II Camp, home to refugees from Côte d'Ivoire, over to the Guinean Red Cross. UNHCR, as well as the International Committee of the Red Cross and local nongovernmental organizations, regularly monitor detention conditions in the country. According to their reports, prisons are overcrowded, and conditions remain inhumane and life threatening. Guineans reportedly intimidate those who sought to file complaints against locals into dropping their cases. Furthermore, asylum seekers do not receive any form of documentation, which renders them open targets for harassment. In the meantime, refugees are often subject to traditional forms of dispute resolution in cases involving rape and sexual assault, typically resulting in impunity or a monetary exchange between families rather than any form of punitive punishment. Similarly, although refugees and asylum seekers have access to Guinean courts, challenging detention remains difficult due to limited resources and a lack of training of prison and judicial authorities. The formal justice system often does not protect victims, charges their families' fees, and is reluctant to arrest Guinean perpetrators.[24]

These conditions prevail despite the fact that Guinea is bound by the Africa-wide Refugee Convention, which was agreed by

[24] See ICRC report on refugees in Guinea at www.icrc.org/web/eng/siteengo.nsf/htmlall/guinea?OpenDocument (last accessed on September 6, 2009).

African presidents in 1969.[25] Meanwhile, there are discernable reasons for the limited applicability of this Convention in current-day Africa. To start with, although it gives political backing to the idea of safe asylum, the 1969 Convention was designed when most African refugees were politically acceptable to their hosts. At the time, they were fleeing from conflicts against colonialism or from wars aimed at overthrowing apartheid in South Africa. Today's African refugees are different in their characteristics. The majority of them are fleeing from civil, often ethnic war, genocide or human rights abuses. Consequently, while most African governments have signed the regional 1969 Convention as well as the international 1951 Convention, few have proceeded to enshrine legal protection for refugees in their local laws. Instead, by and large, protection is accorded on an ad hoc basis. This also means that, at the grassroots level, police or customs officials at border posts are not equipped to deal with refugees at best, or, at worst, are heavily prejudiced against asylum seekers. It is true that strengthening the legal position of refugees at every level is vital. However, the way to achieve this in Africa is open to dispute. Could this be done simply by putting heavier emphasis on the stricter interpretation of the obligations dictated by the original European refugee jurisprudence such as the 1951 Convention, or, are there other ways of ensuring effective protection of refugees through regional and domestic interventions? Given the fact that Guinea is party to the 1951 Convention without reservation, its 1967 Protocol, and the 1969 Convention governing the Specific Aspects of Refugee Problems in Africa, the issue does not seem to be one of jurisprudence but of interpretation and application. Furthermore, the 1992 Guinean Constitution guarantees asylum to foreign nationals mistreated because of political, philosophical, or religious opinion, race, ethnicity, or intellectual, scientific, or cultural activities. In addition, the 2000 Guinean Refugee Law incorporates both Conventions' definitions of a refugee and those recognized under the mandate of UNHCR. It also prohibits expelling or extraditing refugees

[25] This is the Convention Governing the Specific Aspects of Refugee Problems in Africa. Full document can be found at www.africa-union.org/Official_documents/Treaties_%20Conventions_%20Protocols/Refugee_Convention.pdf (last accessed on September 6, 2009).

or asylum seekers, including during appeals. It is also true that Guinea did not confine refugees and asylum seekers to camps or segregated settlements. However, neither does it look after the safety and security of asylum seekers and refugees in urban areas. Similarly, the 1994 Entry and Stay Law provides that authorities issue refugees and stateless persons special identity cards. In addition, the 2000 Memorandum of Understanding between Guinea and UNHCR provides that the Government issues such cards within a month. The 1992 Constitution extends to all persons its protections of access to courts, equality before the law, due process, and proportional punishment. The 2000 Refugee Law prohibits punishing refugees or asylum seekers for irregular entry or presence. The 1994 Entry and Stay Law provides for house arrest for otherwise deportable refugees. This list of formal legal remedies could go on. And yet, there are widespread reports pertaining to the continual harassment of and injury to refugees in the hands of the Guinean security forces and state officials. At the level of their daily existence and livelihood, for instance, the 2000 Guinean Refugee Law treats refugees on par with nationals from countries with which Guinea has the most favorable treaties concerning the right to work. Residents of the Economic Community of West African States (ECOWAS), including refugees from Liberia, Côte d'Ivoire, and Sierra Leone, therefore have the legal right to work without permits or licenses. Meanwhile, refugees generally have great difficulty obtaining employment because employers do not recognize their foreign credentials. Some refugees with businesses complained that authorities extorted false business taxes. Similarly, although the 1992 Constitution offers to all the right to work, to join unions, and to strike, the majority of refugees work without labor protection in fear of deportation. This is, again, despite the fact that refugees in Guinea can engage freely in business, own property, open bank accounts, and repatriate assets when they return, subject to customs' fees. In summary, there is a marked gap between what refugee jurisprudence guarantees in the Guinean context and what actually happens in the daily life of refugees and asylum seekers. In this particular case, the concern is not about the adaptation of international refugee law. It is about the lack of implementation, application and efficient monitoring of it from within the domestic domain, as well as the barring of international organizations from intervening in cases of malpractice.

The second case to be examined is that of China. China has been dealing with a very large number of refugees from neighbouring states for decades. Only in August 2009, more than 30,000 refugees from Myanmar crossed into China, fleeing fighting between the Myanmar army and local ethnic militias in the Kokang region of Myanmar. At present, roughly 9,000 are living in seven camps along the border in China's Yunnan province, while as many as 4,000 had already returned. In addition to these new additions to the refugee population in China, around 11,000 North Korean refugees remained in hiding near the border with their home country for years. China, however, considers them illegal economic migrants and continues to deport North Koreans back to their home country. China allows passage to South Korea via a third country only to those Korean refugees who gain public attention or the protection of a foreign embassy or consulate and only after five to six months of delay. China also denies UNHCR and nongovernmental organizations (NGOs) access to its northeastern border with North Korea. In addition to Koreans, China thus far hosted more than 319,000 refugees from Vietnam, mostly ethnic Chinese, who fled Vietnam during and after the Sino-Vietnamese War in the early 1980s. Their conditions were markedly difficult and they lacked official recognition as refugees. At present, China permits a small number of asylum seekers of other nationalities to remain, mostly in Beijing, while UNHCR determines their status and seeks to resettle them.[26]

Similar to the Guinean case, there is no lack of refugee jurisprudence in China. Indeed, China is a party to the 1951 Convention and its 1967 Protocol. In addition, the Chinese Constitution allows it to grant asylum to those who sought it for political reasons. However, China does not have a procedure for doing so. Instead, there is a high degree of securitization of immigration and refugee regime in the country. For instance, China detains and deports North Koreans who come to its official attention. It also installed enhanced security measures on its border with North Korea, as well as offering rewards

[26] For a full account of the refugee situation in China, see the World Refugee Survey documentation at www.worldrefugeesurvey.org/index.php?title=China (last accessed on September 6, 2009).

of roughly $300 for those who turn in North Koreans. Indeed, China built a barbed wire fence along the Tumen River, which marks the border with North Korea, and installed heat and motion sensors in the desert along its border with Mongolia. In terms of the treatment of refugees once they manage to get into China, the Public Security Bureau holds all detained refugees and asylum seekers, and the detention centers are not subject to any independent monitoring. Refugees and asylum seekers cannot challenge their detention before any court, either. In summary, refugees under UNHCR's protection, along with the unrecognized North Korean asylum seekers, have no official status under Chinese law, and cannot use the courts to pursue their rights unless they hold a visa or residence permit. Under these circumstances, Vietnamese refugees enjoy the most rights. The provincial governments where they live issue identification cards to all those over the age of 16, but not refugees or asylum seekers from other countries. As a result, North Koreans have to use forged identification cards to move within the country. Police outside the Beijing area are not familiar with the certificates that UNHCR issues to refugees, and most do not travel outside the capital for fear of arrest. Authorities also limit the movement of refugees without valid travel documents. China does not issue travel documents to refugees, and those whom UNHCR resettled to other countries rely on travel documents from their home countries or their new hosts. Finally, in terms of earning a living, China allows Vietnamese refugees to work freely. However, other refugees need a passport with a valid visa or residence permit to apply for a work permit. North Korean refugees, who generally left their country illegally, are not able to work. The inability to work legally forces many North Korean women in China to depend on relationships with Chinese men to survive and they rely on brokers or traffickers to link them up. The children of these Chinese men and North Korean women can attend school through middle school and beyond only if their family secures legal documentation. In summary, although we witness a somewhat different set of limitations in the Chinese treatment of refugees and asylum seekers, the overall picture resembles that of Guinea: the overall problem lies not in the lack of ratification of international refugee conventions per se. Rather, China offers different interpretations of refugee jurisprudence in the case of Vietnamese (political) refugees as opposed to North Korean asylum seekers and refugees as well as other groups coming into the country. This is a discretionary choice on China's part and third party observation or monitoring of the situation is rendered practically impossible.

The third and last case to be examined in terms of the variant applications of the 1951 Convention in the Global South is Turkey. Turkey shares borders with three major Middle Eastern countries: Iran, Iraq, and Syria. The most urgent and ongoing refugee problem for Turkey is the Kurdish issue. Following Iraq's defeat by the United States-led coalition at the end of February 1991, Iraq's Kurdish minority, which constituted approximately 15 percent of the approximately 19 million of the country's population, attempted a mass exodus toward the Iranian and Turkish borders. Unable to deal with the refugee flood, Turkey closed its borders after more than 400,000 Kurds had fled into Hakkâri and Mardin provinces. Turkish soldiers subsequently prevented about 500,000 more Kurdish refugees on the Iraqi side of the border from crossing over to Turkey, forcing them to remain in makeshift camps. The humanitarian crisis and the international publicity surrounding it posed a major dilemma for Turkey, which was reluctant to absorb hundreds of thousands of Kurdish refugees and thus add to its own Kurdish minority problem. Turkey also opposed the creation of permanent refugee camps in the border regions, believing such camps would become breeding grounds for militant and separatist Kurdish nationalism, citing the example of Palestinian refugee camps established during the war that followed Israel's creation in 1948. Turkey's preferred solution to the Kurdish refugee crisis has thus been for the Iraqi Kurds to return to their homes with guarantees for their safety.

However, there is more to this story. Turkey actually maintains a geographical limitation to the 1951 Convention and refuses to recognize persons of non-European origin as refugees. As a result, persons in need of international protection in Turkey or arriving at Turkey's borders are prevented from accessing their internationally recognized refugee rights due to specific Turkish asylum regulations. Furthermore, many of those who are in need of international protection are forcibly returned to countries where they may be at risk of persecution. For instance, since Turkey does not recognise non-Europeans as refugees, resettlement in a third country has long been presented as the only option available to Iranian refugees who flee to Turkey in fear of political, social, religious or gender-based persecution. This is how this procedure typically unfolds. Turkish law requires Iranian asylum seekers to apply for "temporary asylum" immediately after their arrival. They are then given a certain period of time to seek resettlement in a third country with the help of the United Nations High Commissioner for Refugees (UNHCR). To be resettled, a refugee must first be recognized by UNHCR, a process that is getting longer and more difficult every year. During this time, refugees receive no humanitarian assistance from UNHCR or the Turkish government and nor are they permitted to work. On the basis of the same principle, Turkish law enforcement officials have regularly expelled Uzbekistani refugees into Iranian territory.[27]

Another twist in the Turkish case is the two-tier reception of asylum seekers depending on their ethno-religious profile. The generalized sub-standard treatment of asylum seekers in general starkly contradicts the reception of people in need of protection or help who are deemed to be of Turkish origin. The Turkish General Assembly repeatedly recommended efforts to be made by Turkey to meet the needs of Bulgarian [Turkish] refugees in its territory and their permanent settlement. Meanwhile, the massive influx of refugees into Turkey as a result of events in Bulgaria in 1989 did not lead Turkey to reconsider its interpretation of who falls within the scope of the 1951 Convention. Instead, the majority of asylum seekers who arrive in Turkey are still treated as "people in need of temporary protection" or as "de facto refugees." It is in this context that Turkey justifies regularly returning refugees to their countries of origin or deporting them to other countries. In 2008, for instance, UNHCR attempted 393 times to interview nearly 3,400 foreign nationals arrested for illegally entering the

[27] For further details of this case, see Amnesty International's www.amnesty.org/en/news-and-updates/news/turkey-expels-refugees-second-time-20081014, 14 October 2008 Report (last accessed on September 6, 2009).

country. Turkey allowed UNHCR access to only seventy-two of these cases, and UNHCR believes Turkey deported those it could not reach without allowing them to seek asylum or refugee status. There is evidence that Turkish border officials regularly return Iraqis apprehended at the Turkey-Greece border to Iraq with no chance to apply for asylum.[28] Turkish authorities also return foreigners stopping in Turkey on their way to Europe if they suspect that the travelers intend to seek asylum. In this vein, again in 2008, Turkish authorities returned 600 Afghanis by plane. In 2008, Turkey received a total of 10,800 asylum applications and granted temporary asylum to 1,100 refugees, who were mostly Iraqis.

In terms of the securitisation of the refugee regime, Turkey does not separate and screen asylum seekers from migrants it interdicts. Asylum seekers have to submit parallel applications to UNHCR in order to receive even temporary protection.[29] Once in Turkey, upon an asylum seeker's registration, UNHCR directs refugees to apply to the Foreigners' Police of the province where the Government assigns them a place of residence. The Foreigners' Borders and Asylum Division of the Ministry of Interior in Ankara then determines, independent of UNHCR, whether applicants have a legitimate need of "temporary asylum". Applicants can appeal negative decisions within fifteen days but the process is not open to public scrutiny. They can also request *interim* measures to avoid deportation but the courts respond slowly and deportations often take place while the courts are considering appeals. A few applicants with lawyers appealed to the European Court of Human Rights (ECtHR). Still, the ECtHR can only order the Government to desist from deporting the applicant pending its assessment and could not intervene with the criteria used for the determination of "temporary asylum." In summary, although Turkey is party to the 1951 Convention, it maintains a critical reservation on its 1967 Protocol. This special

[28] For a detailed account of Turkish refugee and asylum policy and current practices, see the World Refugee Survey Report on Turkey at www.worldrefugeesurvey.org/index.php?title=Turkey (last accessed on September 6, 2009).

[29] Meanwhile, ethnic Turks including Bulgarian Turks and Iraqi Turkomen are free to stay under the 1934 Law on Settlement. For further debate, see Kemal Kirisci, "Refugees of Turkish Origin: 'Coerced Immigrants' to Turkey since 1945," *International Migration* 34 (3) (2009), 385–412.

arrangement markedly limits Turkey's obligations under the 1951 Convention. Similarly, Turkish law protects non-European asylum seekers from refoulement if and only if they register their claims without delay, provide valid identity documentation, and receive resettlement assistance from UNHCR or directly from resettling countries. In addition, the Passport Law of 1950 criminalises entry into Turkey without valid travel documents. Within this framework, Turkey also restricts access to detainees by UNHCR and NGOs. Similarly, Turkey restricts lawyers' access to clients in border areas. It confines refugees and asylum seekers with "special security risks" to the Refugee Guesthouse in Yozgat province. Asylum seekers who apply for protection after authorities detain them as illegal entrants have to remain in administrative detention at foreigners' guesthouses.

On the brighter side of things, Turkey grants refugees and asylum seekers the same political and civil rights as foreign nationals, regarding the freedom to practice their religion, to seek access to court, and to marry and divorce, yet only when they have valid identification documents. Temporary asylum applicants who have registered with authorities and reside in their assigned cities receive an asylum seeker identification card and a residence permit from the provincial Foreigners' Police. Still, although Turkey does not confine refugees and asylum seekers to camps, the Law on Residence and Travel of Aliens requires them to reside in areas assigned by the Ministry of Interior, which sends them to thirty satellite cities. Turkey does not allow UNHCR-registered refugees to live for long periods in major cities either. Furthermore, asylum seekers constitute a separate category and have to report regularly to the local police. Authorities in each city determine the terms of their residence. Asylum seekers and refugees can move freely within their assigned provinces, but have to obtain permission from the provincial Governorate to travel to other provinces. Those who wish to transfer to another satellite city can do so only if they have family members there or if they have a medical condition that is not treatable in their current city of residence. Finally, Turkey restricts exit permits for refugees and asylum seekers to third-country and family-reunification resettlement cases. Nor does it issue international travel documents to refugees.

Finally, in terms of earning a living, Turkey's 2003 Law on Work Permits for Foreigners permits refugees and asylum seekers with valid residence permits to work legally. However, since asylum seekers are eligible only for six-month permits, they can work in temporary jobs only. In addition, the 1932 law reserves certain professions and activities for Turkish citizens, specifically those in the various service sectors such as health care, medicine, law, and public and private security. The vast majority of refugees and asylum seekers work in the informal sector and they do not enjoy the protection of labor laws or social security. It is true that refugees with valid residence permits are eligible for government services. However, limited government health services leave many refugees without medical attention. Refugees have to apply for medical aid to officers from the Foreigners' branch of the police and depend on provincial authorities' discretion and the availability of local Social Assistance and Solidarity Funds. UNCHR contracts with hospitals and pharmacies to provide recognized refugees with medical services only on an emergency basis. Although non-European refugees to whom Turkey grants temporary asylum are entitled to free medical care in state hospitals, and under a 2008 law asylum seekers and stateless persons are entitled to the same right as well, this has not yet been implemented.[30] Overall, the Turkish case is separate from the Guinean and Chinese cases in the sense that the country entertains a highly truncated adoption of international refugee law. Refugees and asylum seekers survive under such circumstances only through ad hoc arrangements, irregular intervention of international organizations and NGOs, through the charitable measures extended by small groups and irregular network of Turkey's already over-utilised and under-funded national education, healthcare and social welfare systems.

Issues from the Global North: The case of European Union

Currently 147 countries have acceded to the original 1951 Convention and the 1967 subsequent Protocol. The majority of these are in the Global South, and yet the engine of international refugee law is

[30] For a detailed discussion on the 1994 Asylum Regulation and other instruments used to regulate refugee and migrant flows in Turkey, see www.va.lv/files/asylum-seekers%20and%20refugees_ali_gitmez-2.pdf (last accessed on September 6, 2009).

still located in the West. This is partly due to the fact that the original, 1951 Convention was used to resettle more than one million displaced Europeans around the world and helped 73,000 civilians to return to their former homes.[31] And yet, paradoxically, the same Europe that gave birth to the 1951 Convention is now home to confusingly diverse and often disconcerting practices as far as modern-day refugees and asylum seekers are concerned. Huge differences exist between national asylum systems across the continent, making the asylum system almost like a "lottery" for refugees. It is true that the recent Hague Programme[32] envisaged "practical and collaborative co-operation" among Member States as an important step in the process of achieving a common European asylum system. It is also true that only recently, the European Commission unveiled plans to allow more refugees from conflict zones into European countries. Still, in 2008, the EU accepted about 5,000 or less than 7 percent of the refugees officially settled worldwide. By the end of 2008, countries in the Global South were hosting 8.4 million refugees, – 80 percent of the global refugee population – with Pakistan alone hosting 1.8 million people. These demographics hardly match with the anxiety European societies exude as far as refugees and asylum seekers are concerned. By any measure, the scale of the refugee settlement operations in Europe is small. However, procedural aspects of the issue are subject to meticulous regulation. Under the new settlement scheme, for instance, EU nations would decide together every year which refugee groups should be given priority for resettlement, and receive more money from a joint fund to give them a new home. The new scheme also calls on the EU to set annual priorities – for example, focusing on

[31] There already was a 1933 League of Nations' Convention relating to the International Status of Refugees and a 1938 Convention concerning the Status of Refugees coming from Germany providing limited protection for uprooted peoples. The 1933 instrument, for instance, had introduced the notion that signatory states were obligated to uphold the principles of the Convention. However, this original Convention lacked teeth as only eight countries ratified it, several of them after imposing substantial limitations on their obligations.

[32] The European Commission's five-year action plan for freedom, justice and security – with detailed proposals for EU action on terrorism, migration management, visa policies, asylum, privacy and security, the fight against organised crime and criminal justice, launched May 10, 2005.

Iraqi or Somali refugees – in coordination with the UNHCR. As a monetary incentive, member states that resettle will receive an extra 4,000 Euros per resettled person from the European Refugee Fund. However, a lot is yet to be done in terms of the treatment of asylum seekers who are not handpicked for settlement from refugee camps where millions are warehoused. The treatment of those who arrive at Fortress Europe continues to merit critical and sometimes urgent attention, let alone the numbers who are granted official refugee status upon application.

In effect, some of the most blatant breaches of the 1951 Convention in the EU occur in the area of non-refoulment. For instance, in general European countries follow the UNHCR recommendations not to return rejected Iraqi asylum seekers to the southern and central parts of Iraq and to return Kurds only to the Kurdish areas in the North if they had family links there. In April 2008, however, Sweden returned to Baghdad a rejected Iraqi asylum seeker from northern Iraq. Similarly, in November 2008, the UK's House of Lords approved the forced return of non-Arab Sudanese from Darfur, reasoning that, even if they could not return to that province, the internally displaced persons squatter camps around Khartoum were not posing a threat to the asylum seeker's life and well-being. In December 2008, Sweden's Migration Board allowed the government to return Somali asylum seekers to Mogadishu, unless they could show specific targeting for persecution, reasoning that the rebels in Mogadishu held no territory and that the situation there did not amount to armed conflict. The Greek coastguards systematically force boatloads of potential asylum seekers out of Greece's national waters and back into Turkish territorial waters, occasionally abandoning them on uninhabited islands. Greek border guards often arrest Iraqi and other Middle Eastern asylum seekers upon arrival, issue all of them automatic deportation orders, and at times detain them incommunicado without registration for several days before returning them to Turkey. Ukraine regularly detains or extradites ethnic Chechen asylum seekers back to the Russian Federation, despite the fact that the UNHCR strongly advises states to refrain from returning asylum seekers without subjecting them to refugee status determinations.

Across the EU, asylum-granting rates continue to vary widely,[33] with newer EU members on the periphery generally having much lower rates. While Austria granted refugee status to 80 percent of Chechen cases, Poland thus far has granted only 20 percent and Croatia and Slovenia none at all. Sweden deemed 90 percent of Iraqis who sought asylum to merit protection, while Greece granted it to almost none. In France and Germany, where the EU's Qualification Directive expanded the scope of grounds for granting protection, the Directive still failed to establish a common standard for determining internal alternatives to asylum. France, for example, did not apply the concept of internal protection to Chechens in any of the sixty cases UNHCR reviewed, whereas Germany and Slovakia considered most of the territory of the Russian Federation acceptable for return. Under the Dublin II Regulation[34], which allocates responsibility to examine asylum claims within the EU and associated States, Sweden returned some 900, mostly Iraqis, to Greece. This is despite the fact that UNHCR continually advises European governments to refrain from returning asylum seekers to other European countries they crossed en route and to examine the cases themselves. Even the processing of standard applications proves to be problem laden. France regularly holds asylum seekers in airport waiting areas and does not allow them to file claims until authorities decide whether they are "manifestly unfounded." Border authorities could deport applicants even while appeals of those decisions are pending. France's new Aliens Bill grants asylum seekers at the border twenty-four-hour suspensions of deportation to file appeals. Meanwhile, the French National Assembly amended the bill to shorten the deadline for filing appeals inside the country from one month to fifteen days, suspending deportation for the appeal only in certain select cases. Again, Switzerland's 1998 Asylum Act allows border authorities to declare claims "manifestly unfounded" and

[33] For a detailed account of all the relevant EU directives on refugees and asylum seekers in Europe, see European Council on Refugees and Exiles documentation at www.ecre.org/topics/asylum_in_EU (last accessed on September 6, 2009).

[34] Council Regulation (EC) No 343/2003 of 18 February 2003 establishing the criteria and mechanisms for determining the Member State responsible for examining an asylum application lodged in one of the Member States by a third-country national. OJ L. 50, 25.2.2003.

refuse to hear them if applicants could not document their identity within forty-eight hours. Slovenia's new Asylum Act also applies accelerated procedures without complete hearings to all applications for asylum *except* those it deemed "manifestly well-founded" or those filed by separated children or persons with special needs. It also allows the government to expel persons appealing negative decisions before the outcome.

Regarding issues of detention and access to courts, according to the Jesuit Refugee Service, the countries of the EU have 224 immigration detention facilities with a total capacity of more than 30,000 people. These centres often held people for as long as 18 months and, in a number of countries there is often no upper limit on length of detention. Many of these detention centers are overcrowded, understaffed, and lacking medical staff and interpreters and some detain unaccompanied minors in solitary confinement. Detainees have almost no access to legal advice. Greece, for instance, systematically detains illegal migrants including asylum seekers, unaccompanied minors as young as ten, torture and trafficking victims, disabled persons, and pregnant women from countries such as Iraq, Afghanistan, and Somalia in sub-standard conditions. Similarly, a doctor with Medicare Services Limited testified that Malta isolated seven or eight detained asylum seekers with chickenpox in a windowless isolation cell. Malta and Cyprus do not require a court order to detain or prolong immigration detention, and in the Czech Republic, asylum seekers detained under the Dublin II Regulation do not have the right to challenge their detention. Lithuania does not limit the duration of immigration detention. The Czech Republic, Poland, and Spain all limit or completely block independent human rights organizations' monitoring of places in their major airports where they hold potential asylum seekers. In January 2008, for instance, the European Court of Human Rights (ECtHR) found Belgium's more than ten-day detention in 2003 of two asylum seekers in the transit section of the Brussels airport without food, beds, or ability to wash themselves or their clothes or to apply for asylum to be unlawful and inhuman. Only the cleaning staff of the company that ran the airport gave them food out of mercy

The right of citizens of EU countries to freedom of movement and residence throughout the EU does not apply to refugees or asylum seekers. Even the most recent EU Directive on long-term residents[35] that granted freedom of movement to some categories of non-EU nationals did not grant such rights to refugees in general, although it counted their time as asylum seekers toward the duration requirement for long-term residence. The EU Reception Directive[36] allows states to restrict the freedom of movement of asylum seekers within their borders. Under the EU Qualification Directive,[37] however, refugees and beneficiaries of other forms of protection would have the same freedom of movement as foreigners generally. Similarly, countries of the EU normally allow refugees to work freely, but restrict work rights for asylum seekers and persons granted subsidiary protection. Moreover, in general, Western European countries often limit asylum seekers to seasonal work or for short periods. Slovenia, for instance, restricts refugees' right to work for one year. Cyprus allows asylum seekers with only subsidiary protection, many of them Iraqis, to work only on farms for the first year. Furthermore, the EU Reception Directive and a Directive on refugee status and subsidiary protection allows states to restrict work rights of holders of subsidiary protection based on the labor market. It is true that refugees generally received public assistance on a par with nationals. Poland, however, offered almost no public relief to Chechens because it granted them only subsidiary protection. In the same vein, the United Kingdom denies childless asylum seekers housing and health services if they applied seventy-two hours or more after arrival with few exceptions.[38]

To summarise, implicit in much current debate on EU migration and asylum policy is the specter of supra-nationalization as a self-evident antidote to the exclusionary and securitized migration and refugee policies of individual European countries. Meanwhile,

[35] Council Directive 2003/109/EC of 25 November 2003 concerning the status of third-country nationals who are long-term residents, OJ L. 16, 23.1.2004.

[36] Council Directive 2003/9/EC of 27 January 2003 laying down minimum standards for the reception of asylum seekers, OJ L. 31/18, 6.2.2003.

[37] Council Directive 2004/83/EC of 29 April 2004 on minimum standards for the qualification and status of third country nationals or stateless persons as refugees or as persons who otherwise need international protection and the content of the protection granted, OJ L. 304, 30/09/2004 p. 12–23.

[38] For further details of individual cases, see the World Refugee Survey report on European Union at www.refugees.org/countryreports.aspx?id=2138 (last accessed on September 6, 2009).

it could be argued that the current process of harmonization of refugee jurisprudence has less to do with the establishment of a common European asylum system and more to do with reducing immigration pressures and compensating for the perceived losses of internal security in the wake of full freedom of movement inside the Union. As the examples discussed in this section indicate, communitarisation of refugee policy is dogged by the legacy of intensive national border-protection mechanisms. European governments have only been prepared to support communitarisation so long as they could have separate protocols that legitimised their non-participation or individual and idiosyncratic readings of communal treaties pertaining to international refugee law. European migration and refugee policies have always been fraught with internal contradictions, which are yet to be resolved. In short, despite the recent common initiatives, the emergence of a rights-respecting model of Europe-wide refugee regime based on the 1951 Convention remains a desire to be fulfilled rather than a program to be realized in the near future.

V THE PROMISE OF LEGAL PLURALISM: COMING TO TERMS WITH THE FRAGMENTED NATURE OF THE INTERNATIONAL REFUGEE REGIME

If state interests, home politics and domestic judiciary interpretations of international law by and large determine the way the 1951 Convention is interpreted and put into practice, what would be the point of purporting principles or even law that are transnational and based on universal ideals? Despite the discussion and cases I presented thus far, I would still argue that nation-state based accounts of international law entertain an oversimplified and short-sighted view of international law in particular and international regimes in general. In contradistinction, more current, alternative accounts of law present us with a more nuanced understanding of international law. One such example is the scholarship on legal pluralism. In this latter context, international law is seen as a complex deliberative process rather than as a set of treaty-based rules cushioned by "soft law" – that is, customary law. In fact, recent debates on legal pluralism go as far as portraying international law as a battleground for multifarious interests and actors only one of which is the nation state, each trying to determine legal or semi-legal outcomes to their benefit at a globally intertwined platform.[39]

In a broad definition, legal monism refers to the pervasive, positivist understanding of law as a unified structure of valid rules and principles contained within a solid institutional framework. Legal pluralism, on the other hand, emphasizes the multiplicity of legal practices and hybridity of socio-political platforms upon which legal edifices are built in the form of institutions, rule-based structures and legal regimes.[40] Therefore, the legal pluralist take on international law acknowledges the inherently plural (though not necessarily pluralist) make-up of international law and pays attention to multiple processes in the making, interpretation and use of such law above and beyond the interests of the nation state. This debate allows for a new understanding of refugee law in a global context, as well. Then, the central question in the study of international refugee law and refugee regime is no longer how to maintain the integrity of refugee jurisprudence as a uniformly applicable system under the rubric of the 1951 Convention. One is forced to accept that quasi-legal decision-making bodies, internal governance systems of large organizations, alternative modes of dispute resolution and arbitration, human rights monitoring organs, non-governmental regulative systems and myriad other forms of governance also produce legal or law-like effects. Therefore, the critical issue becomes how to read this complexity within a regime context that includes, for better or worse, the nation state and domestic jurisprudence as a key actor. State law by and large continues to be singled out by its coherence, internal consistency and its separation from other, non-state related domains. The question is whether legal pluralism, when applied to international refugee law in particular, could produce the desired effect of change

[39] For a promising and hopeful account of the making of international law in the era of transnational politics and global economy, see Janet Koven Levit, "A Bottom-Up Approach to International Lawmaking: The Tale of Three Trade Finance Instruments," *Yale Journal of International Law* 30 (2005), 125.

[40] In Margaret Davies words: "The 'ethos of pluralism' evidenced by [this] scholarship is part of a paradigm shift towards a less positivistic, more open and more responsive concept of law." See Margaret Davies, "The Ethos of Legal Pluralism." *Sydney Law Review* (2005). Also see Neil Walker, "The Idea of Constitutional Pluralism," *Modern Law Review* 65 (2002), 317.

of optics and take our gaze away from the states versus international jurisprudence tension.[41]

Until recently, legal pluralist scholarhsip was divided into two main debates. "Classical" legal pluralism referred to anthropological and socio-historical analyses of legal systems of ex-colonial or post-colonial societies, which had dual or multiple legal systems derived from indigenous, pre-colonial folk, communal or customary law on the one hand and imperial law on the other. In contradistincion, the "second wave" legal pluralism entertained the insight that all societies, whether or not formerly colonised, are composed of multiple "semi-autonomous" fields of normative control and legal discourse. This second debate purports that many forms of law co-exist, the majority of which are non-territorial, non-state, local or international, and horizontal rather than hierarchical in their jurisprudential coverage. No doubt both schools of legal pluralism concentrate on legal plurality and challenge the presumption that state law is indeed a superior source for legal meaning or conduct. However, more attention has been paid to jurisprudential characteristics of plurality of legal regimes in the particular debate initiated by the work of Robert Cover and continued by Gunther Teubner and David Trubek.[42] This, I will call the "third wave" of legal pluralism, whereby legal scholarship developed a rich analytical approach for the study of different forms of law and the struggle amongst them in terms of co-existence within a dynamic normative landscape. This latest debate does not assume that pluralism in law is merely limited to the multiplicity of "semi-autonomous" systems separated by territory, culture, or history. Rather, an attempt is made to theorise law as a process in which

[41] The term "two optics" was originally coined by Robert Keohane. See Robert Keohane "International relations and International law: Two optics," *Harvard International Law Journal* 48 (1997), 487.

[42] See Gunther Teubner, "The Two Faces of Janus: Rethinking Legal Pluralism," *Cardozo Law Review* 13 (1992), 1443; Teubner, "The Anonymous Matrix: Human Rights Violation by 'Private' Transnational Actors," *Michigan Law Review* 69 (2006), 327; David Trubek, Yves Dezalay, Ruth Buchanan, and John R. Davis, "Global Restructuring and the Law: Studies of the Internationalization of Legal Fields and the Creation of Transnational Arenas," *Case Western Law Review* 44 (1995); David Trubek, Jim Mosher and Jeffrey S. Rothstein, "Transnationalism in the Regulation of Labor Relations," *Law and Social Inquiry* (2000); 25 David M. Trubek and Lance Compa, "Trade Law, Labour and Global Inequality." *University of Wisconsin Law School Legal Studies Research Paper Series* (2005), 1001.

legal actors, legal subjects and legal norms are rendered interdependent and effected by power and politics at large.

This particular take on international law seeks for three elements in order to determine the existence of a legal system: a legal concept, a structure or framework capable of supporting its operationalisation as law, and, the political consensus to recognize it as law.[43] This mode of thinking promises to look beyond the debate of "legal norm creation" or "loyal domestic adaptations" in international law. Instead, it dwells on international law's effectiveness and the importance of its multiple constituencies. Consequently, international law is not seen just as a coherent collection of rules, prescriptions and aspirations governing the conduct of states and other international actors through legal processes and jurisdictional negotiations. This intervention also cuts short the somewhat stale conversation about treaty implementation and compliance. In its place, it turns our attention to institutional and system-wide normative characteristics of international law as well as multiple and overlapping regimes enabling its operations. Here, I will narrow down the debate on the applicability of legal pluralism in understanding international law to the specific field of accountability regimes, in particular international refugee law. In this context, the critical issue to focus on becomes which actors and structures matter for the international refugee regime in addition to the 1951 Convention, UNHCR and domestic refugee jurisprudence at the nation-state level. My answer to this question will be, first and foremost, the regimes pertaining to international human rights and humanitarian law. I would argue that only through the intersection of these other accountability regimes and the interaction amongst them that we could entertain a tangible hope for a more faithful adaptation of the 1951 Convention at a global scale.

In almost any given field of international law, establishment of an all-encompassing unitary legal system or regime has long proven to be an elusive goal.[44] Full coherence and efficacy in the overall

[43] Paul F. Diehl, Charlotte Ku and Daniel Zamora, "The Dynamics of International Law: The Interaction of Normative and Operating Systems," *International Organization* 57 (2003), 43.

[44] See Karen Wellens, "Fragmentation of International Law and Establishing an Accountability Regime for International Organizations: The Role of the Judiciary in Closing the Gap." *Michigan Journal of International Law* 25 (2004), 1160 and her "Diversity in Secondary

international legal order could not be achieved by any given set of primary rules. The multitude of "secondary rules" in international law is a constant force to reckon with. Neither could we do away with the proliferation of "third-party forums" or hybrid organs in international law, or indeed diverse ways of law making and adjudication at the national or regional levels.[45] If so, how could we pronounce the international refugee regime as an "accountability regime" that is far-reaching, flexible, adaptable and yet one that does not amount to a cacophony of legal practices or regular breach of the basic tenets of the 1951 Convention? Here, the third wave of legal pluralism debates come to our aid. The customary understanding of the 1951 Convention is that it is designed to be ratified and embedded in the domestic legal realm of individual states. However, this is a far too positive law oriented interpretation of the international refugee regime since it does not take into account the socio-political dimension that is required for the full adoption or even codification of refugee rights. As the case study examples illustrated, the problem is often not that states are not parties to the 1951 Convention, nor that they do not embed refugee rights into their domestic jurisprudence. And yet, the general discourse in the field of international refugee law has become increasingly more focused on centralization and standardization of refugee jurisprudence. My argument here has been that when looked at under the lense of legal pluralism, while the legacy and saliency of the Convention remains, on its own it cannot make or sustain the regime.

Concerns about the increasing diversity of secondary rules and variant interpretations and readings of primary rules of international law abound. In other words, diversification and differences in interpretation are seen as an integral part of an international legal regime and hence, secondary rules are no longer to be considered to constitute a threat to primary ones at least in some corners of legal

Rules and the Unity of International Law. Some Reflections on Current Trends" in L.A.N. M. Barnhhorn and K. C. Wellens (eds.), *Diversity in Secondary Rules and the International Law* (1995), 3–27.

[45] See Jonathan Charney, "Is International Law Threatened by Multiple Tribunals?" *Recueil des Cours, Collected Courses of the Hague Academy of International Law* 101 (1998), 115.

scholarship.[46] Furthermore, as the 1969 Convention binding African states exhibits, it is possible to talk about accountability regimes in international law that can embrace the variations amongst the judgments of international, domestic, regional and transnational legal regimes.[47] What needs to be added to this framework is the possible fruitful results of the intersection amongst different international accountability regimes, such as the refugee regime, human rights regime and humanitarian law regime.

VI CONCLUSION

If we are to talk about the international refugee regime as an accountability regime, there has to be more to it than an identifiable framework for judicial functions or a set of well-defined primary rules such as those dictated by the 1951 Convention. Furthermore, there is a significant difference between substantive and remedial law in both domestic and international jurisprudence. The former is generally understood to stand for statutory or written law that governs rights and obligations of those who are subject to it. Therefore, it defines the legal relationship between individuals and the society, as well as the relationship between society and the state. Remedial law, on the other hand, is a version of procedural law. As such, it comprises the rules by which a court hears and determines what happens in civil or criminal proceedings. In other words, remedial law refers to the method and means by which substantive law is administered. While substantive law defines the rights and duties, procedural law is the body of rules and practices that provides the machinery for enforcing those rights and duties. In the context of the international refugee regime, what constitutes substantive law is the 1951 Convention and its additional protocols. Remedial law, on the other hand, is the domestic, national interpretations and implementations of the international refugee jurisprudence.

As the examples given in this paper revealed, organs of international law are not only fragmented. They also operate at multiple

[46] In Herbert L. A. Hart, *The Concept of Law* ([1961] 1994). See also Hart, "Positivism and the Separation of Law and Morals," *Harvard Law Review* 71 (1958), 593.

[47] See Jonathan Charney, "Is International Law Threatened".

levels of jurisdiction and have to address a variety of claimants, the state constituting one of them. However, as the debate on legal pluralism debate on transnational law indicates, neither the variations in procedures nor oscillations in the competency of judicial organs stand in the way of an international legal regime. Instead, it is possible to argue that in the area of international law, and specifically with regards to accountability regimes such as the refugee regime, administration of substantive and remedial justice has to be undertaken as a balancing act. Public international law is commonly detected to oscillate between a Kantian cosmopolitan ethos and honing of domestic adjudication regarding conflict of laws and other jurisdictional matters at the domestic level.[48] Regimes of trade law, human rights law, environmental law, and of course international refugee law are all testimony to this hard balancing act. The former, cosmopolitan impetus to manage and resolve "global problems" often finds its best expression in the form of institution-building with an international reach and a purportedly universal mandate. In the context of the international refugee regime, this is what the 1951 Convention stands for.

In international law, refugees exist at the mercy of the sovereign states, though no longer the one within which they once had citizenship and hence a legitimate claim for rights and protection. As non-citizens and without membership within the community that they are asking for protection from, they are at a great risk from the discretionary behaviour of formal authorities and thus constitute a global class of vulnerable peoples. This is in addition to their overall status as stateless people. As the debate on legal pluralism illustrates, legal regimes do not exist in isolation or as edifices standing on their own. International refugee regime is not an exception in this regard. It requires the engulfing effects and synergy with other accountability regimes such as human rights and humanitarian law and practices that enhance the life chances of outsiders, marginal groups and vulnerable populations at a global scale. The examples discussed in this chapter pertaining to refugee selection and admission practices both in the Global North

[48] See Martti Koskenniemi, "The Fate of Public International Law: Between Technique and Politics," *Modern Law Review* 70 (2007), 1.

and in the Global South are testimony to the fact that without the intervention and balancing effects of a multitude of accountability regimes coming into the aid of international refugee law, 1951 Convention and its additional protocols and treaties alone could not lead to a genuine exercise of systematic protection for those who suffer from the excesses of the nation state in the post-Welphalian international order.

Index